Children's Literature & Story-telling

AFRICAN LITERATURE TODAY 33

Editor:	Ernest N. Emenyonu
Assistant Editor:	Patricia T. Emenyonu
Associate Editors:	Jane Bryce
	Maureen N. Eke
	Stephanie Newell
	Charles E. Nnolim
	Chimalum Nwankwo
	Kwawisi Tekpetey
	Iniobong I. Uko
Reviews Editor:	Obi Nwakanma

HEBN Publishers Plc

JAMES CURREY

GUIDELINES FOR SUBMISSION OF ARTICLES

The Editor invites submission of articles on the announced themes of forthcoming issues. Submissions will be acknowledged promptly and decisions communicated within six months of the receipt of the paper. Your name and institutional affiliation (with full mailing address and email) should appear on a separate sheet, plus a brief biographical profile of not more than six lines. The editor cannot undertake to return materials submitted, and contributors are advised to keep a copy of each material sent. Please note that all articles outside the announced themes cannot be considered or acknowledged. Articles should be submitted in the English Language.

Length: Articles should not exceed 5,000 words.
Format: Articles should be double-spaced, and should use the same type face and size throughout. Italics are preferred to underlines for titles of books. Articles are reviewed blindly, so do not insert your name, institutional affiliation and contact information on the article itself. Instead, provide such information on a separate page.

Style: UK or US spellings are required, but be consistent. Direct quotations should retain the spellings used in the original source. Check the accuracy of citations and always give the author's surname and page number in the text, and a full reference in the Works Cited list at the end of the article. Italicize titles of books or plays. Use single inverted commas throughout except for quotes within quotes which are double. Avoid subtitles or subsection headings within the text.

Citations: Limit your sources to the most recent, or the most important books and journals, in English. Cite works in foreign languages only when no English-language books are available. Cite websites only if they are relatively permanent and if they add important information unavailable elsewhere.

For in-text citations, the sequence in parentheses should be (Surname: page number). No year of publication should be reflected within the text. All details should be presented in the Works Cited list at the end of the article. Consistency is advised. Examples:

Cazenave, Odile. *Rebellious Women: The New Generation of Female African Novelists*. Boulder, CO: Lynne Rienner Publishers, 2000.
Duerden, Dennis. 'The "Discovery" of the African Mask.' *Research in African Literatures*. Vol. 31, No. 4 (Winter 2000): 29-47.
Ukala, Sam. 'Tradition, Rotimi, and His Audience.' *Goatskin Bags and Wisdom: New Critical Perspectives on African Literature*. Ed. Ernest N. Emenyonu. New Jersey: Africa World Press, 2000: 91-104.

Ensure that your Works Cited list is alphabetized on a word-by-word basis, whether citations begin with the author's name or with an anonymous work's title. Please, avoid footnotes or endnotes. Do not quote directly from the Internet without properly citing the source as you would when quoting from a book. Use substantive sources for obtaining your information and depend less on general references.

Copyright: It is the responsibility of contributors to clear permissions.

All articles should be sent to the editor, Ernest N. Emenyonu, as an e-mail attachment (Word)
Email: eernest@umflint.edu
African Literature Today
Department of Africana Studies
University of Michigan-Flint
303 East Kearsley Street
Flint MI 48502, USA
Fax: 001-810-766-6719

Reviewers should provide full bibliographic details, including the extent, ISBN and price, and submit to the Reviews Editor:
Obi Nwakanma, University of Central Florida, English Department, Colburn Hall, 12790 Aquarius Agora Drive, Orlando , FL 32816, USA
obi.nwakanma@ucf.edu

AFRICAN LITERATURE TODAY

Children's Literature & Story-telling

AFRICAN LITERATURE TODAY **33**

James Currey is an imprint of
Boydell & Brewer Ltd
PO Box 9, Woodbridge,
Suffolk, IP12 3DF (GB)
and of
Boydell & Brewer Inc.
668 Mt Hope Avenue,
Rochester, NY 14620-2731 (US)
www.boydellandbrewer.com
www.jamescurrey.com

HEBN Publishers Plc
1 Ighodaro Road, Jericho,
PMB 5205, Ibadan, Nigeria
Phone: +234 2 8726701
info@hebnpublishers.com
hebnpublishers@yahoo.com
http://www.hebnpublishers.com
www.facebook.com/pages/HEBN-PublishersPlcs
www.twitter.com/HEBNPublishers

British Library Cataloguing in Publication Data
is available on request

ISBN 978-1-84701-132-9 (James Currey paper)
ISBN 978-978-081-518-9 (HEBN Nigeria edition paper)

Designed and set in 10.5/12 pt Berkeley Book by
Kate Kirkwood Publishing Services, Cumbria, UK

Contents

Marjorie Jones
(18 June 1926–6 September 2015)

Obituary Note

As we go to press for the latest edition of *African Literature Today*, we hear of the passing of Marjorie Jones, wife of legendary scholar and critic of African literature, Professor Eldred Jones, on Sunday, 6 September in Freetown, Sierra Leone, at the age of 89. Marjorie was an active participant in the African literary field in her own right and not just the wife of a pioneer critic and scholar of African literature. Readers of *African Literature Today* will recall that when Eldred Jones was Editor and Eustace Palmer Associate Editor, Marjorie served as Editorial Assistant for the journal. This was in the pre-computer age, and it meant that she was responsible for re-typing all the articles and reviews accepted for publication in the journal and playing a very important role during the proof-reading process. When Eustace Palmer left Sierra Leone for the United States in 1992, she and Eldred Jones virtually co-edited the journal until Ernest Emenyonu took over as Editor. What some may not know is that for the last thirty years or so Eldred has been completely blind and Marjorie has been literally his eyes. That meant that Marjorie read all the articles and reviews submitted to the journal to him, and therefore played a very important role in deciding what should be published. She helped to compose the editorials, and was instrumental in seeing each edition of the journal through the publication process. She thus played an unforgettable role in shaping the destiny of *African Literature Today*, and ensured its continuation even during the years of Sierra Leone's civil war.

As Eldred was blind, Marjorie had to read all new publications he was interested in to him. She thus became very well read and very highly informed herself. I remember a very notable incident when Syl Cheney-Coker published his massive novel *The Last Harmattan of Alusine Dunbar*. At the launching ceremony in Freetown, Eldred

Jones was asked to be the keynote speaker and to give his views of the book, which he did superbly. This meant that Marjorie must have read the whole of that extensive novel to Eldred, and read it so well that Eldred was able to give an informed opinion of it which he was able to share with his Sierra Leonean audience. That held true for many other publications.

After Eldred retired from his position as Principal of Fourah Bay College, he continued to teach a course in one of his areas of specialization, Shakespeare, although the students had to go to his home, and although he was almost completely blind by that time. This meant that Marjorie had to read student essays and examination papers to him. I know of at least one situation in which she had to read an entire Master's thesis to him so that he could evaluate it.

Marjorie guided Eldred to conferences, took down his speeches and other contributions from dictation, and virtually co-wrote his recent book of memoirs – *The Freetown Bond: A Life under Two Flags*. As Lynn Taylor of the publishers Boydell and Brewer/James Currey said, Marjorie was the one who ran all over Freetown with a photographer to get just the right view over the harbour for the cover and who described all the photographs in the family albums to Eldred so that they could decide which should be included in the book, and, of course, she oversaw the whole process of production and publication, as she had done with so many of the volumes of *African Literature Today*.

In 2013, she also edited, together with Sheikh Umarr Kamarah, *An Anthology of Krio Poetry*. The volume was published in the Sierra Leone Writers' Series. She was therefore an author in her own right, and, partly because of this, she was elected President of the Sierra Leone Writers' Club. Her entire life was devoted to African literature and largely to the service of her husband. As one colleague has said, it is difficult to think of any other woman, throughout the world, who was more devoted to and supportive of her husband. May her soul rest in perfect peace.

EUSTACE PALMER
Distinguished Professor of English, Georgia College & State University
Associate Editor of *African Literature Today* from Vol. 12 (1982) to Vol. 19 (1994)

Notes on Contributors

Faith Ben-Daniels teaches African and World Literature at the University of Education-Winneba, Ghana. Her research interests are in new forms of African Literature and the diverse traditional forms of oral story-telling worldwide.

Juliana Daniels teaches in the English Department, University of Education, Winneba in Ghana. She is also a doctoral student with the University of South Africa. Her major research interests are African Literature, Children's Literature, Gender and Women's Studies.

Blessing Diala-Ogamba is a Professor in the Department of Humanities at Coppin State University, Baltimore, Maryland. She is the coordinator of World Literature and also teaches English Composition, African and British Literature. She is co-author of *Literary Crossroads: An International Exploration of Women, Gender, and Otherhood*. Her current research interests are World Literature, Immigration and Women issues.

Louisa Uchum Egbunike received her Ph.D from SOAS, University of London, where she also has lectured in Contemporary African Literature. She has published in numerous academic journals and has been an invited guest lecturer at Wellesley College, Massachusetts. She has presented her research at conferences in the USA, UK, South Africa, Germany and Nigeria and is one of the conveners of the annual international Igbo Conference at SOAS.

Eve Eisenberg, a graduate of Duke University, studies Anglophone postcolonial literature, including African Literature, in the English Ph.D program at Indiana University-Bloomington. She has a special interest in the changing roles of literature in postcolonial societies during the turbulent cultural and political changes of the late 20th and early 21st centuries.

Patricia T. Emenyonu, author of *Reading and the Nigerian Cultural Background*, is a Professor at the University of Michigan-Flint with a specialization in African Literature and Women Writers of the African World. She is a member of the African Literature Association where this paper was first presented at the Annual Conference in Johannesburg, South Africa. In addition to teaching and writing, she recently accompanied students on a three-week Study Abroad in Ghana where they had an interactive session with Ama Ata Aidoo, a leading African feminist author.

Wazha Lopang is a Lecturer in the Department of English at the University of Botswana. His area of research interest is oral literature and the gender politics within. He is co-editor of, and contributor to *Amantle*, a book that focuses on Botswana Literature.

Yvonne E. McIntosh is Associate Dean, College of Social Sciences, Arts and Humanities, and Associate Professor of French at Florida A&M University, Tallahassee. Her primary research interests are West African francophone literature and film. She participated in the Fulbright Teacher Exchange Program in France. She also served as the Project Group Leader on three Fulbright Group Abroad Programs: Senegal and Côte d'Ivoire, Morocco and Turkey.

Ikeogu Oke is the author of four books of poetry, *Where I Was Born* (2002), *Salutes without Guns* (2009), *In the Wings of Waiting* (2012) and *Song of Success* (2013), among other works. Since 1988 his poems have appeared in print on both sides of the Atlantic and in Asia in a variety of journals, including *Unity Magazine*, Discovery (published in Braille), and *Prosopisia*. He has performed his poems extensively in Nigeria, South Africa, and was as a special performance-poet guest of Brown University, Rhode Island, US, during the 2014 Chinua Achebe Colloquium. In 2010, Nadine Gordimer, the winner of the 1991 Nobel Prize in Literature, selected *Salutes without Guns*, Oke's second book of poems, as one of the Books of the Year for *The Times Literary Supplement* (*TLS*), describing Oke as 'a writer who finds the metaphor for what has happened and continues, evolves, not often the way we want in our lives in Africa and the world,' and who 'does so timelessly and tellingly, as perhaps only a poet can'.

Rose Sackeyfio is an Associate Professor in the Department of English at Winston Salem State University, North Carolina. Her areas of specialization and research interest are the literature of African-American women, Women's Studies, Cultural Studies and South Asian Women's writing.

Kelvin Ngong Toh holds a Ph.D in African Literature from the University of Yaounde, Cameroun. He is currently a Senior Lecturer at the University of Buea, Cameroun where he teaches African and African Diaspora Literatures and Cultures. His areas of research interest are African Literature, Caribbean Literature, Literary theory, Film and Music criticism and Political philosophy.

Julia Udofia is a lawyer and Senior Lecturer in the Department of English, University of Uyo. Her research interests are Black-Diasporan Literature, African Literature and Gender Studies.

Iniobong I. Uko is a Professor of English in the Department of English, and the current Director of Pre-Degree Studies, University of Uyo, Nigeria. Her research areas include African women's writings, and a cross-cultural study of African and Diasporic women's writings. She has published extensively in learned journals and books, and is the author of the seminal book *Gender and Identity in the Works of Osonye Tess Onwueme*.

Editorial

Children's Literature in Africa:
Time to Rethink Attitudes & Misconceptions

Speaking from a personal perspective, when I hear or see a 'call for papers', I say, that's academic and so that excludes me, a writer. ... Unless people in academia offer courses in children's literature and critics and teachers take up the writing of papers on the genre, it is not going to come from the story-tellers. It is for the academicians to write about what the story-tellers produce. And if they don't, it says a lot about the scholars and critics not story-tellers or writers of children's books.
– Sindiwe Magona

The quote above is part of the reaction of the versatile South African author, activist, social worker and veteran writer of children's books, Sindiwe Magona (who was interviewed for this issue of *African Literature Today*), on being told that the response by scholars to this issue on children's literature and story-telling in Africa, was abysmally poor to say the least. Part of this situation can be traced to attitudes to, and misconceptions of the genre, Children's literature. The attitudes range from indifference to outright negativity. Some critics and scholars tend to see the genre as something quite trivial, nothing to reckon with, and undeserving of quality-time or the rigorous endeavours of eminent scholars of literary criticism. To emphasize this, some scholars on lecture circuits, and lecturers in classrooms have albeit unwittingly, chosen to refer to the genre as 'Children Literature'.

Classified as something for children (like games for children or tales told to children about Santa Claus in some other places), it implies that adults need not take it seriously.

Any wonder why some publishers print and produce their children's books not just in ridiculously tiny sizes with hardly legible prints but also using cheap paper, and if there are illustrations at all, they are hardly ever in colour. There are mismatched edges and other evidence of hasty and shoddy production. On their scale of priorities in terms of commitment and allocation of resources, books for children are at the bottom of the ladder. And in our citadels of learning some promotion and tenure committees disqualify children's books as fulfilling the requirements of scholarly productivity, and those that accept them for assessment score them irreverently low! And when it comes to birthday, Christmas and other such occasions, some parents would rank books much, much lower than balloons and other toys as gifts.

It is time however, to rethink these unhealthy attitudes and ludicrous misconceptions. Good books for children are as important as nutritious breast-feeding that nurtures and enhances physical and mental growth and development in infancy.

Traditionally, Africans are a story-telling people, and the story-telling begins with children. From time immemorial African societies have used 'story' (variously called folktale, myth, legend, fable, oral performance etc), for purposes of acculturation and entertainment.

Elsewhere (Emenyonu, 2004), I had elaborated on the use of the folktale for the inculcation of essential community and societal values during the formative years of the child:

> Folktales are rich and authentic sources of raw African values. Used deliberately to inculcate positive values, they were therefore, necessarily didactic and morality-laden and driven. Children generally grew up under the tutelage of their mothers who at chosen times and places told them folktales in which enshrined community values were explicitly extolled … Some of the values espoused were direct, blunt and uncoated, the narrator often using a particular story to reinforce a moral issue of the moment. Some stories advocated instant justice through a revenge or retaliation of an evil act, or the deployment of a *deus-ex-machina* who killed off miscreants and hardened criminals. Good invariably must prevail over evil, and right over wrong. Wit and cunning (The sharp use of common sense) must excel over brute force and abusive might. Hard work must yield good results and be rewarded. Honesty always paid off. Falsehood and fraud were anti-social behaviours and must never escape severe punishments. Corruption in any form or manner was strictly frowned upon and the 'soul that sinned' died instantly to serve as deterrent to others. (427-8)

The socio-cultural and political environments of today make the desire to impart these values in the upbringing of children not only highly desirable but extremely pertinent. The impact of oral performances on contemporary African fiction for adults has over the decades been traced and established, primarily because at its inception in mid-20th century, African writers took issue with social and political injustices and wrote stinging works to protest against them. They include attacks on slavery, colonialism, neo-colonialism and corruption among others. Writers of children's stories have in their fiction exposed and condemned in various forms and manners anti-social behaviours such as child abuse, wars (especially the involvement of children in wars), child trafficking, child marriages, gender inequalities and patriarchal institutions that espouse gender inequities. Good and appropriate Children's Literature is not in short supply in all regions of Africa. What is lacking now is the teaching and reading of these works to achieve the traditional purposes and functions which made folktales and other oral performances part of the upbringing of children in African societies. Scholars and critics must pay adequate attention to the genre through research and presentations at conferences. Effective implementation of these will not only result in positive impacts on the behaviour of children in their formative years, but will also help in no small way to establish a viable reading culture in African countries.

This issue of *African Literature Today* on 'Children's Literature and Story-Telling in Africa' is a call to return to tried and tested practices in the use of literature to achieve purpose-driven and morality-laden lives from infancy through adulthood. This calls for the collaboration (and co-operation) of various agencies and individuals – governments, educators, teachers, parents, publishers, non-governmental agencies, libraries etc. We echo the call by Sindiwe Magona to make Book fairs for Children's Literature a norm rather than the exception in the operations of publishers of children's books in various languages in all parts of Africa. Massive quantities of Children's Literature have been produced in African indigenous languages throughout the continent. These need to be translated, first, into other African languages and, second, into non-indigenous African languages. Parents need to recognize the age-old importance of reading for young infants and story-telling that are part of the nurturing of the spirit of the child. It is not too early for mothers to recognize this even while unborn babies are in their wombs. Educators should restore (where not in place yet) the scheduling of 'the story-hour' in the school curriculum. Publishers should see the production and circulation of Children's books as their essential contribution towards the improvement of social and moral development of African people from infancy through adult life. Teachers should take interest in ensuring that Children's literature is taught with full commitment and dedication like any other subject in the curriculum. Writers and illustrators of Children's books should see their roles as highly pertinent to the successful implementation of producing books that can compare favourably with the best children's books elsewhere in the world. Libraries should design with resourceful initiatives Children's literature sections in their establishments. Governments, foundations and philanthropic organizations should assist with generous endowments the production and distribution of Children's books across all regions in the African continent. These supports and endowments should be viewed as invaluable investments in the lifelong education of African peoples. Successful implementations of Children's literature projects and programmes are actions directed towards the enhancement of literacy on the continent of Africa. No child anywhere in Africa should be left behind in these lofty schemes.

Contributors of articles in this issue have endeavoured to explore in theory and practice various dimensions of these ideals in the works produced for children in different regions in Africa. Rose Sackeyfio, Iniobong Uko, Blessing Diala-Ogamba, Patricia Emenyonu and Louisa Egbunike have discussed aspects and perspectives of literature produced by Nigerian authors. Faith Ben-Daniels and Juliana Daniels have focused on the nature and state of children's literature in Ghana. Kelvin Ngong Toh and Eve Eisenberg's articles focus on children's literature in Cameroon which cuts across national linguistic boundaries. Wazha Lopang in his article deals with the 'Trickster Tale' as a 'recurring decimal' in African oral narratives.

Yvonne McIntosh's 'The Journey Quest in West African Folktales' explores the journey motif in the quest for identity in African Children's literature, while Julia Udofia takes issue with the nature of contemporary literature designed for African children with special reference to the inclusion of children in armed conflicts as characters.

While we were going to press in 2014 with *African Literature Today 32: Politics & Social Justice*, the news of the death of Nobel Laureate Nadine Gordimer (1923-2014) was announced. We are grateful to Ikeogu Oke for the special Tribute which we promised in this volume in memory of Nadine Gordimer, whose contributions to twentieth-century African literature, and particularly to the battle against the obnoxious apartheid system, make her a heroic giant in African literature of protest against social injustices and crimes against humanity.

WORKS CITED

Emenyonu, Ernest, N. 'Selection and Validation of Oral Materials for Children's Literature: Artistic resources in Chinua Achebe's Fiction for children'. In Emenyonu, Ernest N. (ed.) *Emerging Perspectives on Chinua Achebe*, Volume 1. Trenton, New Jersey: Africa World Press, 2004.

Culture & Aesthetics in Selected Children's Literature by Akachi Ezeigbo

ROSE SACKEYFIO

In the 21st century, the role of African children's literature is pivotal in connecting the past, present and future generations through the expression and celebration of cultural heritage. For the African child, the world today represents myriad challenges to success such as urbanization, migration and displacement, generational conflict, and tension between tradition and modernity. These realities collude with the ever-present barriers of race and class for African people. The voluminous works produced by Akachi Adimora-Ezeigbo, explore diverse and timely themes that have earned critical acclaim in the literary world. Her children's literature reifies her commitment to African-centred and authentic literature that fulfils multiple roles in society.

As a prolific writer across genres of poetry, the novel, and the short story, her literature for young readers is a connecting thread to oral traditions of story-telling for the purpose of acculturation and socialization of youth. The potential impact of this genre on young readers is invaluable because literature, as a mirror of life, may convey didactic elements as well as aesthetic appeal to the young mind. This chapter will examine select works of children's fiction by Akachi Adimora-Ezeigbo to highlight conflicts between tradition and modernity within urban and rural settings in Nigeria. Through the lens of childhood, the author has woven significant ideas about character formation, African values and cultural continuity. Children universally represent the future and writers for this audience have a commitment to use their artistry in ways that foreground the preservation of African cultural integrity in a globalized world of fractured identity and misplaced values.

In contemporary Nigerian literature, one of the foremost writers of children's literature is indisputably Akachi Adimora-Ezeigbo whose prolific outpouring of creativity has earned her prestigious literary awards and critical acclaim. To date, she has produced five novels, twenty-two books for children, four collections of short stories and two plays. Akachi Adimora-Ezeigbo is a writer, activist and professor at the University of Lagos, Nigeria. As one of Nigeria's leading contemporary writers, she has won the coveted ANA Spectrum Prize (2001), the Zulu Sofola Prize (2002) for women writers, the Flora Nwapa Prize (2003) and the WORDOC Short Story Prize in 1994. She was awarded the Cadbury Poetry Prize (2009), ANA (Atiku Prize 2008) and in 2007 she, along with Mabel Segun, won The Nigeria Prize for Literature for *My Cousin Sammy*. In 2012, *Roses and Bullets*, an epic novel about the Biafra War, was shortlisted for the Wole Soyinka Prize for Literature.

Ezeigbo's books for children place her squarely within the canon of writers who, in the decades after Nigeria's independence, amplified the exigencies of nation-building as a catalyst for relevant literature for children on whom the nation's future depends. Ezeigbo's works for children display a commitment to nation-building through the inculcation of values and ideals that energize and re-invigorate Nigeria's youth. She has used her creative artistry to recapture and preserve the best and most positive African values that define Nigeria's cultural heritage. As a master story-teller she conveys cultural authenticity and aesthetic appeal of the Nigerian landscape to captivate the minds of young readers.

The use of culture as a guidepost serves three important functions: first, it creates the bridge between oral tradition and literature and like earlier writers for children and youth, Ezeigbo has drawn from the inexhaustible repertoire of oral tradition. Second, African cultural values are still relevant in modern settings and her children's books reflect this idea. Third, cultural content from Nigeria and other African cultures is rich in didactic elements, a feature that is intrinsic to African oral tradition. In much the same way as oral artists of the past, Adimora Ezeigbo has effectively adapted salient features of Nigerian folklore to address contemporary issues in the world of the Nigerian child of the 21st century.

Osayimwense Osa in *African Children's and Youth Literature* (1995) highlights the evolution of Nigerian children's literature as a mirror of the nation's political history because the works are produced in response to the political flavour of the post-independence era. For example, Osa recalls the sentiments of Cyprian Ekwensi, who, writing in the early 1960s is a pioneering figure in children's literature. Ekwensi stated that Nigeria as an emergent nation state must produce books to replace the family gathering under the moonlight tree, commonly known as 'Tales by Moonlight'. Decades ago he observed that the transformation of the Nigerian environment through urbanization and industrialization eroded the possibility of telling folktales as an expression of informal education within a traditional setting. His seminal work in 1962, *An African Night's Entertainment*, is essentially a long folktale in print. As a classic of Nigerian children's literature, it is representative of works that not only adapt the art of the folktale, but are also a response to the dearth of indigenous literary production. His purpose was to counter foreign books that were the legacy of colonial education which some critics might call mis-education.

Two decades later, in 1981, Chinua Achebe echoes these same ideas in an essay called 'Chinua Achebe: At the Crossroads' (192) where he emphasizes the role of literature as an instrument for uniting the country and affirming its nationhood. With regard to Achebe's profound impact upon the literary world through his novels for adults, his contribution to children's literature has not received the attention it deserves. Ernest Emenyonu asserts that careful study of Achebe's children's fiction soon reveals that he has blazed another trail in modern African literature, for through these stories, he has opened a new vista of experimentation for writers in cultures with rich oral traditions to draw from (430). Emenyonu goes on to assert that Achebe uses the Nigerian setting and his Igbo cultural background to introduce his new mission of cultural reorientation and rejuvenation for children and young adults who are secondary sufferers of the legacies of colonialism and neo-colonialism (430). Achebe's vibrant contribution to children's literature includes four children's books, *Chike and the River* (1966), *How the Leopard Got His Claws* (1972), *The Flute* (1977), and *The Drum* (1977). Of note is the recreation of popular folktales among his people as well as other ethnic groups within Nigeria and beyond. Both Ekwensi and Achebe are forerunners of modern children's literature (albeit in English) whose ideas foreground post-colonial literary theory as a lens of analysis for this important but under-researched genre.

Ezeigbo's continuation in the tradition of earlier Nigerian writers is a signal for readers, critics and scholars to celebrate her enormous contribution to literature for children. She began writing in the 1990s and stands firmly on the shoulders of her fellow writers for children who began in the 1960s. And, like her forerunners, Ekwensi and Achebe, Adimora's works for children display a commitment to nation-building through the inculcation of values and ideals that may animate and inspire Nigeria's children and youth. In Patrick Oloko's 2008 volume of essays, *The Fiction of Akachi Adimora-Ezeigbo: Issues and Perspectives*, Susan Arndt, noted literary critic of African women's writing, interviews Ezeigbo where she credits the authenticity of her cultural moorings as the inspiration for her craft. She recalls being in the company of Igbo women storytellers, young and old, and in her youth, having been fed and nurtured on the folklore of her people.

Ezeigbo recalls the numerous stories she imbibed in her childhood that helped to structure her vision as an artist and critic and to enrich her understanding of her culture and traditions from her Igbo heritage. She recalls that it is the women from her community to whom she owes her extensive knowledge of folklore, the art of story-telling and the power to create and structure tales (2008: 17). As a contemporary writer, Ezeigbo's works skillfully adapt themes that resonate with cultural continuity while maintaining culturally derived content. Her talent as a writer shines brightly through multi-layered themes that are appropriate for young readers. An excellent example of this creative technique is in her award-winning novel *My Cousin Sammy* (2007). This book is a clever blend of the old and the new, the urban and rural divide, a feminist perspective on gender roles, and very importantly, cultural values and traditions.

Ezeigbo is well known as a feminist writer and, as in other books she has written, the protagonist in *My Cousin Sammy* is a girl named Ene, who is a bright and precocious character. In terms of aesthetic appeal, the reader cannot help but admire this girl because of her compassion, sensitivity and intelligence in the face of family conflict and unsettling events. Her family lives in Lagos and she has a brother named Adaka. The urban-rural divide is vividly conveyed as Ezeigbo describes Ene's parents' bias against the Nigerian rural environment that is devalued when cast against the sophistication of Lagos. Ene's cousin Sammy arrives from his village to live with her family because he has lost his parents. Onukaogu and Onyerionwu observe that: 'the conflict begins as Sammy confronts the challenge of his transition from village life to the urban world: and extends to when he loses his way from school and falls into the hands of a youthful gang of delinquents' (241).

The author's presentation of tension between the values of city and country, along with dangerous pitfalls for youth is an important message for young readers. The ambiguities of urban lifestyles underscore the need for balanced and informed perceptions of development in Nigeria and in other African societies and the potential corruption of youth. Literature, as a window of reality must rise to the challenge to counter societal and global trends that clash and disrupt African cultural heritage.

The reader is quickly drawn into the storyline from the perspective of the female narrator. Sammy is awkward, out of place, and underexposed to his new environment. He is laughed at because he eats with his hands, speaks English differently and is having trouble fitting in. Ezeigbo contrasts the absence of cultural continuity in the urban environment when Ene is surprised to learn that in addition to English, Sammy speaks two Nigerian languages, Edo and Igbo that he is also able to read. Sammy tells Ene proudly that his father taught him and that he speaks Igbo in the village with his grandmother. Here, the writer makes a profound statement about connecting the past, present and future generations, something that is easily lost when people migrate to urban areas. Ene tells her cousin Sammy that her parents did not teach her Igbo and that English is spoken at all times in their home. Her family rarely visits their village and hardly communicates with their relatives, symbolic of diminished linkages to the past, their culture and traditions.

As the story unfolds, several lessons are embedded in the narrative about diligence, resourcefulness, consequence of bad behaviour, miscommunication and family conflict. Perhaps the greatest strength of this book is the transformation of all the characters as they gradually develop cohesive bonding and begin to embrace their Igbo identity. Both Ene and Sammy's intelligence somehow guides the adults to more nurturing behaviours such as spending quality time, speaking their language and renewal of kinship ties to relatives in their village. Spending more time with their grandmother denotes an appreciation of the past as a connecting link to the future. This idea is captured in the Adinkra symbol from Ghana called Sankofa which literally translates: 'recover your past in order to go forward into the future'. The generational link to the past is skilfully woven into the book. The family comes together after they weather illness, and the possible loss of Sammy who actually gets physically 'lost' in his new environment in a way that worries and frightens Ene and her family. Ezeigbo suggests potential dangers and the tangible risks of urban life as well as the allure of dubious characters that people the underbelly of a sprawling city like Lagos. The obvious symbolism of Sammy getting 'lost' in the city is a subtext of the work's didactic elements.

A feminist reading of the work highlights the agency and a strong sense of self displayed by Ene, the eleven-year-old protagonist, a self-directed critical thinker who uses reason and logic to navigate her conflicting environment. She struggles to make sense of her world and sometimes takes risks. When her family responds unkindly to Sammy's difficult adjustment, she is welcoming, caring and sympathetic. She displays the best of her character at the risk of punishment and the disapproval of her parents. When her cousin gets into trouble, she seeks him out, offers advice and behaves like a sister. Such admirable qualities in a female protagonist model positive character traits to both male and female children who read this book. In this way, conventional socialization for rigid gender roles can be transformed in society as children are introduced to a different perception of what it means to be male or female.

In addition, Ezeigbo portrays Sammy as knowing how to cook as opposed to Ene, a female who cannot and who is embarrassed at her ignorance. The author makes the point that practical knowledge in the domestic arena holds merit for both male and female children and must not be neglected in pursuit of western education or over-reliance on domestic labour. In the midst of her embarrassment, Ene thinks to herself that it is not her fault that she doesn't know how to cook: 'Her Mum did not teach or encourage Adaka and me to cook', but told them to read their books and work hard to pass their exams to get into university (54). As an independent thinker, she reasons that if Sammy could cook, so should her brother and herself. She decides to spend time with Sammy and the house-help in order to learn how to cook. The story is told with realism, honesty and aesthetic appeal and is more than deserving of the literary prize given to Akachi Adimora-Ezeigbo. The work narrates the transformational elements that exist within all of us as human actors on the stage of life. Ene is indeed a lovable character whose qualities reflect the admirable ideals for childhood behaviour that is universal.

Another book with a female at the centre is *The Prize,* published much earlier in 1994. Although shorter than *My Cousin Sammy,* the message is effective in a well-crafted tale as the reader enters the world of an eleven-year-old girl named Onyema. Her greatest wish is to win a scholarship to secondary school. An appealing feature of this book is the rural setting which draws a stark contrast to the story's message about the value of education. In life and in literature, aspiration to progress, education, careers and upward mobility is commonly associated with urban settings. Although village life is usually characterized by a lack of sophistication, illiteracy and a bleak future, an important lesson to children reading *The Prize* is that despite humble beginnings, discipline and hard work are the real key to success in life.

The lofty aspirations expressed by Onyema are cast against a patriarchal authority that threatens her ambition. Her father has arranged for her to marry early instead of continuing her education. Throughout Africa and in many developing nations, the practice of choosing to educate a male child rather than a female is a reality that perpetuates gender inequality and ultimately poverty of girls and women. Ezeigbo raises consciousness about this practice and the feminist elements in the work are expressed through the qualities of strength and determination of Onyema and her mother. Onyema tells her mother she is 'tired of her life' because she doesn't want to marry Onyia (10). She says she will run away if forced to marry. She aspires to become an engineer but is ridiculed by the boys in her class. The boys proudly discuss their plans to become doctors, pilots or accountants. One of them tells her laughingly that '...she will be an engineer in his brother's kitchen' (16). This true-to-life conflict connects to Tsitsi Dangaremgba's classic novel, *Nervous Conditions* (1988) wherein the female character Tambudzai's brother can attend school but she cannot. She is determined to earn the school fees by farming. Her father asks her whether she can 'cook books for her husband' (15). Onyema is defiant in her resolve to become educated. Her mother secretly helps her apply for the scholarship while she studies almost day and night for the qualifying examination. The story has a happy ending and her father is impressed by Onyema's intelligence. He is clearly proud of her and this makes her success even sweeter. The idea of overcoming obstacles and standing by one's principles is worthy of emulation by children and young adult readers. In the portrayal of male characters, Ezeigbo underscores the idea that social transformation of gender roles is possible in society. In *The Prize*, the depiction of culture or rather unproductive cultural practices such as child marriage is treated as an obstacle to progress and the narrative structure is a critique of rigid and inflexible gender patterns. In order for any society to develop and make genuine progress, the talents and skills of both females and males are mandatory in the socialization of children in contemporary society.

Another of Ezeigbo's books that is set in a rural environment is *Alani the Troublemaker.* The story opens in Kaduna where Alani has not been successful in the first term of secondary school. Instead of working harder, he gradually earns a reputation as a troublemaker. He is punished for playing a prank on his teacher and his performance in school continues to deteriorate. When his mother talks to the principal, the reader learns that the real cause of his difficulties is the death of his father in a car accident. His mother decides to enrol him in a secondary school in her village where her brother lives. Ezeigbo introduces a realistic story of a child coping with death. Alani has not worked through his grief over the loss of his father and because he has no outlet for his suppressed emotions, his behaviour becomes rebellious. His mother is unable to cope with his emotional needs because of the demanding nature of her life in the city.

Ezeigbo illustrates the strength of the African extended family pattern within a wholesome rural setting. As the story unfolds, Mr Abuna, Alani's uncle, resolves to take charge of his education and upbringing. In addition, Ezeigbo develops yet another cultural element through introducing the continued belief in ancestors to watch over their living family members from beyond. When Alani's uncle mentions his father perhaps watching his activities, it sparks his desire to make him proud by working hard. Ezeigbo, by infusing a traditional spiritual belief in the presence of ancestors, invokes the idea of continuity with the past as an anchor for success in the future. With his uncle's encouragement and supervision, Alani begins to thrive in the midst of family cohesiveness and a renewed sense of belonging. The story ends on a jubilant note when by the end of the school term he takes second place among his classmates in school. This story is a compelling account of the potential for children's success within an unlikely environment. The challenges faced by the young protagonist bring to the surface latent or dormant potential for positive character development through a nurturing extended family.

Ezeigbo skilfully highlights the idea that urban life does not offer automatic success or solutions to family problems. The work also suggests that fast paced, demanding and stressful city life is a less than ideal environment for nurturing children and moulding character. The young narrator observes that in the village 'There was time for everything in the Abuna family. There was time for work, and time for meals. There was time for study and time for play' (53). As Alani's character is transformed, not only is he highly intelligent, he demonstrates courage, bravery, resourcefulness, obedience and a strong work ethic that earns success in school. Ezeigbo's portrayal of village life is never romanticized or overrated, but is described realistically to engage the young reader.

The range of themes and issues explored in Ezeigbo's fiction for children is broad in scope. The young protagonists, whether female or male, encounter experiences drawn from the world of the Nigerian child. Her stories interrogate patriarchy, the value of education, the need for positive character development, and the value of preserving ties to a rich cultural heritage that is rooted in rural settings. The young protagonists learn meaningful lessons and begin to embrace values that will guide their future success. In *My Cousin Sammy*, and *Alani the Troublemaker,* the experiences and ideas that derive from cultural elements in rural environments is pivotal in the socialization of adolescents. Ernest Emenyonu, in *Selection and Validation of Oral Materials for Children's Literature* (2004) offers meaningful insight into the significance of village settings in oral literature.

He describes how the new era has set in motion a breakdown of 'the old cherished moral order and codes of behavior'. Although the article was published in 2004, the ideas are relevant and timely today. At present, globalization has exacerbated these changes through technology, exposure to western media, materialism and continued corruption of traditional values that conflict with fast-paced urban realities and demands upon Nigerian society, as well as African families throughout the continent. Emenyonu notes that established writers such as Ngugi wa Thiong'o and Chinua Achebe articulate a challenge for the committed artist to reassert his or her creative imagination and cultural reaffirmation through the rediscovery of the folktale tradition as a valid form of instruction and entertainment. Ezeigbo, along with other contemporary writers, adapts elements of oral literature in her works.

Ezeigbo's books for children display her commitment to use her craft to effect social transformation. These ideas are best conveyed in the classic and often cited text, *Recreating Ourselves: African Women and Critical Transformations* (1995) by Molara Ogundipe-Leslie, who in the chapter, 'The Female Writer and Her Commitment' articulates the mandate for creative writers to write authentically about females from a gendered perspective:

Ezeigbo upholds the charge to women writers to project female protagonists in positive ways as a departure from male-centred children's books. This represents feminist expression with full potential for positive impact upon young minds. The portrayal of girls as leading characters is revisionist in scope because of the full range of strong and exemplary characteristics, values, ethical and moral principles and female agency that is not only aesthetically appealing but also socially relevant for the 21st century. Emenyonu (2004) corroborates the timeliness of socially conscious children's literature and the dilemma it poses for committed writers. He draws the readers' attention to Achebe and Ngugi who both address the moral crisis and value disorientation which have engulfed the younger generation in Africa. A decade later, in the era of globalization and rapid change these ideas appear prophetic and it is rather unsettling to consider these realities amidst the uncertainties of modern life for future generations.

Ezeigbo has risen to this challenge in a compelling array of works for children. Her stories are told in a lively and engaging style that will captivate young readers. The aesthetic elements of all the children's books reveal the talent of the writer to enter the world of children and to see life through their eyes. Finally, Ezeigbo's literature for children is significant because of the portrayal of female characters in an effort to deconstruct prevailing gender bias, patriarchy and the devaluing of women and girls in Nigerian society. In this way, the artist uses literature as part of the socialization of females and males in the interest of gender equality. The portrayal of positive role models, the agency of female characters, and of girls who are intelligent, is a strong and commendable effort towards social and cultural transformation. Ezigbo's distinguished career as a writer is founded upon her commitment to preserving cultural integrity and promoting the best qualities among youth that will strengthen Nigeria in the 21st century.

WORKS CITED

Arndt, Susan (2008). 'Paradigms of Intertextuality: Orature and Writing Back in the Fiction of Akachi Adimora-Ezeigbo', in Patrick Oloko (ed.) *The Fiction of Akachi Adimora-Ezeigbo: Issues and Perspectives*. Lagos: African Cultural Institute, 17-65.

Dangaremgba, Tsitsi (1988). *Nervous Conditions*. Seattle: Seal Press.

Emenyonu, Ernest (2004). 'Selection and Validation of Oral Materials for Children's Literature: Artistic Resources in Chinua Achebe's Fiction for Children', in Ernest Emenyonu (ed.) *Emerging Perspectives on Chinua Achebe*. Trenton NJ: Africa World Press, 474-54.

Ezeigbo, Akachi-Adimora (2007). *My Cousin Sammy*. Lagos: The Book Company Limited.

——. *Alani and the Troublemaker*. Lagos: Lantern Books.

——. (1994). *The Prize*. London: Heinemann.

Khorana, Meena (1998). 'To Build a Nation Where Peace and Justice Reign: Postcolonial Nigerian Young Adult Literature', in Meena Khorana (ed.), *Critical Perspectives on Postcolonial African Children's and Young Adult Literature*. Westport and London: Greenwood Press

Ogundipe-Leslie, Molara (1994), 'The Female Writer and Her Commitment', *Recreating Ourselves: African Women and Critical Transformations*. Trenton, NJ: Africa World Press, 57-67

Onukaogu, Allwell Abalogu and Ezechi Onyerionwu (2004). 'Children's Literature in 21ˢᵗ Century Nigeria' in Emenyonu, *Selection and Validation of Oral Materials for Children's Literature*. Lagos: Kraft Books, 232–55.

Osayimwense, Osa (1995). 'Cyprian Ekwensi: Pioneer African Writers for Children and Young Adults' in *African Children's and Youth Literature*. New York. Twayne Publishers, 1-24.

Contemporary Nigerian Children's Literature

A Study of Ifeoma Onyefulu

INIOBONG I. UKO

The reality confronting many contemporary African societies is that many of their values have been lost over the years, and more are steadily fading off through the combined impact of colonization, Western education, foreign religions and civilizations, modernity and globalization. Nigeria is prominent in this context. As a result of these trends, recent generations of Nigerians, particularly the children, hardly know about the traditional practices of their people, or realize the critical essence of those practices, or appreciate the uniqueness and pride in being Nigerian, living in Nigeria, and the difference involved in being a Nigerian in the diaspora. To check this trend, and to ensure that the Nigerian spirit is not obliterated among future generations of Nigerians, Ifeoma Onyefulu recaptures in her writings for children, Nigerian cultural values, traditional practices and mores, patterns of education and other inheritances. This study examines the sociological perspective of Onyefulu's corpus of children's stories to establish the essential role that each story performs in the establishment and sustenance of the Nigerian experience and spirit, even among Nigerian children raised in the diaspora.

Story-telling is oral tradition, and it is essential in many cultures. As in other parts of the world, story-telling has been practised all over Africa. The stories, which usually include tales of exploits, folktales, legends, epics, riddles, also seek to preserve the history and customs of the people. This study focuses on story-telling in Nigeria as captured by Ifeoma Onyefulu, a Nigerian who is resident in England. The study gains relevance from the fact that Onyefulu makes considerable use of real life photographs to support her narratives, thereby injecting reality into her stories and making the readers confront the objects of the stories. Story-telling is a significant practice in Nigeria because Nigerians in the remote past had no form of writing by which to preserve their stories about their land, the people and their evolution as well as their traditions. Consequently, the databases for the preservation of the stories were all oral and passed from person to person and from generation to generation. Other forms of preservation of the people's values were through mnemonics, carved symbols, sculpture and other material story-prompts, and ancient scripting. Story-telling in Nigeria serves to 'interpret the universe, resolve natural and physical phenomena, teach morals, maintain cultural values, pass on methods of survival, and to praise God' (Octavia Utley http://teachers.yale.edu/curriculum/viewer/initiative).

Children's stories in Nigeria constitute a special category because on the one hand, they provide entertainment and explain the origins of certain practices, beliefs, taboos, myths and other phenomena in everyday life. On the other hand, these narratives endow animals with human features to convey wisdom. Despite the strangeness of these features, they stick in the minds of the child audience and make a lasting impression. Significant within this framework are trickster tales in which storytellers use animals to help people understand human nature and human behaviour. The background to these tales derives from the fact that primordial people in Nigeria lived in close proximity to (wild) animals that shared their land and environment. The tales are generally meant to be both entertaining and instructive to reveal the values that bind the people together. Also, the nature of the stories makes their origins ubiquitous, with nobody claiming authorship because the stories belong to everyone and occur everywhere. Even though the stories may be similar between and among other cultures beyond Nigeria, there are still slight variations since they were not documented but disseminated by word of mouth over generations.

Ifeoma Onyefulu was born and brought up in Eastern Nigeria. After studying Business Management in London, she trained as a photographer, a vocation that has given life and vibrancy to her stories. As an expatriate now living in London with her husband and two sons, she has 'successfully introduced English-speaking audiences to the range and variety of village life in her homeland through her picture books for young readers' (http://biography.jrank.org/pages/1257/Onyefulu-Ifeoma-1957.html). Onyefulu's books have been praised for their invaluable contributions to the teaching of the universality of some experiences, as well as for their use of pictures in the portrayal of Nigerian rural life. The brightly coloured photographs that she uses to illustrate the stories that depict true events in her natal family in Nigeria not only evoke the relationship between and among the people in her stories, but also highlight the customs and realities of everyday life in contemporary Nigeria.

Her highly acclaimed children's books counter negative images about Nigeria (and Africa in general) by celebrating both traditional village and urban Nigerian lives and values. Her books largely demonstrate cultural diversity. *A is for Africa*, her first book for Frances Lincoln publishers, was chosen as one of the best information books of 1993, and was nominated for the 1994 Kate Greenaway Medal (http://franceslincoln.com/ifeoma-onyefulu). Onyefulu twice won the Children's Africana Book Award: Best Book for Young Children in the USA with *Here Comes our Bride* in 2005, and *Ikenna Goes to Nigeria* in 2008. According to Onyefulu, 'I love people very much, and having grown up in Nigeria where one is never alone, this type of hunger for company comes naturally. Therefore, my interest in people has increased since I left my country' (http:/biography.jrank.org/pages/1257/Onyefulu-Ifeoma-1959.html).

This study involves a survey of seventeen of her children's stories. Ten stories are in a collection entitled *The Girl who Married a Ghost and Other Stories from Nigeria*. Six of the ten stories in the collection are fable, set in the animal kingdom. Four stories are about humans, celestial as well as supernatural beings. Seven others are true life stories about Igbo concepts and practices as recounted by Onyefulu's children, who approach the Nigerian reality with European orientation, or by other children in her wider family. In each of these categories, Onyefulu shows a world where the different entities cohabit, have disagreements and conflicts, and then develop their diverse strategies to resolve them. She depicts the Nigerian environment as composite, with human beings relating closely and actively with supernatural beings. She demonstrates that in spite of the various factors that have interfered with the Nigerian reality – dislocations, transatlantic slavery, colonialism, wars – the people remain united even in their struggles to survive.

In the fables, Onyefulu obliquely reveals the common animals and birds in the Nigerian environment: the lion that is the mythical king of the forest, the elephant, monkey, giraffe, tortoise, goat, serpent, squirrel, lizard and the parrot, among others. These animals symbolize human characters and the different traits that people exhibit while relating with others. The dexterity with which the author approaches the narration of the fables depicts the specific stereotypes by which the animals are identified in Nigerian cosmology: the tortoise is highly innovative, cunning, industrious and tenacious. In the story *The Great Eating Competition*, Tortoise violates the major rule of the competition, but no animal notices it because as he eats the spicy food, he sings along with the other animals the song he has taught them. Diverting their attention from himself, Tortoise eats up the spicy food, becomes the champion and earns the shiny gold chain which Lion, the King, offers as the prize.

Tortoise appears again in the story *Lazy Dog and Tortoise* in which his innovative spirit urges him to try to resolve the problem of acute water shortage in the animal kingdom. The binary model of the inflationary and deflationary technique is applied in this story, because as Tortoise takes a practical step to provide water in the jungle, he is inflated, while Dog is deflated as he is portrayed as lazy and evasive. He refuses to join his friend, Tortoise, to dig the well to find a spring, but Tortoise mobilizes the other animals and succeeds in his heroic ambition of ending the misery faced by them because of lack of water.

However, in *Pig's Money* and *The Famine,* Tortoise is a negative role-player as he is deceitful, insincere, and selfish in his dealings with other animals. In *Pig's Money*, Tortoise lures Pig into lending him two thousand naira (the Nigerian currency), which he promises to refund but in reality does not intend to. By portraying the dual attitudes of positivity and negativity of Tortoise in the different stories, Onyefulu accentuates the trickster motif by which Tortoise is described in Nigerian/African oral tradition. The stories present the common stereotypes of the animals: Lion is powerful and fearful; Giraffe is calm and sensible, and her height gives her an advantage over other animals; Snake is known for telling tall tales in the jungle; Monkey exaggerates stories, and so on.

Other stories demonstrate the interaction between human characters and celestial beings: prominently, the ghost. In *The Girl who Married a Ghost*, the arrogant Ogilisa rejects all the suitors that come to marry her, and accepts a strange man. She realizes too late that the man has taken human body parts from people to whom he returns them and he ends up being a terrifying sight, which Ogilisa fears. She runs back to her parents. In this story, the author shows that Ogilisa understands the song of warning by Bird, but this may seem very strange and incomprehensible to children raised outside Nigeria and Africa who are not familiar with the mythic aspects of life. *The Wrestler and the Ghost* also depicts Ojadili who gets so carried away by heroism that he challenges a ghost to a wrestling match. This unnecessary sense of pride and the severe combat that ensues combine to teach Ojadili the virtue of humility.

Indeed, while the issues that the stories expound are highly instructive and enlightening, some of them lack verisimilitude. They are nevertheless generally accepted as valid and handed down from generation to generation. Specifically, the story *The Child Who Never Went Out* borders on the mysterious, as a child is formed from palm-oil. The ancestral spirit instructs Ngozi, the mother, in her dire quest for a child:

> Tomorrow morning … go to the market and buy the finest palm oil you can find. Wait until midnight, and then pour the oil on the ground in front of your house. When you wake in the morning you'll find a child standing on your veranda. But you must never, never let this child out in the sun. Remember, oil melts in the heat. (21)

This focus on the mysterious palm-oil girl, Apunanwu, raises sobering questions that cannot be answered rationally. The potential of relating what is real with what is left to the imagination demonstrates the dynamic nature of Nigerian folktales.

For Onyefulu to operate safely within the domain of the Nigerian folktale, she deploys the major characteristics of this narrative tradition. Prominently, the opening formula introduces each story, as follows:

> 'Many years ago' is the opening formula for the stories *Lazy Dog and Tortoise*, *The Girl who Married a Ghost* and *Talented Grasshopper*

> 'There was once a man …' is the opening formula for the stories *The Child who Never Went Out*

> 'There was once a lizard…' opens the story *Why the Lizard Nods his Head*

> 'There was once a very special man…' begins the story *The Wrestler and the Ghost*

> 'A long time ago…' introduces the stories *The Great Eating Competition*, *The Famine* and *Who Stole Python's Eggs?*

> 'Many, many years ago…' serves as the introduction to *Pig's Money*.

Furthermore, Onyefulu is careful to situate the stories within traditional settings. They take place in rural environments where the different entities – humans, animals, birds, ghosts etc – relate and interact freely. Some stories are set in the jungle where Lion is the king of the animals.

The author displays dexterity in her portrayal of time in the tales. In the collection's first narrative, *The Great Eating Competition*, Lion instructs Parrot to announce to all the animals that they should attend a meeting at his (Lion's) palace at six o'clock the next evening. The omniscient narrator explains that 'Lion knew that meetings were best held at sunset, when a cool breeze blew gently through the jungle and everyone was more relaxed' (9). By referring to six o'clock, Onyefulu uses what is familiar to her audience to introduce what may be unfamiliar. This is apparent in the total absence of the reference to clock time in subsequent situations.

In the stories, references are made to 'at daybreak…' (*The Child who Never Went Out* 22), 'one morning…', 'next morning…' and 'the sun was just rising from behind…' (*Lazy Dog and Tortoise* 35); 'when the sun was blazing down…' (*Pig's Money* 52); 'as the sun was disappearing…' (*The Famine* 62), and 'one cloudy morning…' (*The Famine* 66). These phrases reflect Onyefulu's skill in referring to time using traditional codes. These are a significant feature in Nigerian orature since the people mutually recognize and understand the codes as authentic.

Significantly, although some of the stories reflect surrealism, they are relevant for the lessons that can be gained from them, which the author clearly states at the end of each story. In the first of the collection, *The Great Eating Competition*, Tortoise outsmarts the other animals and successfully eats the heavily spiced food, earning the gold chain. The moral from that story is 'Be very observant'. That Tortoise is able to assess the situation, learn from the mistakes of the other animals that failed before him, and introduce a song to occupy the other animals, indicate Tortoise's high intelligence and the high premium that traditional Nigerian society attaches to songs. In *The Child who Never Went Out*, the lesson is 'Always listen to your parents and do as they tell you' (30). While *Lazy Dog and Tortoise* teaches that 'Laziness won't get you anywhere' (38). The moral from *The Girl who Married a Ghost* is 'Don't be too choosy because you never know what you might get' in the end (48). *Pig's Money* teaches that one should stay calm, otherwise one will be like the angry Pig who still has not been recompensed by Tortoise, his debtor (56), and the lesson from *The Famine* is 'You mustn't be greedy. You must share what you have with others, especially those who have none' (69).

Indeed, the moral lessons – the obvious and the implied ones – are essential in Onyefulu's motive for writing the stories. They reveal what she derived from the stories when her mother and grandmother told them to her, and what she seeks to teach her readers. Besides the morals, Onyefulu injects local colour into the narration of the stories to give them authentic Nigerian identities. She also translates into English most of the Igbo expressions that she uses. Local colour is also apparent in the anecdotes and analogies, which project such Nigerian values as communal living, cooperation, credible personhood, love and sharing, etc.

As an oral traditional element, song is used in the stories for diverse motives. In *The Great Eating Competition*, Tortoise introduces a song with a chorus that the other animals sing in response:

> Chant: Osili ofe n'osika! (Whoever cooked this sauce is a great chef)
> Chorus: U ... Ah!
> Chant: Onye osili ñi n'osika! (Whoever cooked this meal has outdone himself!)
> Chorus: U ...Ah! (15-16)

All the animals like Tortoise's song, and sing it with great joy and gusto. Tortoise, therefore, creates a sense of brotherhood among the animals.

Onyefulu also recreates traditional Nigerian life and values through stories of real events, which are recounted by children including her son, Ikenna. Ikenna's stories are accounts of his experiences while visiting Nigeria at different times with his mother and brother. The author uses different stories to expose different aspects of Nigerian life, beliefs and traditional practices. By portraying real experiences and capturing live images of the people, objects and events, Onyefulu authenticates the message of each of the stories.

In *Ikenna Goes to Nigeria*, Ikenna describes with appropriate pictorial support his visits to Lagos, Abuja, the Federal Capital Territory, Nkwelle, Onitsha and Oshogbo. These expositions subtly reveal the attractions in each location and the customs of the people. Through Ikenna's uncle, Mazyi, Ikenna knows about the history of Ikoyi: many Europeans lived there in colonial times, but now it is occupied by rich Nigerians. Ikenna is delighted to know and bond with his cousins in Lagos, and other family members as well as his grandparents in Onitsha, his great-uncle in Nkwelle, and some more relatives in Abuja. Ikenna's visit to Oshogbo coincides with the celebration of the *Osun* festival, which is usually marked once a year at the king's palace. His mother explains that the festival offers women an opportunity 'to pray to the goddess *Osun* to have children or to give thanks for the children they have had' (28). The celebration involves much singing, drumming, dancing as well as the special form of dance, on stilts.

In *Saying Goodbye*, Ikenna explains the various activities that constitute the funeral ceremony of his maternal great-grandmother, popularly called Mama Nkwelle. Fortunately, she was a good woman, and everyone in the village feels so too about her. She died at the age of one hundred and two. Ikenna witnesses the display of love and unity among the people as many gifts are presented to Mama Nkwelle's family.

Here Comes our Bride is the story of a traditional wedding ceremony in Nigeria. It is set in Benin City, and narrated by Ekinadose, a young boy of about eight years old. He is fascinated by the word *ugieoromwen,* which means marriage, because it implies festivities, gifts, pleasant exchanges, new dresses, and so on. Ekinadose is eager to have his aunt, Efosa, married to Uncle Osaere, a medical doctor, who often visits her. Many of Ekinadose's friends have attended marriages and described the excitement of such an event to Ekinadose. He keenly desires to attend one, and Aunt Efosa and Uncle Osaere's event is promising.

Onyefulu carefully shows the various stages that are involved in the typical traditional marriage process in Nigeria. First, the groom's family members visit the bride's family to commence a relationship. Second, a list of things is given by the bride's family to the groom's to procure and deliver to the former on an agreed date. This is aimed at testing the ability of the groom and his family to care and provide for the bride and the children that she will deliver into the groom's family. The items listed are as varied as the implication of each of them.

Chidi Only Likes Blue is a story told by Nneka in a conversational mode with her brother, Chidi. The story reveals that Chidi only likes this colour because it is the colour of his best shirt and of the sky. Their mother senses that Chidi does not know the names of other colours, and this motivates Nneka to name and explain them, and how they apply in the Nigerian environment. She names specific colours, states how they are represented, and presents full visual support for each. The technique that Onyefulu deploys in the narration in *Chidi Only Likes Blue* is unique because throughout the story, Nneka is teaching Chidi the different colours. Even though Chidi has been exposed to several other colours, he still likes blue and prefers it to the other colours.

The story *Ogbo: Sharing Life in an African Village* expounds the concepts of unity, group-affinity, sharing, and helping, which characterize African and Nigerian life. The narrator, Obioma, a six-year old girl from Akwuzu village, explains that 'Ogbo', also called age group or age grade, comprises every person born within a five-year period, and membership is not defined by family background or status. This reality allows everyone to have a friend and belong to his/her *ogbo* all through life. Each *ogbo* has a responsibility to the community, and each member of an *ogbo* owes obligations to other members of his/her *ogbo*.

In *Emeka's Gift: An African Counting Story*, Onyefulu initiates a process of teaching children how to count. She does that skilfully in the course of narrating stories. For instance, Emeka is introduced as 'one boy who was not too small, but not too big either, set off to visit his grandmother in the next village. His name was Emeka' (1). A bold portrait of Emeka is also presented. The following series of stories narrate diverse issues concerning Emeka and what he is exposed to as he journeys to visit his grandmother.

Significantly, for each item that is counted from number one to number ten, Onyefulu offers a brief description of its origin, its essence among the people, its mode of operation or how the people regard or use it.

While *Emeka's Gift* teaches numbers, *A is for Africa* teaches the English alphabet. Just like the former, *A is for Africa* has each letter introducing a concept that is essential within the African and Nigerian environments. It offers a description of the notion and value that each alphabet represents. For instance:

> **Aa** is for Africa, a great continent of many countries and peoples. … They may dress differently and speak different languages, but Africa is home to them all. (1)

The critical context of Onyefulu's story-telling is as extensive as it is insightful. Apart from the collection of stories in *The Girl who Married a Ghost and Other Stories from Nigeria*, the seven other of her children's stories discussed here enjoy the support of her own family's snapshots. This technique is significant in different ways: it creates an immediate impression of what is being described; to use these informal photos is an effort to make the issue real, not merely to be imagined and represented; it convinces the reader about the authenticity of the concept. Onyefulu may have been compelled to do the above because of her task of depicting Nigeria to her foreign audience. It explains why she actually uses herself, her children, and her close relatives as characters in the stories. Thus, some of the stories enact real life events – such as the burial ceremony of Onyefulu's grandmother in *Saying Goodbye*. Through this technique, Onyefulu transcends the challenge of being inspired only from what she imagines, as she creates a confluence of the real and the imaginary in the course of one story.

She easily captures the interest of children by the titles she selects for some of her stories. The title 'A is for Africa' parodies the age-old English nursery rhyme 'A is for Apple…', and redirects it to a traditional African, and specifically Nigerian motif, by making each alphabet represent a value that is typically Nigerian. This engages the foreign reader, possibly inspires questions, and establishes awareness. In *Emeka's Gift*, the story tells of Emeka's attempt to find a gift to take to his grandmother, before he sets off to visit her in the next village. The author notes the features that Emeka encounters in the course of his walk through his village: some of these are two of Emeka's friends playing *okoso*, three women going to the market, four new brooms are kept for sale, five children are dressed up in large straw hats, and so on.

In the end, Emeka cannot find anything suitable for his grandmother, but the latter is elated to receive him as 'the best present of all!' (15). In this way, counting is fun, just as common traditional items found in a typical rural Nigerian community are highlighted. Prominent among the techniques used by Onyefulu in writing the stories is her effort to help the foreign reader to appreciate the items presented and also to try to call the names. In *Ogbo: Sharing Life in an African Village*, the narrator is the six-year-old girl, Obioma (pronounced o-bee-O-ma), who lives in a village in Nigeria called Awkuzu (aw-koo-zoo), and she belongs to an *ogbo* (or – Bo) or age group. Throughout the story, the author takes time to describe the pronunciation of the name of each person or an object that is introduced:

Obioma's big brother, Ifeanyi (ee-FAY-ny-ee)
Obioma's uncle, Chike (CHEE – kay)
Obioma's auntie, Ngozi (un-Go-zee)
Obioma's grandfather, Nnam Ochie (nam-OH-chee-eh)
The village *ilo*, (ee-lo) or village square
Ifeanyi's small drum, *ogene* (o-gay-nee)
Obioma's mother's *ogbo*, Obinwanne (o-BEEN-war-nay)

Onyefulu dexterously translates into the English language the name of each *ogbo* to show the import of each name to the specific group:

Obinwanne (o-BEEN-war-nay) (for women) – the kind heart of a sister
Igwebike (ee-WAY-BEE-kay) (for big men) – together is strength
Amuoko (ah – Moo-O-Koo) (for young men) – lighting a fire
Asammanuboko (a-sam-anoo-Bo-ko) – for elderly men – beauty

This technique of transcribing the sounds in a word to facilitate pronunciation also dominates *Chidi Only Likes Blue: An African Book of Colours*. The narrator is Nneka (Pronounced n-Ek-a), whose little brother is Chidi (CHEE-dee). In this story, Onyefulu both teaches the major colours as well as the features and values that they represent in traditional Nigerian life and community.

Nneka's Great Uncle is a chief chosen by the king, or *igwe* (ee-gweh). Only the chiefs are allowed to wear the special red caps. *Gari* (GAH-ree), the staple food of Nneka's people, is obtained from cassava roots. It is yellow. Green is the colour of leaves, particularly the leaves from the plant *akwukwouma* (ar-kwoo-kwo u-ma) which Nneka's mother's friend, Mrs. Okoli uses to wrap up foods like *moi-moi* (moy-moy) for cooking. By this means, the author introduces the colours, the object that portrays each colour, and how the object may be obtained as well as its significance in the community.

In several of the stories, Onyefulu offers an initial page titled 'Author's Note', 'A Note from the Author' or 'Introduction'. This serves as an introduction to the specific story, the idea(s) and impression(s) raised and the implications for Nigerian traditional life. In *Ogbo: Sharing Life in an African Village*, a map of Africa is also presented with Nigeria situated to show the location of the country in which the practice is observed. In the note, the author also makes important statements about herself and her motive. In *A is for Africa*, she explains: 'I wanted to capture what the people of Africa have in common: traditional village life, warm family ties, and above all, the hospitality for which Africans are famous. This book shows what Africa is to me ...' In *Saying Goodbye: A Special Farewell to Mama Nkwelle*, the Author's Note reads, 'I am proud to be able to tell my own children that I have had the privilege of seeing my grandmother dance ... I will always remember Mama Nkwelle and this book tells how we said goodbye to her.' In the Introduction to *Here Comes our Bride: An African Wedding Story*, Onyefulu comments on the Nigerian regard for marriage as not just about the union of two people, but of two families. That fact, on the one hand, prepares the reader for what to expect, and on the other, demonstrates the marked difference between how marriage is conceived in Nigeria and in other cultures of the world. In *Ikenna Goes to Nigeria*, a map of Africa is presented, and an enlarged map of Nigeria, with indications of the towns – Ikeja, Lagos, Nkwelle Onitsha, Oshogbo and Abuja – which Ikenna visited during his stay in Nigeria.

In the collection *The Girl who Married a Ghost and Other Stories from Nigeria*, the Introduction gives insight into each of the ten stories. The author explains:

> When we were children, in our village in Eastern Nigeria, I and my brothers and sisters were told lots of stories by our mother, grand-parents, aunts and uncles, and sometimes family friends. We were catapulted from our familiar surroundings into strange worlds where spirits ruled, and where animals could talk and reason...

The stories were all about moral values. They were certainly not about happy endings, although some were funny. Nevertheless I learnt a lot from them (6).

Onyefulu's words reveal that Nigerian stories are both entertaining and functional, and even though they are transmitted orally from generation to generation, their essence is well entrenched in the consciousness of the people. Recognizing that a dominant component of her audience is foreign, Onyefulu strives to have them identify with the concepts and ideas that each story depicts. In so doing, she teaches the major motifs and myths that abound in the Nigerian culture. She makes bold to have some characters often express themselves in Igbo, her mother tongue, followed by her explanation of the meaning in English.

It is vital to note Onyefulu's consciousness that good children's literature, as Mabel D. Segun affirms, 'arouses a child's imagination and extends his [or her] horizon, it gives him [or her] a knowledge of the past in relation to the present and imbues him [or her] with those ideals and values that are necessary for national development' (1992: 32). Also, to write effectively for children, the author has to use illustrations effectively because, as Elizabeth Ashimole affirms, '[the illustrations] breathe life into [the] words … [and] there exists a symbiotic relationship between them' (1992: 74). Through Onyefulu's expertise in the portrayal in each story studied in this paper, it is obvious that she overcomes the difficulties attributed to the writing of children's literature, for she is able to 'enter into the child's world and interact with him [or her] with understanding and lack of condescension…' Onyefulu is readily categorized among successful writers who have a childlike side to their personalities (Segun 1992: 32).

In conclusion, by writing the stories discussed above, Ifeoma Onyefulu not only performs a didactic role, like most writers of Nigerian literature: she effectively recreates Nigeria in the young minds of her children and her foreign audiences. Although her children are fairly well exposed to Nigeria, they are raised in a foreign culture. This is true for numerous other children living elsewhere, who have no idea about Nigeria and what it truly implies to be a Nigerian. This author recreates several aspects of Nigeria: the myths, the traditional funeral or marriage rites, the various cultural practices, the socio-political values, and the emerging new culture that reflects the contact of the foreign with the traditional culture. As Chinua Achebe asserts, in her role as writer of children's literature Onyefulu demonstrates that 'the [African] writer cannot expect to be excused from the task of re-education and regeneration that must be done. In fact, he [or she] should march right in front. For he [or she] is … the sensitive point of his [or her] community' (1990: 45). It is important that Onyefulu sustains her consciousness of Nigeria and the Igbo cultural values with which she was raised before she settled in the United Kingdom. This constant attachment with her past is the major feature that makes Onyefulu both outstanding and relevant. As she draws her materials from the Nigerian cosmology, she also teaches Nigerian values and contributes to the reorientation of children (and adults) on what constitutes the Nigerian reality.

WORKS CITED

Achebe, C. (1990). 'The Novelist as Teacher', in *Hopes and Impediments: Selected Essays.* New York: Anchor Books, 40-45.

Ashimole, E. O. (1992). 'Nigerian children's literature and the challenges of social change' in Ikonne, Oko and Onwudinjo, eds, *Children and Literature in Africa.* Ibadan: Heinemann.

Onyefulu, I. (2007). *Ikenna Goes to Nigeria.* London: Frances Lincoln Ltd.

———. (2004). *Here Comes our Bride.* London: Frances Lincoln Ltd.

———. (2002). *The Girl who Married a Ghost and Other Tales from Nigeria.* London: Frances Lincoln Ltd.

———. (2002). *Saying Goodbye: A Special Farewell to Mama Nkwelle.* London: Frances Lincoln Ltd.

———. (1997). *Ogbo: Sharing Life in an African Village.* London Frances Lincoln Ltd.

———. (1997). *Emeka's Gift: an African Counting Story.* London: Frances Lincoln Ltd.

———. (1997). *Chidi Only likes Blue.* London: Frances Lincoln Ltd.

———. (1993). *A is for Africa.* London: Frances Lincoln Ltd.

Segun, M. D. (1992). 'Children's Literature in Africa: Problems and Prospects', *Children and Literature in Africa.* Ikonne, Oko and Onwudinjo, eds. Ibadan: Heinemann. 24-42.

Utley, O. (2008). 'Keeping the Tradition of African Story-telling', Retrieved 3/7/2014. http://teachers.yale.edu/curriculum/viewer/initiative.

Search for Identity

The Journey Quest
in West African Folktales

YVONNE E. McINTOSH

The theme of the journey quest permeates world literature. It is especially prevalent in oral literature: such orature (Chinweizu 1988) is an essential part of the West African tradition: it permeates the culture by influencing religion, dance, music and various aspects of socioeconomic realms of life. The main goals of oral literature are to pass down the history of an ethnic group, teach its moral values and the importance of group solidarity. Griots, among others, transmit their cultural traditions from generation to generation and traces of these traditions are still apparent in literature. Literary genres of orature include poetry, proverbs, songs, epics, folktales, legends, riddles and myths. This article will focus on selected folktales from West Africa and the importance of the journey quest encountered in them.

The theme of the journey in folktales is one way by which cultural values are transmitted to children. Whether the hero embarks on this quest voluntarily or not, it leads him in search of a seemingly unattainable task. However, the hero often succeeds in finding not only the sought-after object but also conquers fear and other obstacles which lead to the discovery of his or her identity.

As a basis of analysis, the article uses the stages of the heroic quest outlined in Joseph Campbell's *The Hero with a Thousand Faces,* published in 1973. According to Campbell, these stages are Departure, Initiation and the Return. Applying these steps helps to unlock the mystery of the journey quest in certain West African folktales, enabling greater understanding of various aspects of West African culture and heritage.

Four folktales are examined to this end. 'Le Pagne noir' (The Black Cloth), by Bernard Dadié of Côte d'Ivoire, illustrates the journey quest of a young girl who is sent to accomplish an impossible

31

task by her stepmother. '*Le Cercueil de Maka-Kouli*' (The Casket of Maka-Kouli) is told by the Senegalese writer, Birago Diop. A young man strives to reclaim his birthright, stolen by a family 'friend'. The third tale is '*L'Héritage*' (The Inheritance) by Birago Diop, which recounts the journey quest of three brothers searching for the meaning of their dying father's last gift. The fourth and final folktale, also by Birago Diop, '*La Cuiller Sale*' (The Dirty Spoon) tells of the journey of a young girl, Binta, as she tries to satisfy the whims of a menacing stepmother.

In '*Le Pagne noir*', Aïwa's mother dies in childbirth. Soon after, her father remarries. Aïwa is a beautiful and happy young girl whose singing and beauty charm everyone except her stepmother. Her stepmother searches for her and tries in many ways to break Aïwa's spirit but she never succeeds. For example, Aïwa is given the most difficult tasks: she is the first to get up in the morning and the last to go to bed. Her stepmother becomes increasingly enraged by her beauty, her lovely voice, her never complaining, and her constant smile. All of these attributes irritate the stepmother tremendously, until one day, she conceives a plot that she thinks will get rid of the girl forever. She gives Aïwa an impossible task: she hands her a black garment and commands her to make it become as white as porcelain. So Aïwa departs, as would the hero, to do a seemingly impossible task.

In '*La Cuiller Sale*', Binta also deals with the wrath of an unscrupulous stepmother. The stepmother treats Binta horribly, beating her and yelling at her. Binta's father is intimidated by his wife and offers his daughter no relief from the torments she suffers. Binta does all the household chores while her stepsister, Penda, spends her time doing her makeup and playing with her toys. Binta sometimes escapes from the house to go to her mother's grave, praying and pleading for her mother to help her out of her dire situation. Finally, the stepmother can no longer tolerate Binta. When the latter neglects to wash a wooden spoon properly, she is thrown out of the house and ordered to go and wash the dirty spoon in the sea of Danyane. Binta has no idea where this sea is located and her stepmother refuses all help.

In the tales '*Le Cercueil de Maka-Kouli*' and '*L'Héritage*' one finds two instances where sons either must fight for their inheritance or must learn the significance of their inheritance. '*Le Cercueil de Maka-Kouli*' begins with an exposition of Demba Sall's life. Demba Sall, a devout Muslim, is a dedicated friend and family man.

Realizing that his days are numbered, he wishes to secure the well-being of his family. Because his son, Seydou, is too young to receive his inheritance, Demba entrusts his son's birthright to a long-time friend, Malick Gaye, with the understanding that Malick would give his son's belongings to him once he comes of age. However, Demba starts to feel uneasy about his friend's trustworthiness so he leaves written instructions about his wishes with his wife, Fatou. Shortly after he dies, Demba's premonition comes true, for Malick keeps the son's inheritance. Two years after Seydou comes of age, Fatou informs her son that it is time he claimed his birthright. Therefore, Seydou goes to Malick's home to claim his belongings but Malick insists that he is the rightful heir. Upon hearing this, Seydou shows Malick the written proof that he is indeed the true heir. Unfortunately, the will falls to the ground and Malick quickly throws it into the fire.

After this incident, Seydou goes before the chief of the village to accuse Malick Gaye of stealing his birthright. The chief of the village of Maka-Kouli is also the village's spiritual leader, renowned for his wise and just decisions. During the trial, both Seydou and Malick recount their versions of the events before the chief and the village, after which the two men notice a large casket set before them. The chief instructs them as to what they must do in order to prove who is the legitimate heir of Demba Sall. The two households, that of Seydou and his mother, and of Malick and his wife Oumou must, in separate turns, make a circle around the village while carrying the casket. Thus both men are sent on a journey to accomplish a seemingly impossible task.

In 'L'Héritage' three brothers must work together to solve the mystery of their father's last wishes. The first paragraph of the story sheds light on what the *héritage* or 'inheritance' will be. The father has led a life of hard work, wisdom and good deeds – the benchmarks of a productive life. Before he dies, Samba, the father, shows his three sons, Momar, Birame and Moussa, their inheritance which is contained in three *outres*, or goatskin leather bottles. The sons, one by one, arbitrarily pick one of the three containers. After the mourning period has passed, the sons open their bottles. Momar discovers only sand. Birame finds pieces of cord in his. Moussa finds nuggets of gold and gold powder. Moussa does not understand why he, the youngest, would have received the gold. Momar, the eldest, has no idea why he received the container of sand. Birame, the middle son, reminds them that their father did not have time to tell them who was to receive which container – they were picked out randomly. Thus begins their journey to discover the meaning of their inheritance. They go to the oldest man in the village who tells them that Kém Tanne, the wisest man in the region, will be able to tell them the meaning of their inheritance. As in the case of Aïwa, Binta and Seydou, the three brothers' journey is by necessity and a resolution seems impossible.

Thus, all of the heroes commence the first part of the quest: the Departure. The first stage of the departure is the 'Call to Adventure'. This is the first segment of the mythological journey. Typically, according to Campbell, it 'signifies that destiny has summoned the hero . . . to a zone unknown . . . maybe a distant land, a forest, a kingdom underground . . . but it is always a place of strangely fluid and polymorphous beings, unimaginable torments, superhuman deeds and impossible delight' (1973: 58). Aïwa's and Binta's call to adventure came when their respective stepmothers gave them an impossible task: Aïwa must have the black cloth turn as white as porcelain and Binta must go to a far-away land to wash a dirty spoon. They will both face unknown zones and torments. Seydou and the three brothers were also called to embark upon an unknown adventure in order to receive their inheritance.

Another stage of the Departure is receiving 'Supernatural Aid'. For those who accept the journey, they have 'a protective figure who provides the adventurer with amulets against the dragon forces he is about to pass' (1973: 69). Aïwa is protected not only by her departed mother but also by the various creatures that help her along the way. Binta is first assisted by various creatures she encounters along her journey. Then she is aided by an old woman, *la Mère des bêtes* 'the mother of the beasts', who possesses supernatural powers. This woman tells her that she has arrived at the sea of Danyane: Binta will now be able to accomplish her task. Seydou is accompanied by his mother who comforts him and gives him counsel along the journey. Malick is accompanied by his wife who also attempts to help him on his way. Upon their journey to find Kém Tanne, who possesses supernatural powers, the brothers encounter many strange and extraordinary figures. Kém Tanne and these supernatural beings 'represent the benign, protecting power of destiny . . .' (1973: 72).

The next stage of the Departure is 'the Crossing of the first threshold'. The hero must pass over this to continue the journey – even if the first obstacle is life-threatening. Campbell emphasizes that '[t]he adventure is always and everywhere a passage beyond the veil of the known into the unknown; the powers that watch at the boundary are dangerous; to deal with them is risky; yet for anyone with competence and courage the danger fades' (1973: 82). Aïwa's first challenge arises when she comes upon a stream. She plunges the black cloth in the water but it refuses to get wet. She does not get discouraged, but continues her journey. Binta encounters many strange creatures but her kindness conquers her fears and she succeeds in finding the old lady who helps her to find her way back home. Seydou and his mother lift the casket and begin to circle the village. However, midway they become exhausted because it is so heavy, and they have to sit down and rest. But this does not deter them: they continue the test.

The brothers witness many strange things along their journey to find Kém Tanne who will, in turn, unlock the secrets of what they saw along their journey. For instance, they see a fat bull, covered with sores. This represents a man of honour who, despite all his trials and tribulations, maintains his good character. The sores (the bad things in his life) cover his body but do not sully his good self. The brothers also notice a three legged *biche* 'doe' on their trip, but they fail to capture it. This doe represents the world and life that man is constantly pursuing until the day he dies. Each hero crosses this threshold of the unknown and succeeds in getting to the next step of the journey quest.

This step entails the hero entering into 'the belly of the whale': he must go inward to be born again, symbolically, a 'life-renewing act', in Campbell's terms (1973: 91-2). The heroes go inward in that they proceed into unknown territory. Seydou's entire journey takes place in a forest. As for Aïwa, during her months and months of searching for water to wet the cloth, one day she is enveloped by a forest where she is pushed about and stumbles as she makes her way. After this ordeal she leaves the forest and comes upon a clearing where she sees a banana tree, overhanging a pool of very clear water. She plunges her cloth into it and finally the cloth is soaked. Binta journeys in a strange land seeking the mysterious sea. Searching for Kém Tanne, the three brothers journey far and encounter many strange creatures.

After the departure, in Campbell's analysis, the second stage of the hero's adventure is the 'Initiation': the stage where the hero must survive a succession of trials (1973: 97). Shortly after the departure of the protagonists, they undergo various trials. When the casket becomes too heavy for Seydou and his mother, they must rest before continuing their journey. The three brothers face many unknown situations that they cannot explain, but they continue their search for the one who can unlock the secret meaning of their inheritance. Aïwa walks for months, encountering gigantic vultures, chimpanzees who talk, ants who salute each other, as well as facing her ordeal in the forest, but she does not abandon her journey. At each step, she continues on her way with a smile on her face. Binta encounters many challenges and dangers but she never forgets to be kind and gracious to all the beings she meets along the way.

On the road of trials and tribulations, the hero must make 'atonement with the father' (1973: 130). This stage is difficult, for the hero must abandon the attachment to ego itself. Campbell comments, 'One must have a faith that the father is merciful and then a reliance on that mercy. It is in this ordeal, that the hero may derive hope and assurance from the helpful female figure' (1973: 130) Near the end of the tale, Aïwa sings another song to her mother for help, and is rewarded Her mother appears, takes away the black cloth and gives her a white one – a cloth that is as white as porcelain. Similarly, Binta meets an old mysterious woman who lives beside the sea that she went searching for, in order to wash her spoon clean. The old woman also bestows many riches on Binta for her kindness and humility. During their rest periods from carrying the heavy casket, Seydou asks for his mother's forgiveness for allowing the crucial evidence to be destroyed by Malick, and reveals all that happened at his adversary's home. It is through this confession to his mother that Seydou will be vindicated. The brothers journey on together to unlock the mystery of the containers they inherited from their father. They are rewarded for their struggle and are told the meaning of all they have seen during their journey. During this stage of the initiation, the child grows up and becomes an adult. He must go through the trials and tribulations in order to conquer his innermost fears.

In the next stage of the initiation, the hero comes to the realization that 'instead of thinking only of himself, the individual becomes dedicated to the whole of *his* society' (1973: 156). Rebirth makes us more than what we were (1973: 162). Seydou thinks of his mother's grief and asks for forgiveness, thus, he becomes an adult. He is thinking of someone other than himself. Aïwa pleads and sings imploring chants to her mother asking for help, realizing that she cannot succeed on her own power and strength. Binta does not capitulate during her journey to find the far away sea. She continues through her trials and tribulations and maintains her generous spirit. The brothers continue their long journey in search of the wisdom of an elder and never doubt that they will succeed in their task. All of the heroes break through their personal limitations, thus, growing and developing spiritually. The many obstacles and trials help the hero to conquer his fears and his limited horizons, going forward to the 'ever-expanding realization' (1973: 190). This is the ultimate gift.

The third and final stage of the adventure of the hero is the 'Return'. As Campbell explains, 'When the hero's quest has been accomplished, through penetration to the source, or through the grace of some male or female, human or animal, the adventurer still must return with his life-transmitting trophy' (1973: 193). Though some heroes refuse to return, our heroes do indeed return. Seydou returns to the village to face the chief's ultimate decision. Aïwa returns home after her task has been completed. Giving her stepmother one of the white burial robes of her departed mother brings an end to her suffering. Binta returns home with riches from her journey and is indeed a success in the eyes of her former tormentor. The brothers are informed of the meaning of their containers: there is nothing mysterious inside them. Moussa has the gold but he cannot eat it. The sand of Momar represents all the land and the crops. Birame's pieces of cord symbolise that he can have everything that is attached to a cord, for example, the herd of cattle. However, none of the items they have inherited is worth anything without the other, for they must work together to be prosperous. The wise man tells them to return home and hang the containers in their rightful place, and to not forget anything that they have seen or heard on their journey. They must continue the legacy of their father.

There is then a 'magic flight' home (1973: 196). This final stage of the adventure is supported by all the powers of a supernatural patron. All the heroes return home successfully. Aïwa presents one of the white burial garments of her mother to a stupefied stepmother. Binta lays out many riches for her family; riches bestowed upon her by the old woman who rewarded her for her kindness. Seydou's return is widely anticipated: he completed his circular or perfect journey of knowledge around the village where his truth and Malick's lies are uncovered, for there was a man hidden inside the casket who heard Seydou's truth and Malick's lies. Now the wise village chief blesses Seydou's truth, and he is reinstated as the rightful heir. Malick's lies were not blessed; he has fled the community. The brothers realize the meaning of their inheritance through the wisdom of Kém Tanne. They return home and work together successfully.

Through the boon or gift, the hero restores the world. Seydou receives his inheritance. The brothers have understood the importance of the family. As for Aïwa and Binta, they are released from their stepmothers' tyranny.

'The crossing of the return threshold' is another stage of the Return. The hero's return is described as a coming out of a supernatural zone. As Campbell comments, 'Nevertheless, and here is the great key to the understanding of myth and symbol – the two kingdoms are actually one' (1973: 217). The supernatural world and the real world are one and the same. Thus the voyages of the heroes were journeys of self-realization or self-knowledge. Their journeys also involved searching for a token or object. The heroes brought back with them not just a casket, a white cloth, a clean spoon and the meaning of the containers, but their journeys also brought back the power of the truth. This truth not only helped them, but was in turn generated throughout the whole community.

The 'Freedom to Live' is the last segment of the 'Return'. It is evident that the various trials are symbolic of life's journey: it is a quest that helps an individual to become self-aware and to become cognizant that there is a greater power.

In conclusion, the adventure of the hero leads to the knowledge that one must go beyond one's limitations. One must go pass the fear of the unknown, step out in faith and trust that a power greater than the self will be present throughout difficult times and ensure a safe passage home. This knowledge is very empowering and helps in attaining goals that were thought to be unreachable. These African folktales are the vehicles that illuminate this path of self-realization. Their stories signify universal truths are passed on to children through the lessons imparted by oral literature.

The journey quest is a device which the storyteller uses, so that the reader of the tales or the spectator of the oral story may discover his or her own identity, achieve self-realization, or find a reason for being. The search is not really for the 'lost' object: the quest helps one become a better person by casting off the vestiges of one's own limitations.

The mythic journey is a narrative device to teach children how to face the future – the unknown – with the confidence that finding the full self will, in the end, help to improve one's community, and society as a whole. These are some of the lessons imparted by West African folktales. And in the words of a traditional West African saying, 'I put these words into the universe so they may spread throughout humanity.'

WORKS CITED

Campbell, Joseph (1973). *The Hero with a Thousand Faces*. Princeton NJ: Bollingen Series XVII.

Chevrier, Jacques (1986). *L'Arbre à Palabres: Essai sur les contes et récits traditionnels d'Afrique Noire*. Paris: Hatier.

Chinweizu (1988). *Voices from Twentieth-Century Africa: Griots and Towncriers*. London: Faber and Faber.

Dadié, Bernard B. (1970). 'Le Pagne noir', in *Le Pagne noir, contes africains*. Paris: Présence Africaine.

Diop, Birago (1973). 'Le Cercueil de Maka-Kouli', in *Contes et lavanes*. Paris: Présence Africaine.

———. (1969). 'La Cuiller Sale', in *Les Nouveaux Contes d'Amadou Koumba*. Paris: Présence Africaine.

———. (1969) 'L'Héritage', in *Les Contes d'Amadou Koumba*. Paris: Présence Africaine.

Trends in Ghanaian Children's Literature

FAITH BEN-DANIELS

The art of story-telling is widespread in Africa and traditional folktales are found all over the continent's diverse cultures. Indeed, folktale culture forms part of African night entertainment in the rural communities. Interesting characters feature in almost every tale. For instance, there are tricksters such as the spider, Ananse, among the tales of the Akan of Ghana. The tortoise, the hare and the rabbit are also tricksters in other parts of Africa. Folktales have been the embodiment of entertainment and education for Ghanaian and other children across Africa.

However, there is a need to investigate the relevance and role of these folktale characters as well as their influence and presence in the entertainment and education of the Ghanaian child. In a society that is gradually moving away from the traditional performance art of story-telling, it is important to explore current literatures for children to identify writers who write purposefully for the contemporary Ghanaian child.

In his novel, *First Term Surprises*, Lawrence Darmani depicts the lifestyle of children in second cycle institutions. He writes a series that follows the three terms of the Ghanaian educational calendar. The novel breaks down the school activities as the writer weaves his story around the curriculum for each term. Although it is a work of fiction, it establishes an authentic storehouse of information reflecting the educational and social life of the Ghanaian teenager in school. In Ruby Yayra Goka's novel, *The Lost Treasure*, the author takes young readers on a journey to a different part of Ghana where the child is not in school but engaged in illegal work. Again, a work of fiction passes down authentic information inbetween the lines of artistic creativity. On the other hand, Meshack Asare's novel, *The Cross Drums*, intertwines traditional myths and folktale cultures from the North of Ghana to tell a story that includes child heroes of whom the Ghanaian child would be proud.

These examples indicate the existence of a kind of literature that meets the needs of Ghanaian children. However, one must delve into the various types of supplementary materials used in teaching literature to the Ghanaian child. It is equally important to draw the attention of educators and all education stakeholders to the imperative of including relevant Ghanaian literature in mainstream curricula by showing the lack thereof and the factors that perpetuate it. The following is an account of such an attempt.

In order to achieve the above-mentioned goal, books written by the authors cited above were read in order to judge the relevance of the material to children's literature. Two schools were used as case studies for determining the extent to which Ghanaian children's literature is employed in schools. The first school, Adankwame District Assembly School, was chosen because it is a state-run school in a rural location. The choice of the second, Pentecost Preparatory School, depended on the fact that it represents privately-run educational establishments in urban areas. This particular school not only seeks to attract the children of rich parents; the proprietors also have in mind attracting middle-income earners and working-class families.

In Ghana, the traditional art of story-telling has paved the way for contemporary children's literature. Writers directly or indirectly adapt from the repertoire of traditional tales for retelling in print, with or without colourful illustrations, depending on the target group. The group of Ghanaian writers studied here is devoted to writing for children of all ages, but this has not always been the case for Ghanaian children's literature. In its present state, this kind of publishing has come a long way.

Over the years, as culture evolved, the art of traditional story-telling by the fireside at night, whether related by grandmothers, mothers, elders or peers, has gradually lost its place. This could be partly explained by urban migration as a result of economic and social challenges. In contemporary Ghana, more people are migrating from the rural communities in search of jobs and basic social amenities that are absent outside cities. Economic challenges that render it more difficult to provide the basic essentials for family put a lot of stress on the average Ghanaian. Thus, traditional story-telling has gradually become a luxury. This notwithstanding, there is an urgent need for children to hear stories, which serve as both entertainment and education.

Ghanaian writers have emerged intent on keeping the art of story-telling for children alive. Aba Brew-Hammond, author of *A Boy Called Wiser-Than-You*, *The Rabbit and His Singing Hoes*, and *Why God Created Everybody* counts among these writers. She publishes paperback folktales from the North, Upper-West and Upper East Regions of Ghana, retold for children. Her migration of traditional folktales from their rural hearth, where performance is physical, spontaneous and affective, to the written form retains two essential functions: entertainment and education for the child. In her story, *A Boy Called Wiser-Than-You* (2007), entertainment is achieved through the actions of *Wiser-Than-You* in the narrative. For instance, when the chief who dislikes the boy sends for his mother and gives her guinea corn with order to brew a local alcoholic beverage, *pito*, within a day, it is *Wiser-Than-You* who saves his mother. He accomplishes his task by going to the chief's palace to plant some gourd seeds. When the chief confronts him, he explains:

> "I know you are very wise and everything about you is extraordinary. That is why I have come to plant my gourd seeds here so that they will grow fast, bear fruits for me to cut, prepare and dry, all by the end of today when they are required for use." "Are you crazy?" the chief asked him. "How is that possible? A gourd plant needs at least a year to mature and be made into calabashes. Don't you know that?"

As the chief insists that it is not possible, Wiser-Than-You asks, "Sir, why then did you ask my mother to brew pito in one day?" (2007:3). The boy's question draws the chief's attention to his innate intelligence and also to the fact that the task assigned to the boy's mother is impossible. Throughout the story, the chief tries to outwit Wiser-Than-You but always fails, until the end, when his hatred for the boy causes the death of his own son.

The Ghanaian child learns a moral at the end of this story: one cannot always have one's way. Consequently, there should be mutual respect for one another; also, wisdom is not the sole preserve of the elderly. A child can also have it. One also needs to accept the fact that there will always be others better and smarter; jealousy must be avoided. Instead, we must learn to appreciate those among us with extraordinary abilities and help nurture them. The moral lessons highlighted are discussed at the end of the story in the same way found in traditional oral narrative performances. For Aba Brew-Hammond, the migration of traditional story-telling into print form must retain the original purpose, that is, instruction and entertainment.

The Senegalese griot, D'Jimo Kouyate, in his essay 'The Role of the Griot', explains the griot's function as a traditional instructor:

> In the evening, after dinner, the stories that are usually told by the griot are called *tahlio* (tah-lee-OH), which means it is not reality but an imagined event between humans and animals and some kind of spirit. These are the stories that are told for entertainment. A griot has special ways of telling these stories so that they are very entertaining, even though the griot's main intention is not to entertain but to teach the people to know themselves. (1989: 180)

D'Jimo Kouyate's explanation above echoes the instructional aspect of African story-telling performances, that is, the teaching of moral lessons. This important function is not lost on Aba Brew-Hammond who adapts it in her stories for children. In *The Boy Called Wiser-Than-You*, as in many others, she keeps alive traditional story-telling for contemporary Ghanaian children and contributes to Ghanaian children's literature.

Another writer who migrates traditional folktales and myths into print form is Meshack Asare, a German-based Ghanaian author who has written many stories for children. His works include *Sosu's Call* (1997), *Nana's Son* (2000), *Meliga's Day* (2000), and *The Cross Drums* (2008). In creating these narratives, the writer integrates traditional story-telling elements into the creative process. For instance, in *The Cross Drums*, Asare introduces his young readers to his fusion of traditional tales and the ethnographic history of Northern Ghana.

The story evolves from a traditional tale of the history of enmity and later friendship between twin villages. Hostility which originated with adults is resolved by the love between two young boys, Atimbilla and Meliga, both princes. Through the help of a hermit dwelling in the nearby caves, the boys become proud owners of a set of twin drums. It is with the aid of these instruments that the conflict between their twin villages reaches a resolution. After a conflict between the two villages that leads to the loss of lives, the boys fail to see each other for a long time. Atimbilla misses his friend. He begins to play his drum and is happy when he receives a response from Meliga:

Belem-bebem! Belem-bebem! Belem-Bebem! Like floodwater that carries everything along, it all rushed out of him in the voice of the drum: the fields where they graze their animals and play, the rocks and trees and bushes. It was the voice of the air and winds and storms, of thunder and lightning; of goats and sheep and squirrels... It echoed the happiness that was cast freely into the air like birdsong, for all to share and happiness too that had turned sour from being trapped in the hearts of those who feared one another. It echoed how much he missed Billa, his friend. (2008: 92-93)

The two boys finally meet in the field separating their two villages. They are followed by children from both places as they play their drums and dance. Soon they are followed by adults, and finally, by the chiefs, of the twin villages:

The enemy chief took a stride closer, the dagger glinting in his hand. Even children were still and adults held their breaths. Then something happened. The enemy chief sheathed his dagger again, raised it over his head and tossed it far behind him. He did not look where it fell. The smiling chief Abuguri searched under his smock and brought out a dagger. He too threw it far behind him...the two chiefs continued towards each other until they met. Then they stopped and looked straight into each other's eyes. They were like that for a few moments before Billa's father, the enemy chief Akuguri, spoke: "If the elephant cannot dance, they go to the mice and learn from them", he said. "Now you and I must learn to dance", said chief Abuguri, Meliga's father... (2008: 102-4)

This story not only refurbishes pieces of traditional retellings from Northern Ghana; it also teaches the child through a moral lesson at the end of the story. The story exposes the child to the various ethnic conflicts that plague the Northern, Upper East and Upper West parts of Ghana. After reading this story, the child appreciates the virtues of love, peace, unity and tolerance for others. The child understands in simple terms the role of these virtues in the creation of a homogenous society.

The reading of the story itself also provides entertainment for the child. In addition, it showcases the purity and innocence of childhood. After reading this story and discovering that it is actually an adaptation of the mythical history of a group of people from Northern Ghana, a child feels proud that others like him or her were responsible for the peace that the two communities finally enjoy after years of fighting each other. The figure of the child as an important member of society who has a role to play is highlighted by Asare.

Indeed, Aba Brew-Hammond and Meshack Asare offer the consolation that although the popularity of the oral narrative performance culture has diminished, they are adapting its elements as well as repertoires for print, which means easy access to children. While Aba Brew-Hammond makes a direct adaptation of traditional folktales, Asare's approach is rather indirect, as seen in *The Cross Drums*, where he recreates his own version of the story by the fusion of more than one traditional myth from the North.

However, this does not mean that all writers of children's literature in Ghana are adapting from traditional folktales. Others are educating and entertaining children through creating stories based on the experience of the contemporary Ghanaian child. An example is Ruby Yayra Goka, whose fiction for children includes: *The Mystery of the Haunted House* (2011), *The Lost Royal Treasure* (2012), *When the Shackles Fall*, (2013), and *A Gift for Fafa* (2013). Ruby uses Ghanaian topography coupled with her observation of the contemporary Ghanaian child in her stories. She also creates serial characters found in all her stories. In so doing, she creates child heroes and heroines for the Ghanaian child, who represent their youthful expectations. For instance, in the story, *The Lost Royal Treasure*, we encounter serial characters, Koku, Kakra and Payin. In this story they are out on an adventure with an uncle, Professor Kumah, engaged in an archeological expedition in the Bepoase area, in the Western Region of Ghana.

This region is blessed with the most valuable natural mineral resource, gold. It is home to big mining companies such as AngloGold, Gold Fields and Newmont. In the story, Ruby presents Bepoase realistically, as a place rich in gold, but the actual social issues affecting mining towns and villages are also exposed. One example of such social issues is the use of child labour by illegal miners, locally referred to as 'Galamsey' operators, who employ children to help in the sifting of debris containing gold. This is a lucrative business for both the children and their parents. Thus, children living in these areas prefer going to the goldmines than to school. Ruby clearly shows this in her story through the young boy, Yaw.

A typical case is the little town of Tontonkrom, located in the Bekwai district of the Asante Region of Ghana. This is a mining town teeming with small-scale miners, mostly Chinese and illegal workers from the indigenes of the area. A visit to the town reveals that children as young as seven are absent from class, in search of gold. During a discussion with one of the inhabitants of the town, a young wife of one of the chiefs of the town named Juliet, she was asked why children were allowed to mine. She responded:

> Why waste time in school when you are going to school because of money? Once you search one pit, you can make a thousand cedis by the close of day. Is that not the reason why we are going to school? For money? (Tontonkrom, 14 February 2014)

It is obvious that with this mind-set, it is quite challenging to convince children to remain in school. Juliet gives an example of a teacher who was posted to the town and who himself abandoned the classroom in pursuit of gold. She explained, "He is now into Galamsey and making it big time!" (Tontonkrom, 14 February 2014).

Juliet's response confirms the facts woven into Ruby's fiction: these are pertinent issues that Ghanaians grapple with daily as a nation. Ruby identifies the role of children in this issue, weaving it beautifully as a theme in her narrative. We meet the young boy, Yaw, who is a native of Bepoase, and in search of his brother whom he believes has gone to Accra. When he meets Koku and Kakra for the first time and tells them of his missing brother, Koku suggests he should seek the help of his teacher to report his brother as missing. However, the reader learns:

> Yaw sneered, "I don't go to school." Koku and Kakra look at each other in surprise. He looked about a year older than they. Why was he not in school?" Kakra asked what they were both thinking, "Why not?" The boy removed his wallet from his back pocket. It was stuffed full of fifty cedis notes. "Why would I want to go and waste my time in school when I can be working?" (2012:. 74 -75)

Koku and Kakra are curious as to what kind of job the young Yaw is doing, so Yaw takes them to his work place:

> Koku was not sure if this was the same river they'd encountered in the mountains. But there were fewer rocks and lots of pebbles and sand. Uprooted palm trees, bushes, and heaps of red earth were scattered along the bank. Many pits and trenches had been dug. The water here was dirty and brown. Groups of men, women and children were spread all over its banks... some of the children were carrying the sand and pebbles from mounds to the shallower end of the river where the water was clearer... some of the children, were naked with others clad only in shorts or singlets. (2012:76)

As a child reads this story, he would identify himself or herself in it. For instance, Koku and his friends living outside Accra are a representation of Ghanaian children living in the new developing communities bordering the capital's metropolis and other urban areas. Simple activities such as hunting for fruits, riding bicycles along dusty roads and playing football in the local community pitch are brought into the story. The young reader in Accra, and other metropolitan areas in Ghana will recognize the similarity of the characters. Besides, he or she becomes aware of another child who lives in the rural communities in Ghana and works instead of going to school. Likewise, the child in a rural mining community identifies himself or herself with the story in appreciation of the circumstances. Education and entertainment take place just as in traditional folktale. There is education in the information that the writer presents to the child about the geographical location of Bepoase and its wealth in gold. There is entertainment in the enjoyment of reading the book and the suspense it creates, besides benefiting from the relevant educational information.

So far, we have seen evidence of writers writing for children. However, after writing, the target audience or market must have access to the work. This presents its own challenges to writers in Ghana. The distribution of books in Ghana is increasingly becoming problematic. In the past, one effective means of distribution was through schools. A book distributor and publisher, Florence Agyemang, explained that writers and publishers get their books into the hands of children through school authorities. The process involves approaching the school authority, preferably, the head of the school, with samples of the books, and to market them as supplementary readers. The head takes his time to go through the books, with the assistance of some of his teaching staff. Once they have vetted the contents of the book and deemed it fit for consumption by the pupils, or students, they inform the writer or publisher that they are ready for business. Normally, the books should not be more than the equivalent of US$2.00 (six Ghana cedis). This is the standard price for schools. However, some institutions decide to add a little to it for profit, so they sell the books to the children for a slightly higher price, between eight and ten Ghana cedis. Furthermore, the distributor or publisher pays the school 12% of the proceeds. This practice has helped to get more books into the hands of pupils as well as second-cycle students. For instance, school children now know of authors such as Maamle

Wolo, Irene Matie-Bates, Lawrence Darmani, among many others writing in this field.

However, due to the present government's political campaign to increase educational quality and access, there has been considerable government interference in this sector. Monitoring teams have been set up, whose duty is to visit schools to investigate fee break-downs. As a result, those with a long list of billing items are penalized. The Heads are either asked to withdraw their services voluntarily or involuntarily. In order to save their jobs, they have in turn started to cut down on their billing items. Of course, one major area on the list that suffers the most relates to supplementary readers. This is affecting the distribution of literature to pupils and second cycle students.

Another area of concern is the book purchasing culture of parents and guardians in Ghana. For instance, in government schools, text books and supplementary readers are provided by government from kindergarten right up to junior high school. As a result, the practice of parents and guardians buying books for their wards is almost non-existent. Parents and guardians consider this purchasing to be the government's responsibility. However, when the government provides the books, parents have to come and sign for the collection of the books by their wards. This is done to cater for any financial obligation that might arise if the books given to the child are destroyed. According to agreement the child must read and then return the books at the end of each term. Parents see this as a huge responsibility that they are not prepared to shoulder. They do not come forward to guarantee for their wards and thus, the children do not receive the books. The books are also not properly kept by the school because there are no libraries. At Adankwame District Assembly Primary School, they are stored in the backroom of the Headmistress' office because parents refuse to come and stand as guarantors for their children's borrowings. The parents claim they do not want to do so because the children will either tear the books apart or not read them at all (Adankwame, 18 February 2014). Asked what measures have been taken to ensure that the books get to the children, the Headmistress replied:

> We talk to the parents during PTA meetings, but very few step forward to guarantee for their children. The fear that the kids will destroy the books and they will have to pay for the damages makes them scared. This whole thing boils down to poverty. You are thinking of what to eat, why waste money on story books? (Adankwame, 18 February 2014)

Three parents of children at the school were asked to explain their reluctance in this matter. The first parent, a farmer by profession replied:

> My children are very stubborn. In the evenings they do not stay at home. They are always going to watch movies. If I guarantee for them, they will not even read the books! (Adankwame, 18 February 2014)

The second parent, a single mother replied:

> If I take the books for my children, and they destroy them, where am I going to get the money to pay for the damage? (Adankwame 18 February 2014)

The answer of the third parent, a trader, was:

> My children will not read the books. They will end up destroyed and I will have to pay for the damage, so why bother? (Adankwame, 18 February 2014)

All these responses reveal an economic reason why the parents refuse to guarantee for their children to borrow the books: the financial implication if the books are damaged.

For the sake of balance, I also visited Pentecost Preparatory School. This school falls under the category of privately-owned International Schools. I chose this school because it also falls under the category of Second Grade International Schools where the majority of the children are from working-class families and do not attend government schools. The school did not have a collection of supplementary readers provided by government, but they had a library that was scantily stocked with story books and text books from Europe and the Americas. There was not a single work by an African writer on the shelves. The library itself was in a very bad state. In fact, it has not been in regular use. Some of the children I spoke to who had the privilege of reading story books were more familiar with *The Famous Five* than with Ruby Goka's adventure series for teenagers or Meshack Asare's books for children. And they came by such books just by chance. In fact, the room was in a state of disarray and it was obvious that the place was not in regular use. The books on the shelves, which were all foreign, were very old editions.

The explanation is social. The education of children in private schools is biased towards Western formal educational models. After all, it is the only way to ensure an increase of student population and make money. Consequently, the schools are advertised as using the Froebel and Montessori models which go with reading more Western than Ghanaian or African materials.

My interaction with the two groups revealed several issues about the government's role in the final decision of which books get into the hands of children. First, the government needs to clamp down on the excessive purchasing of books by public schools purely on the basis that they look politically correct. The adverse effect of this is that the supply of Ghanaian and African children's literature is cut off. Second, children in rural public schools do not have access to books because of the conditions attached to borrowing them. As a result, the child does not have the chance to read about himself and his world. Third, even though public basic schools in urban centres offer the opportunity to read, students are reading more Western literature than Ghanaian or other African. In addition, as they climb up the educational ladder to public second cycle institutions, the opportunities for accessing children's literature from writers in the latter categories begin to reduce due to government interference.

However, irrespective of these constraints, Ghanaian and African books must get into the hands of children. This is because they need to be educated, entertained and represented. With regard to education, for instance, Asare's story depicts typical life in the Northern, Upper East and Upper West regions of Ghana. In these areas, children take care of livestock such as goats and sheep. Public school hours, in some areas run the shift system – some children go to school in the morning from 6 till 11 in the morning, while others go from 11:30 till 5:30 in the afternoon. This means that some children will tend to the livestock in the morning while others are in school and *vice versa*. Thus, the little boy or girl living in an urban area is made aware of another kind of Ghanaian child with a lifestyle different from his or her own. Conversely, when the boy or girl up north, upper east or upper west, reads this story, the child sees him or herself reflected in the narrative, and is proud of their achievement in the story.

This reminds one of Christopher Myer's article in the Sunday Review of the *New York Times* online, posted 15 March 2014. His article is entitled 'The Apartheid of Children's Literature'. He observes: '…of the 3,200 children's books published in 2013, just 93 were about black people, according to a study by the Cooperative Children's Book Center at the University of Wisconsin.' Myers goes on to relate his interview with a young boy whom he describes as being 'at that age when the edges of the man he will become are just starting to press against his baby-round face'. In Myer's conversation with the boy and other boys his age he comments that they are not featured in the books published in the year 2013:

> "Yep, it's a few thousand [in that year]."
> "And in all of those thousands of books, I'm just not in them?"
> "Well...um...yes."
> "Are there books about talking animals?"
> "Oh, sure."
> "And crazy magical futures?"
> "Absolutely."
> "And superpowers? And the olden days when people dressed funny? And all the combinations of those things? Like talking animals with superpowers in magical futures ... but no me?"
> "No you."
> "Why?"
> "Because you're brown." (*New York Times*, 15 March 2014)

Myers goes on to explain that although publishers produce great mission statements that stipulate how they intend to promote children's literature, the reality is otherwise. Actually, literature depicting children of 'color' is on the low side. This is what he refers to as the apartheid of children's literature. And he explains:

> We adults – parents, authors, illustrators and publishers – give them in each book a world of supposedly boundless imagination that can delineate the most ornate geographies, and yet too often today's books remain blind to the everyday reality of thousands of children. Children of color remain outside the boundaries of imagination. The cartography we create with this literature is flawed. (*New York Times*, 15 March 2014)

Although Myers refers to American society, his 'apartheid of children's literature' reflects the challenges on the Ghanaian scene. Although Myers blames the publishers, in Ghana the blame would be left at the doorstep of government and parents who are unwilling to put the needs of their wards first, to be able to read about themselves in the literature available to them.

This research reveals the strides Ghana has made as far as Ghanaian Children's Literature is concerned. There are writings for all age groups of children. This means that Ghana does not face a challenge of creativity that will appeal to all age groups of children. However, what Ghana suffers from is the culture of reading and the acceptance of its own literature among parents, children, educational curriculum developers and all other stakeholders involved. The practice of government providing literature of Ghanaian origin to basic schools is laudable. However, the government needs to look into extending this practice to second cycle schools. It also needs to monitor the literature consumed by children in privately-run schools. This will go a long way to ensure that the efforts being made by Ghanaian writers of children's literature would be appreciated in order to encourage them to do more.

Although Myer's essay deals with US society, the issue of representation and identity that he raises is relevant to every society. Children's literature should be a means of identification in such a way that the child builds self-esteem and confidence. On the other hand, it should be a map revealing the child's society and also the world beyond its boundaries. It should be the train, the bus, the taxi by which the child travels into their own world and the world outside that world. It should be the key to self-actualization and realization for the child.

As such, in a country like Ghana where writers are doing all they can to represent the Ghanaian child in literature created for them, Myer's 'apartheid' seems to be creeping in, due to the challenges that face the distribution of children's literature on publication. There is the challenge created by governmental policies, the challenge created by parents and guardians who are unwilling to support their children in order to have access to literature materials. Then there is the worst – children with access to literature reading children's literature that do not identify or represent them. All of these are examples of the kind of 'apartheid of children's literature' that Myers describes regarding his own society.

However, all is not lost. Writers in Ghana are determined to keep writing for children. For instance, with the support of the Ghana Writers' Association, writers such as Ruby Goka organize book readings at senior high schools, and in 2013, the Ghana Association of Writers launched an Outreach Programme, which organizes authors' book readings in schools.

This is not to say that we have done it all as far as children's literature in Ghana is concerned. However, the path has been lit by the work of new writers. Perhaps in the next decade we will see more children's literature, so that we will not embrace Myers' conclusion, with reference to Ghana, that there is an alarming apartheid of children's literature. In this regard, future research will consider the impact of Ghanaian children's literature on intellectual, social and academic development. It will also examine whether the scope of Ghanaian children's literature in schools has been widened.

WORKS CITED

Asare, Meshack (2008). *The Cross Drums*. Ghana: Sub-Saharan Publishers.

Baker, Jnr. Houston A.(1989). 'Animal Tales and Lore', in L. Goss and M. Barnes, eds, *Talk that Talk: An Anthology of African American Story-telling*, New York: Simon & Schuster, 99-102.

Brew-Hammond, Aba (2007). *A Boy Called Wiser-Than-You and Other Tales*. Accra: Woeli Publishing Services.

Courlander, Harold, (1996). *A Treasury of African Folklore*. New York: Marlowe & Co.

Darmani, Lawrence (2012). *First Term Surprises*. Accra: Step Publishers.

Darmani, Lawrence (2012). *Entertainment Night*. Accra: Step Publishers.

Goka, Y. Ruby (2011). *The Mystery of the Haunted House*. Accra: Sub-Saharan Publishers.

Goka, Y. Ruby (2012). *The Lost Royal Treasure*. Accra: Kwadwoan Publishers.

Goss, L., M. Barnes, E. Marian (1989). *Talk that Talk. An Anthology of African-American Story-telling*. New York: Simon & Schuster.

Hutchison, Kwesi (2012). *Ananse Folktales From Ghana*. Ghana: Ed-Jay.

Kouyate, D'Jimo (1989). 'The Role of the Senegalese Griot', in L. Goss, M. Barnes, E. Marian, *Talk that Talk: An Anthology of African-American Story-telling*, 179-181.

Myers, Christopher (2014). 'The Apartheid of Children's Literature'. *Sunday Review, New York Times*.

Oti-Agyen, Philip (2007). *The Development of Education in Ghana*. Kumasi: Hannob Press.

Primus, Pearl A. (1989). *The Storyteller.* New York: Simon & Schuster.

Folktales
as African Children's Literature
A Study of Archetypal Symbols in Selected
Igbo Folktales

BLESSING DIALA-OGAMBA

Folktales help us to appreciate how literature reflects our society and worldview. In the past, stories were spoken and passed down from generation to generation throughout the world. Stories could be told by everyone, and the audience would be made up of mainly children. Both adults and children would gather at designated places in the evenings for story-telling performances. The purpose of folktales has always been mainly for the education and entertainment of children. However, the evolution of print technology has changed the mode of delivery. People no longer gather by the fireside in the evenings to tell and listen to folktales. With this change and with modern education, books were printed and children were taken into consideration in terms of a book publishing market. The folktales that were usually told were put into print and read to children. In the African setting, especially in Igbo society, folktales are told to children right from infancy. The evolution of print technology has not taken away completely the idea of oral tales from the Igbo society. Children have story-telling periods in schools where folktales are read aloud or recounted by their teachers. There are television story times for children where adults tell stories and children gather to listen and respond to them and the songs that accompany them. In reference to this change, Ernest Emenyonu (2002) pertinently observes that the telling of folktales in the traditional mode and format has all but disappeared in the face of rapid urbanization and modernization. Television, radio, movies, filmstrips, videos, and other visual forms have become popular entertainment in the home. Emenyonu comments that it is becoming rare even in remote villages to find the traditional moonlit settings or the around-the-fire, after-the-evening-meal gatherings where folktales were told by fathers, mothers, uncles, aunts, elder brothers or elder sisters, and through which esteemed cultural values were transmitted by word of mouth from one generation to the other (2002: 585).

Emenyonu cites the economic situation today as one of the reasons for the lack of communal gatherings in the evenings for story-telling. Many villages have become semi-urban locations where people from other communities rent homes and commute to work from places closer to their work. Akachi Ezeigbo further notes:

> Indeed in the traditional past, children were entertained and instructed with folktales. In most cultures the world over, there was a rich tradition of story-telling for children and even adults. This tradition has been overtaken by the written culture. Some writers have tried to write down and preserve the oral tradition in books which are marketed for children with the intention of instructing and entertaining them, for example, the ubiquitous tortoise tales which have found their way in some storybooks (2013: 282).

It is, however, important to note that there are some homes where mothers, grandparents and other relatives still tell stories to their children as a way of imparting knowledge, morals and values. It continues to be important for mothers and grandparents to do so, because of the affection between parents and children. Emenyonu also observes that the bond of affection between mother and child in the Igbo culture is a very strong one. When the washing-up after the evening meal is finished, children sit round the fireside to be entertained by their mother till bedtime (2002: 3). It is this kind of bonding that Nwoye has with his mother in Achebe's *Things Fall Apart* (1958). As mothers nurture their children in their formative years, the children imbibe the folktales they hear and learn important lessons of life from them. These tales, whether oral or written can be analysed using the same various approaches that are applied to adult literature. This article focuses on archetypal symbols in selected children's folktales in Igbo society in Nigeria, and how the archetypal symbols in folktale reflect the values and norms of Igbo society.

Archetypes are mostly derived from the beliefs of a people. An archetype is as a recurrent narrative design, with patterns of action, character types, or images which are said to be identifiable in a wide variety of works of literature, as well as in myths, dreams, and even ritualized modes of social behaviour. Such archetypes are held to reflect a set of universal, primitive, and elemental forms or patterns, whose effective embodiment in a literary work evokes a profound response from the reader. Wilfred Guerin et al. (1989) explain that archetypes are universal symbols and go further to quoting Wheel-Wright's definition as

> ...those [symbols] which carry the same or very similar meanings for a large portion, if not all, of mankind. It is a discoverable fact that certain symbols, such as the sky father and earth mother, light, blood, up-down, the axis of a wheel, and others, recur again and again in cultures so remote from one another in space and time that there is no likelihood of any historical influence and causal connection among them. (1988:118)

These recurring symbols are not only found in myths, but also in folktales as will be seen in the examples provided later.

Folktales are traditional tales passed down from generation to generation. They provide answers to some cultural, spiritual, psychological and supernatural beliefs of a people. Folktales in Igbo society and in other African societies are specifically told for the delectation and education of children. These stories are rich and authentic sources of African values in traditional African societies. In past times, they were used for purposes of acculturation and were, therefore, necessarily didactic and morality-laden (Emenyonu 2002: 584). The fact that folktale is situated in traditional culture and society is also affirmed by Helen Chukwuma when she states that the oral tale

> is entirely an imaginative enactment very earthbound with man in its centre. The oral tale shows man in his many forms and in the various situations of life that show up the best and worst in him. It can be said that there is a certain naturalistic element in oral tale in that it portrays the baser aspects of man: his greed, villainy, utter lack of sensitivity and his egotism. Amidst this clutter of vice and deceit, some virtue finds its way through and triumphs but not without a grim struggle. (2002: 32)

Even when animals and spirits are depicted in a tale, the parts they play are human and children can learn from these acts and relate them to real people. Folktales are usually simple stories about beasts, woodcutters and princesses who reveal human behaviour and beliefs while playing out their roles in a world of wonder and magic (Kiefer 2010: 225). For convenience, the stories discussed below are divided into three groups as recognized by Chukwuma in her work, *Igbo Oral Literature:* the animal tale, the human tale, and the mixed tale (2002: 32).

In some animal tales, the animals are equipped with magical powers. The first of this category tells of Tortoise, the archetypal trickster animal in Igbo folktales as well as in other traditions. In most stories involving the tortoise, we see his tricks and greed play out, emblematic of humanity's insatiable delight in this behaviour. In many tales, animals are personified. They possess human strengths and weaknesses, behave like humans, and also extol human qualities such as hard work, or perseverance, as well as their faults, wickedness, jealousy and other traits. These human qualities that animals exhibit are used to teach children some life-long lessons about Igbo society.

In the tale entitled 'Tiger Slights the Tortoise', the theme of insult and revenge are explored to teach children the consequences of these actions, using animals as characters. The tiger invites all the animals to work on his farm, except the tortoise, because he believes the tortoise is too weak to do so. The tortoise feels slighted and decides to distract the animals with his music. The tiger sends his son to remind his wives to bring food and drink for the workers. His son hears the music and stops to dance, forgetting his errand. Tiger's wives arrive at the same spot with food and drink and stay to dance as well. After waiting for a long time, the tiger goes to look for his wives and son, and prepares to spank them. However, when he gets to the same spot, he hears the music and cannot help but join in the dancing. Meanwhile, the animals back on the farm, who are now tired of working without food, decide to abandon their labours and go home. When they come to the scene of dancing, they join in. Suddenly the music stops. Tortoise comes out to tell Tiger that he may think he is too weak to work on his farm but he has enough strength to distract his workers.

This story teaches children and even adults the importance of inclusion and equal opportunity. No one should be neglected in society. Although the story teaches a lesson, we find archetypal symbols of neglect, power, revenge, and weakness in this story. These themes are found in many other stories where a powerful person neglects a weaker person. The tiger is depicted as a powerful and strong animal who does not want to deal with the weaker tortoise. The tortoise feels publicly slighted and decides to take revenge on the tiger by distracting his workers. In real life, the only thing that a weak person can do is to distract attention, or create a deception, just as Tortoise succeeds in doing. He does this to show that even though he is not strong, there is something he is good at. However, the tortoise uses this distraction as a cover up for his laziness. The tortoise is always known to be a trickster in Igbo society so when a story is told about him, children will always pay attention, wanting to know what his plots and plans are, and how he will avoid any demanding task. Okpewho explains that tricksters represent what is feared but secretly coveted: tricksters may be condemned for moral depravity, selfishness and lack of a sense to reciprocity but on the other hand, they may inspire a mild sense of admiration for their wit, craftiness and ability to achieve the seemingly impossible (2002: 263). The setting of the story, on the farm, symbolizes hard work and food. Tortoise is not good at farming, but because he knows that there will be food, that is, entertainment at the farm which he will not be a part of, he decides to distract the workers from fulfilling their obligations to Tiger. Music here is an archetypal symbol that can be used to send both positive and negative messages as well as for entertainment. Here, the music is used to entertain and to distract Tiger's workers.

Another trickster tale, 'Why the Tortoise Cracked its Shell', is about famine in the land of the animals. While they do not have food to eat, the birds fly to the sky to get food and remain very healthy. One day the tortoise begs to be allowed to travel to the sky with them and has them pluck a feather each to attach to his body. On reaching the sky, he asks each of them to assume a name, which they do. He takes the name 'All of you'. The people of the sky bring a lot of food for their guests and the tortoise asks for whom the food is meant, and they reply "All of you". The tortoise then tells the birds that he has to eat first since his name is 'All of you', and later, they can eat whatever is left. He eats and leaves the bones for them. The birds get angry and leave Tortoise in the sky after collecting all the feathers they loaned to him. However, the parrot has pity on him and takes a distorted message from the tortoise back to his wife telling her to bring out all the hard objects in his home instead of the soft material requested by the tortoise. She does so and Tortoise falls on the objects, cracking his shell.

This story reminds humans that it is not right to repay good with evil because there will definitely be consequences. Children can relate to the Tortoise's punishment, because it helps them think before they react negatively to good deeds. This story also exposes the tortoise's tricks and greedy nature. The narrative also contains the archetypal symbols of undertaking a journey from the land to the sky: creative energy and consciousness (Guerin et al.,1989: 119). Tortoise is also transformed into a bird in order to find food, but his greed gets the better of him and he comes home disfigured by breaking his shell. He has to get help to patch his shell together by spending money he does not have. We can therefore deduce from this story that the tortoise is conscious of his manipulative nature and employs it to deceive the birds who do him a favour by taking him to the sky to get food.

The second story is a human tale entitled 'The Disobedient Sisters'. Here, there are two sisters who do not obey their parents. The parents warn them not to play outside, then go away to a distant market leaving both girls at home. They ignore their parents' warnings and go outside to play with other children. The 'Beasts of the Sea and Land' invade the field where the children are playing. The Beast of the Sea carries off one of the girls, Omelunmma, while the Beast of the land abducts her sister, Omelukpagham. They are separated: Omelunmma is sold to a young man who loves her dearly, but her sister is sold to one wicked person after another. Then, by chance, Omelunmma's husband buys a maid for her from the market who turns out to be her sister, Omelukpagham, who now has a baby. Because both sisters have grown up, they fail to recognize each other. Omelunmma treats her sister harshly, punishing her when her baby cries, or if she does not finish her chores on time. One day, as the baby cries, Omelukpagham sings a lullaby to her child that explains how she and her sister ignored their parents' advice and were carried away by the beasts. A neighbour overhears the song and tells Omelunmma when she returns from the market. The next day, Omelukpagham sings again to her little one. Her sister hides so she can hear the lullaby herself to make sure that it is really her sister Omelukpagham. She hears the song from her hiding place and comes out to embrace her, apologizing for mistreating her. They live together happily ever after.

Children will learn from this story the importance of being obedient, and the consequences of disobedience. There are some archetypal symbols of the beast: wickedness, stubbornness, while there are also the positive effects of the lullaby and the journey undertaken by the heroine, Omelukpagham.

The title, 'The Disobedient Sisters', alerts the listener that there will be consequences for disobedience, seen in the beasts carrying away the sisters. We notice that the two sisters have different destinies because of their names. One marries a good man because of her name Omelunmma, ('one who does well') and she enjoys a good life with her family. The other is destined to suffer because of her name Omelukpagham ('stubborn one'). She is sold from one person to another and they all punish her, including her sister, who fails to recognize her. The story exposes the fact that people's names can sometimes be a blessing or a curse – a traditional Igbo cultural belief. Moving from place to place is an archetypal journey, one that Omelukpagham undertakes unknowingly but which helps her in her process of transformation and initiation. She survives all the hardships and ends up in her sister's place without recognizing her. She therefore determines to change by comforting her niece when she cries, and taking punishment for not finishing her chores. Here, she turns into a good person which eventually benefits her. In the process of stopping the baby from crying, she sings a lullaby that unfolds her life story, thus portraying the effectiveness of music which is used as an archetypal symbol in a positive way to reunite the sisters. She uses the music to disclose the story of her life and the fact that being disobedient has negative consequences. This story is similar to all children's stories with disobedience as theme.

A similar example is the story of 'The Disobedient Daughter Who Married a Skull'. This is another mixed tale because the skull is not human. Akweke (which means a precious stone) refuses to marry the men recommended by her parents or those who are not strangers. She meets a very handsome man and insists on marrying him without realizing that he is a skull who has borrowed different body parts from his friends. Before they get back to the man's house, he gives back the body parts, revealing his true self to Akweke who becomes afraid of living with him. However, she is kind to the skull's mother who in turn, fortunately, helps her to return home before she is eaten by the skull's friends. With the help of magic, the skull's mother invokes a gentle breeze to take Akweke home to her parents. Before Akweke escapes, the mother makes her promise to obey her parents which the girl does. Her parents are happy to see her again and she quickly agrees to marry her father's choice of a friend, and they live happily ever after.

In this story, the archetypal skull symbolizes that Akweke would have died if she were not rescued quickly. Here, we also see the archetypal symbol of magic used to transport Akweke from the thick forest, the abode of the skull, to the land of the living. Magic can be used either negatively or positively to teach lessons, but in this tale it is used positively to rescue Akweke. The skull's mother uses invocation to get the gentle breeze to take her home. The main character travels from land to forest, and back to land, portraying a frightening setting in this archetypal journey. The forest means that she will live with wild animals, the skull, and be killed, or if she is lucky, she will be saved. Once the skull transforms from a human being to its magical form, one quickly realizes that the story is taking a different turn and anything can be expected. The skull, a non-life object, symbolizes death.

The next example is 'The Story of the Leopard, the Tortoise, and the Bush Rat', in which there is a great famine in the land of the animals and all the animals are weak and thin with the exception of the tortoise and his family, who are fat and do not seem to suffer. At the beginning of the famine, the leopard eats the tortoise's mother which makes the tortoise angry, so he determines to seek revenge. The tortoise has discovered a shallow pond, goes there to fish, and brings home enough food for his family. The leopard sees the tortoise coming back with a heavy basket on his back and demands to know what is in it. Indeed, the leopard smells the fish and insists on eating the catch with the tortoise. The tortoise agrees and devises a game in which they will tie one another with a rope. The tortoise tells the leopard that when the one being tied says 'Tighter!' the rope should be loosened, but when he says loosen the rope, it must be tightened. The leopard plays the game on the tortoise first, but when it is the turn of the tortoise, he switches the game and refuses to loosen the rope. Thus, the tortoise ties the leopard to a tree and eats some of the catch on his own. After eating to his satisfaction, he takes the remainder to his family, but not before he reminds the leopard why he is punishing him. The leopard begs other animals passing by to release him but no one will do it, for fear that they too will be eaten by the leopard. However, a rat, sympathizing with the leopard, decides to untie him, but not before he has dug a hole so he can run away quickly. He frees the leopard who instantly attacks him, but his claws only scratch the back of the rat, who escapes death by diving into its hole. However, his scars remain forever in his furry back.

The leopard is seen as a strong beast that is not kind to other animals when he is hungry so that no one ever wishes to help him. The tortoise again is a trickster and master of revenge. He shows that it takes time to work out a plan but if one has enough patience, a person will be able to avenge any wrong done to them. Here, the moral of the tale is that patience is a virtue. The rat demonstrates intelligence by digging a hole for his refuge knowing that the leopard will pounce on him, since he is very hungry. This story also reveals the value of having an alternative or back-up plan in place when one is engaged in something important. It demonstrates the Igbo value of not putting all one's eggs in one basket.

In 'The Flute', which is a mixed story of human and spirit, a young boy goes to a farm with his mother, where he carves a flute that he will play with when he gets home. However, he leaves it behind. Once home, he realizes his mistake and insists on going back to fetch his flute because he had invested a lot of time in carving it. His mother is worried that the spirits will be in the forest at that time of night and that her son may be killed. She gives him some food to take on his journey. He gets to the farm safely, and finds the spirits playing with his flute. He tells them that he has come back to retrieve it. They ask him for some of his food and he obliges. They hand the flute to the boy, but ask him to play them a tune before taking it away. He plays sweetly, praising how kind and beautiful they are. They are overjoyed, and in addition to allowing him to have his flute back, they send a cool breeze to take him home with a basket of different kinds of beautiful things, including more food. They tell him to open the basket only when he gets home. There, he opens the basket and his house changes into a beautiful place with lots of food.

Now, the mother's co-wife notices this change and discovers what happened. She takes her own son to the farm and asks him to carve a flute. She makes sure that the boy forgets his flute and when they both get home, she sends him back to the farm to fetch it. However, when this boy sees the spirits playing his flute, he becomes furious, refuses to share his food, and insults them, telling them how ugly they look. The spirits give him his flute with a wild wind as well as a basket of destructive items to take home. On his return, the wind destroys his home using the destructive items while his mother looks on, and weeps.

This story teaches children the importance of appreciating the good fortune of others and of being respectful to others. In Igbo culture, it is believed that when one appreciates the good fortune of others, good things will come one's way. The co-wife exposes her greed by telling her son what to do in order to transform their lives, but this archetypal symbol of transformation is only destructive of her home. In contrast, the first boy's family is transformed in a positive way from poverty to wealth. Another archetypal theme of greed, and its consequences, are also portrayed in this story. In Igbo society, greed is considered negative and several stories portray its harmful consequences on a child's education.

The next narrative example is 'The Greedy Wife' also a mixed tale, about humans and the sea god. There is a King who has two wives and children by both women. The younger wife has a beautiful daughter, but the first wife does not like the younger wife because of the attention she receives from the King. One day, the first wife takes the younger wife's daughter to the stream and abandons her there. The sea-god comes out and carries off the girl into the water. Her mother goes to the stream crying and pleading in a gentle tone that her daughter be given back to her. The sea-god takes pity on her and releases her daughter, as well as giving her many presents. On seeing all the gifts, the first wife takes her own daughter to the stream and leaves her there hoping that she will come back with equal good fortune. The sea-god takes her, but her mother returns to demand the girl's return. The sea-god releases her, but hands over only destructive gifts. On returning home, the first wife quickly snatches the concealed gift from her daughter, opens it and all the destructive items inside destroy their house as well as injure the mother and girl. Eventually, the King hears of his first wife's evil schemes, and sends her away, but lives with the younger wife happily thereafter.

Water is considered the symbol of the mystery of creation; birth-death-resurrection; purification and redemption; fertility and growth. It is the commonest symbol of the unconscious (Guerin et al., 1989: 119). In the tale discussed above, both children are taken into the river which symbolizes rebirth and redemption for the first girl, but death and destruction for the second. The first child and her mother are innocent, so they get a positive reward from the sea-god. The second child's mother has evil intentions, so the sea-god punishes her and exposes her evil intentions. The King also banishes this wife and her daughter to prevent them from scheming up some other evil against the younger wife and her daughter. The lesson is evil is always punished, not condoned, according to Igbo cultural norms.

In 'The Tortoise and The Magic Drum', one day, the tortoise decides to go looking for food because he is hungry. He climbs a palm tree to eat some palm fruits. Accidentally, one of the fruits falls into a crab's hole. The tortoise quickly delves into the hole to get his fruit but he sees an old woman eating it. This old woman is a spirit; she tells the tortoise to take a drum hanging on a rope in return for her having eaten the palm fruit. The magic drum will supply Tortoise with food and drink whenever he plays it. The tortoise is happy with the gift and he plays the drum, requesting delicious food which immediately appears. On reaching home, he invites his friends and neighbours to a feast. His guests arrive and they have a great spread of good food to eat and are very happy with Tortoise. The next day, Tortoise is unhappy because the drum no longer provides food. This time, the tortoise throws a palm fruit into the hole on purpose. The old woman, being a spirit, knows about the tortoise's scheme, and gives him a larger drum after asking him what happened to the first one. Tortoise is happy that his plan has worked. On getting home, he beats his drum only to find masked creatures coming at him from all directions to whip him in punishment. He fakes death and the evil sprites go back into the drum. Tortoise recovers and calls another feast inviting his friends and neighbours once more. Because of their first good experience, more people attend the feast. He beats the drum, but then he goes into hiding. The evil sprites come out to whip every single guest, then swiftly disappear, back inside the drum. After a while, the guests get up to go home and Tortoise comes out laughing, saying, 'If you accompany me in enjoyment, you must also endure malicious punishment' (274). The guests go home, swearing never again to have anything to do with the tortoise.

This story signifies the greed and insatiable nature of Tortoise. The second time round, his trick is discovered because he is dealing with a spirit who can divine his intentions. Igbo society believes that whatever one does, there is a higher being somewhere monitoring one's actions. Therefore caution is required at all times. This confirms the Igbo belief that 'Nothing under the sun is hidden.' The archetypal symbol of the magic drum is conveyed in this story as the drum can produce positive as well as the negative things depending on how it is used and the intentions of the person who touches it.

'The Hated Wife' is not a fable about animals, but of a king and his wives. There was once a king who married many wives and they all have female children. Eventually he marries a young and beautiful wife who eventually bears him a son. The other wives do not like this woman because of the attention she receives from the King, so they decide to lie to the King, claiming that the young wife's child died at birth. The young wife continues to raise her child without the King's knowledge. However, the King no longer takes care of his young wife because the other women do not let her get close to the King. The boy is eventually taken away from his mother by the King's first wife, who raises him. One day, the King sees a boy playing with his other children and tries to find out who he is. All the wives except the hated one claim the child as theirs. This ruse brings confusion in the King's palace, and he decides to find out who is the boy's true mother. He tells the wives that they should prepare delicious soup and bring it to the arena. The boy will be asked to taste all the soup and whichever bowlful he likes best and chooses to eat, the King will identify the woman who prepared it as the boy's mother. They all agree and set out preparing their soups. The King buys meat, fish and other condiments for the wives without giving any to the hated wife. The hated wife uses crayfish and whatever vegetable she can afford herself to make her soup. She brings her bowlful for the boy to taste just as the other wives do. After tasting the other wives' soup, the boy goes to the 'hated wife' who is sitting a little bit away from the others because they will not let her come close to them. He tastes the soup and sits down beside the woman to finish it. When the women are confronted with the result and questioned, the other wives eventually tell the King the truth. The King apologizes to the 'hated wife' and takes both mother and son to live with him in his palace.

This human tale portrays the archetypal symbols of greed, jealousy and evil intentions which have been seen in humans through all time. The jealous wives are disgraced publicly, thus elevating the status of the hated wife. The story takes place in the King's palace, where many intrigues take place without the King's knowledge. In spite of all the women's manipulations, the boy is able to identify his mother.

'The Wicked Step-Mother' tells of a boy whose mother dies and whose father marries again. The step-mother mistreats the boy and uses him as a houseboy. One day, she buys 'udara' fruit from the market and does not give any to the boy but only to her own children. The boy picks up the fruit seed and plants it beside his mother's grave. He comes to the graveside often, to sing in request that the 'udara' should grow and it does. In the song, the boy reveals that his step-mother bought the 'udara' fruit and gave it to her children, leaving him out. He ends the song with the words that humans are visitors in the world, and after their stay here, they will go back to where they came from. He sings that the 'udara' should bear fruits and ripen, and it does so. He sings that the 'udara' fruit should fall and it does so, so he picks it all up and eats. On hearing this song, his dead mother rises from her grave and kills his step-mother.

When narrated, this song has a call and response structure to it, and children respond to the refrain while waiting anxiously to find out the ending of the story. The archetypal step-mother is always punished or meets a sad end, and the victim is rehabilitated. However, in this story, the victim is helpless, and seeing that his father does nothing to alleviate his sufferings in the house decides to plant the fruit beside his mother's grave and goes there to sing his song. In this way, he complains to his mother about his misfortunes believing that she will come to his rescue; indeed, she does. The setting is a compound occupied by humans, but the characters are both humans and spirit (the dead mother) who appears in the story to kill the step-mother. The moral of this tale is that victimization or oppression is a bad thing. The archetypal victim is always rescued and the villain punished. Emenyonu has observed that, some stories advocate instant justice through revenge and retaliation for an evil act, or the deployment of *deus ex machina* who kills off miscreants and hardened criminals (2002: 584). Instant justice is seen in the death of the step-mother.

Folktales are always didactic and especially appropriate for children. This is why they are still important today in Igbo society. Folktales serve various social functions whether they are about humans, animals or both. Chukwuma observes that people identify with some animals as friends and companions and others as enemies. Forest animals, big, ferocious and wild are their own friends, whereas smaller animals as dogs, birds, are tame and harmless, but more importantly, they serve the welfare of humanity (2002: 33). The characters in animal tales are types because they lack depth, while those in human tales are more developed. In some mixed tales, humans work with animals, but there can be tales with a combination of spirits, humans and animals, as it is believed that all these characters operate and communicate within the same sphere.

According to Kofi Awoonor, the folk tale was subjected to the 19th-century evolutionist interpretations of human history, as in the works of E. B. Taylor and Sir James Frazer. Folklore became the compendium of beliefs, customs and culture of both early man and still have value for descendants today (1975: 73). Studies of folklore are confined to the archetypal analysis of some the symbolism of this genre, rather than the question of origins or of authorship. The adaptations of folktales to contemporary social situations have been illustrated in this paper to depict the values and customs of the societies in which the stories are told. The totemic link between animals and man has also been studied. Awoonor asserts that the animal heroes are seen to

> ...possess certain primordial qualities of cunning necessary for survival in an uncertain world. Besides, they partake of a spiritual essence of the universal dynamic force. Above all, the animal hero always shares an aspect of everyman [sic]; he is wise, at times greedy, at times generous, he marries, procreates, cheats, attends his relatives' and neighbors' funerals, gets drunk and beats his wife, and dies. He is everyman of the folk tradition, the archetypal hero who succeeds or fails by his guile or preternatural wisdom or when aided by benevolent spirits and his personal deity. (1975: 75)

Characters in folktales are not well developed, but one-dimensional, and their motivations are uncomplicated, unlike characters in novels. A jealous or wicked character does not change. A character in a folktale is either good or bad. Human characters interact with animals and spirit, but they all know their boundaries. The setting is not static: it can be in the land of the spirit, the river, or the land of the living, or both in the land of the spirit and the living; the setting is ample in scope. The plot is always simple and uncomplicated. Children can always relate to the plot and replicate the tales after they have been told. Amini Courts observes in an article written for a field work study on folktales, '...norms and values are imparted to all, especially to the young. Despite [...] similarity of subject matter and theme, they provide detailed lessons for life for those who hear them' (1990: 24). Folktales teach children to be patriotic, obedient, and conscious of their surroundings. Igbo society believes in the education of a child through folktales, because they impart the values, culture and norms of the society. Uche Ogbalu expresses these qualities when she writes:

> ...the folktale narrator lives in the community with others. He takes materials for his tales from his experiences in the community so the events of Igbo folktales are not strange to his audience. Igbo folktales contain the people's culture, world-view, norms, spiritual life, their

hopes and aspirations. In short Igbo folktale contains Igbo man's total way of life. It is the recreation of the folk's activities in the society. (2011: 56)

Children, on the other hand, benefit from this re-creation of the people's way of life through folktales with the excitement, entertainment and education they gain. Folktales also help children to expand their imagination and hypothesize about societal/world affairs as they grow into adulthood.

WORKS CITED

Achebe, Chinua (1958). *Things Fall Apart*. London: Heinemann.
Akachi Ezeigbo, Theodora (2013). 'Folklore, Education and Youth Development: Molding the Minds of Children with Igbo Core Values', in Chinyelu Ojukwu, ed., *Critical Issues in African Literature: Twenty-First Century and Beyond*. Port Harcourt: University of Port Harcourt Press.
Awoonor, Kofi (1975). *The Breast of the Earth*. New York: Nok Publishers.
Chukwuma, Helen (2002). *Igbo Oral Literature: Theory and Tradition*. Port Harcourt: Pearl Press.
Courts, Amini (1990). 'Images of Women in Folklore: A Multicultural View', in *Multicultural Module Field Test Edition*. Baltimore: Coppin State University.
Emenyonu, Ernest (2002). 'Selection and Validation of Oral Materials for Children's Literature: Artistic Resources in Chinua Achebe's Fiction for Children', *Callaloo* 25, 2: 584-596.
———. (1989) *Literature and National Consciousness*. Owerri: Heinemann.
Guerin Wilfred, Earle Labor, Lee Morgan et al. (1996). *A Handbook of Critical Approaches to Literature*. New York: Harper & Row.
Kiefer, Barbara Z. (2010). *Charlotte Huck's Children's Literature*. Boston: McGraw-Hill.
Ogbalu, Uche Janet (2011).'Appreciation of Igbo Folktales and Songs versus Realism', *Unizik: Journal of Arts and Humanities* (UJAH) 12, 1: 55-75.
Okpewho, Isidore (1990).*The Oral Performance in African Literature*. Ibadan: Spectrum Books.

Whose Literature?

Children in Armed Conflict
& Modern African Fiction

JULIA UDOFIA

The United Nations defines a child as a person under the age of
eighteen. The 1999 Constitution of the Federal Republic of Nigeria
(as amended) also considers as of full age a person who is eighteen
years and above, so that the term children refers to young people,
toddlers and teenagers up to and including the age of seventeen.
Therefore, in defining children's literature, many genres are
covered: works of art such as prose narratives, drama and poetry;
traditional narratives such as myths, legends, fairy tales, riddles,
folk tales and ballads; and lullabies created specifically for the
listening pleasure of children, from the instant they can with joy
leaf through a picture book or listen to a story read aloud to them
right up to the age of seventeen.

However, the above definition negates the fact that in many
parts of the world, oral tales, songs and drama are enjoyed together
in a community irrespective of age, that is, by both children and
adults after the day's work, and it also overlooks the kind of
literature created by children themselves. It recognizes the fact
that in children's literature, children are the target audience so that
the uniqueness of this genre lies in the primary audience that it
addresses. Since it is produced largely with the interest and needs
of children in mind, the content of this literature is limited by
the experience and understanding of children, so that the ideas,
relationships and language are simple, not complex, and suitable
for children's enjoyment. Implied also is the fact that the characters,
especially the central ones, are children, since the literature is
largely about them.

In its early stages written children's literature in Africa was
limited in scope with regard to the issues explored in protecting
the child from the harsh realities of life. However, in recent times,

69

children's literature in Africa has shifted away from this need to the depiction of a grittier realism, as in its adult counterpart. This is no thanks to the grim realities of present-day Africa where violence, militancy, terrorism and their attendant pain and suffering have become the order of the day.

Ngugi wa Thiong'o observes that human history seems to consist of two main stages – a movement from the state of nature to a higher consciousness; from relative stability in a rural culture to a state of alienation, strife and uncertainty of the modern world (1978: 46). Thus, it would seem that as African societies moved from the state of nature, which experienced relative peace and stability and showed more love and care to children, to the state of alienation and uncertainty of the modern world, strife, armed conflicts, including neo-colonial struggles have taken the upper hand. The result is that violent wars are fought in many parts of the continent – the Sudan, Ethiopia, Eritrea, Zimbabwe, Somali, Rwanda, Angola, Algeria, Sierra Leone, Nigeria, Congo, Mozambique, Uganda, Libya, Namibia, Kenya, and so on. The list is endless.

However, what is more disturbing about these wars is the fact that they are fought using children: a situation which the United Nations describes as the involvement of dependent, developmentally immature children and adolescents in armed conflicts they do not truly comprehend; to which they are unable to give informed consent; and which adversely affects their rights to unhindered growth and identity. This point is made by a boy-soldier in Ken Saro-Wiwa's *Soza Boy* when he confesses:

> ...true true I do not know why we are fighting the war. The Chief Commander General has not told us why we are fighting. The Soza Captain did not tell us why we must go inside the pit. I just carry gun, fight... (1986: 114)

Amnesty International estimates that over 300,000 children are involved in armed conflicts worldwide, while the *Indian Express* (10 February 2014) reports that not less than two million children have been killed and six million injured or disabled in armed conflicts in the last decade. These children, who are usually aged between six and sixteen, suffer this fate while wandering about in hunger in search of families who have been separated from them by war. As they stray into the areas of the fighting soldiers, they are ambushed, held captive and forced to accept the option of fighting against the enemy or die. Some are lured by promises of jobs, as is depicted in the case of Toma, a teenage soldier in Helon Habila's *Measuring Time* (2007). Thereafter, they are indoctrinated into the world of war and its associated practices: robbery, rape, homosexuality, sodomy, arson, and even village massacres. They are also given dangerous weapons – knives and powerful weapons like the AK 47– and taught methods of self-destruction such as suicide. In addition, they are made to perform other adult tasks, acting as porters, carrying loads of up to sixty kilograms or more, standing guards, manning checkpoints, acting as messengers or spies, laying and clearing land mines, stealing and foraging for food, as well as performing household tasks: cooking, cleaning and washing. To help them cope with the effect of soldiering, they are introduced to hard drugs, smoking and alcohol. Any attempt to run away, disobey orders, or argue with their superiors leads to serious punishments: beating, imprisonment, threats to life or ultimately death by bullet. The girls are especially vulnerable because, in addition to being made to perform adult tasks like cooking and washing for the soldiers and any other thing the soldiers command them to do, they are also sexually abused.

The effects of these experiences are far-reaching. They include physical, spiritual, emotional, mental and psychological consequences not only to the children but to the society as a whole. Thus, African writers, including those who create children's literature have taken it upon themselves to bring to the attention of readers the grim reality of our modern times, such as that depicted in Uzodinma Iweala's *Beasts of No Nation* (2005), which is the focus of this article.

Derived from the title of one of Fela Anikulapo Kuti's music albums whose philosophy centres on challenging the beast in African humankind, *Beasts of No Nation* explores the modern reality of child-soldiering in a genocidal civil war. Narrated by Agu, one of the child-victims and the central character in the work, the novel gives a first-hand account of the present-day practice of using children in armed conflict. Note that the African setting of this novel is unnamed, thus deliberately representing the widespread situation of boys fighting men's wars; a practice that is going on in many parts of Africa and elsewhere today.

The novel begins with Strika, a boy-soldier of about ten years of age, as he pulls another boy, Agu, out of his hiding place into the middle of a war. Agu, aged twelve, had hidden because he thought he would be safe after being separated from his mother and only sister, and also having witnessed the killing of his father by enemy soldiers. However, the fate of war was to prove him wrong as Strika drags him before the Commandant, a ruthless leader controlling a troop of soldiers. Agu is given the choice of joining the army or being killed. As part of his initiation, and to prove that he is not a spy, Agu is given a machete and ordered to hack a man (an enemy soldier) to death. The Commandant assures Agu: "It's just like killing a goat. Just bring this hand up and knock him well well" (21). With this last order, the Commandant closes his hand over Agu's as the boy holds the machete, and brings it down on the enemy's head. Agu knows that what he has been plunged into is evil, and in his conscience, he takes on the blame. In order to justify his action, he reasons:

> I am not bad boy. How can I be bad boy? Somebody who is having life like I am having and fearing God the whole time.... I am soldier and soldier is not bad if he is killing, so if I am killing then I am only doing what is right. (23-4)

It is worth noting that this depiction of conscription and indoctrination is reminiscent of all such cases in Africa where child-soldiers are involved. In Delia Jarret-Macaulay's *Moses Citizen and Me* (2005), Citizen, an eight-year-old boy who is conscripted into the Sierra Leonean government army is forced to murder his grandmother as an act of initiation. The most pitiable part of Citizen's case is that the grandmother was the one taking care of him after he lost his parents to the war. Afua-Iwum Danso corroborates this when he observes in his book, *Africa's Young Soldiers* that 'Recruiters deliberately destroy the bonds between their new recruits and their families and communities in order to end resistance from the communities and block the possibility of the children returning home' (2003: 31). Danso notes the Mozambican and, especially, the Angolan case where children living at the borders and conscripted to fight for the National Union for the Total Independence of Angola (UNITA) were forced to kill their relatives and neighbours, or raid and loot their own villages as a mark of initiation into the war.

The children are also forbidden to use their birth names, traditional names, or any other names related to their past experience with their families or communities. They are instead given war names or names that identify them with their roles in the war. This is evident in *Beasts of No Nation* where some of the boys are given such names as Rambo, Strika, Preacher, Griot, etc. This is intended to sever their links with their people, eliminate the desire to escape and rejoin their families and communities and accept their new world and roles. To get them fully involved, they are also told many untrue things about the people they are fighting; enemies they do not even know, and indoctrinated into believing that the so-called enemies killed their parents and took away their loved ones and therefore must die. Thus, anybody the boys come across, man or woman, boy or girl or even a sucking baby is an enemy and must die.

And so, without any training whatsoever, the children are plunged into war; forced to dance a dance they do not understand. Ini Uko (2008) corroborates this point when she observes that in the case of the Nigerian/Biafran war, young soldiers who were conscripted to fight on the Biafran side were not only poorly clothed and fed, but also lacked adequate care from the officers. To make them stronger, braver and to make them forget their homes and families, they are shown war movies and given hard drugs such as cocaine and marijuana. These take away their humanity and turn them into devouring beasts who are eager to kill without mercy.

Danso notes in the Liberian civil war case that, under the influence of gun juice, women were raped by friends of their sons, while a particular child-soldier, fighting for Charles Taylor's National Patriotic Front of Liberia (NPFL), was forced to bayonet his pregnant sister to show his loyalty to the force. Jude Onwuhanze comments:

> ...children were either killed or maimed. Young women were raped until some of them collapsed and died. Some pregnant women they said had their wombs cut open and their unborn babies brought out and publicly executed. (2008: 80)

These children become so addicted to the drugs that life without them seems almost impossible. John Sherman, in his *War Stories* (2002) tells of a young boy, Pius, who, having been introduced into smoking by the soldiers with whom he stayed as a child-labourer, went to the extent of lying about his age in order to be given cigarettes to smoke. Below is the excerpt of the conversation that ensued between Pius and Sherman on one of such occasions:

> "How old are you?" I ask him
> "Fifteen"
> "You are not, I say, smiling down at him"

"I'm ten years"
"You're too young to smoke". (72)

The soldiers also beat the children and even kill them when they are annoyed. This makes the children afraid. They also turn them into sex machines. Narrating his experience with the Commandant in one of their homosexual encounters, Agu describes what happened after the Commandant had told him to remove his clothes:

So I was removing them. And then, after making me be touching his soldier and all of that thing with my hand and with my tongue and lip, he was telling me to kneel and then he was entering inside of me the way the man goat is sometimes mistaking other man goat for woman goat and going inside of them. (85)

The girls are not left out of this ordeal. In his book, *Measuring Time*, Helon Habila captures the sexual abuse experience of a girl in the Liberian civil war case where a major raped a girl who, in addition to cooking and washing for the soldiers and doing every other thing they commanded her to do was also made to satisfy the soldiers' sexual demands.

It is significant that even though Agu and his fellow boys have been engulfed in war for some time now, the reader is not given any idea of which country the story is set, who the competing factions are, or what the reason for the war is. Neither is the reader told which side Agu is conscripted into. There is also no identifiable plan of attack or pattern of the Commandant's movement or military objective being sought. The soldiers simply move about like mad men destroying and looting whatever they find in the places they raid, all in the name of fighting the enemy; a situation which is reminiscent of the kind of madness Odia Ofeimun talks about in his poem, 'And Where Bullets have spoken':

What prayers, pray where bullets have spoken
A plague rolled by madmen. (1980: 21)

J. P. Clark also notes in his poem, 'The Casualties' that madness had become:

...wandering minstrels who, beating on the drums of the human heart, draw the world into a dance with rites it does not know (Senanu 1976: 136).

The soldiers have thus, turned into devouring beasts eager to kill all the time. Agu, in fact, describes the Commandant and his troops as little better than scurrying ants, and as the killing continues, Agu can no longer differentiate a man from a goat because: "Nobody is having nose or lip or mouth or any of the thing that is making you to remember somebody. Everything is just looking like one kind of animal and smelling like chicken or goat, or cow" (45). Griot also describes his mother who was blown apart as 'meat'. In fact, throughout the novel, we find people being referred to as 'this thing', 'dog', 'goat', 'sheep', and so on.

The boys have seen evil and partaken of evil. According to Agu, they have not seen anything that pleases the eye since the war began but only death, pain, hunger and suffering. In his words, they have even taken unborn babies out of their mother's wombs. In one of their sojourns, while looking for enemies to devour, Agu laments:

> So much time pass us now. I am not seeing road or village or children for too long, I am seeing war, one evil spirit sitting in the bush having too much happiness because all the time he is eating what he wants to eat and seeing what he wants to be seeing – so he is just laughing .... (118)

All this has far-reaching repercussions on (both real and fictional) boys and society. Physically, the children have been displaced and orphaned at very tender ages, leading to hazardous wandering, hunger, sickness, malnutrition, starvation etc. They also suffer physical injuries, especially given their young age and inexperience, including loss of hearing, limbs, voice and sight. La Mamo, a child-soldier in Helon Habila's *Measuring Time* for instance, lost his eye while fighting in the Liberian civil war. Narrating his story to his brother, La Mamo said: "We were in ambush by another group and Samuel Paul was killed, and other ten people. I escaped narrowly. I lost one eye" (130). Similarly, Josiah in Ishmael Beah's *A Long Way Gone: Memoirs of a Boy Soldier*, who because of his very tender age (seven years) was given a stool to stand on, was killed the very first day of fighting. Strika also became mute after witnessing the killing of his parents, while Agu was unable to lie down the first time the Commandant committed sexual rape on him. So, he had asked Strika if his anus was also hurting that badly the first time he did it.

All these experiences impede the educational, vocational and intellectual development and potentialities of the children. When he was a little boy, Agu's mother had already taught him how to read and write before his father formally enrolled him in school where he was well loved by his teacher who encouraged him to study hard so as to become a doctor or engineer. Preacher too had intellectual potentialities as he was always seen carrying his Bible suggesting that he could at least, read. In addition to the formal education the boys received at school, the community also offered some training that would help develop them as responsible adults, such as the age-grade dance. However, all these came to an end with the outbreak of the war and consequent conscription into the army. In the camp, no form of education is provided. Rather, the children are taught the ways of brutality, including bringing out unborn babies from their mothers' wombs.

However, it is not only the educational and intellectual poten-tialities of the children that are thwarted. The boys also lose their once peaceful and serene environment and are plunged instead into a life of chaos, violence and confusion. Before the war, nature was kind to the people and vice versa. The birds and other animals lived in harmony with one another, the palm trees brushed the skies, and night came bringing people back to their homes after a hard day's work. But all this came to an end with the outbreak of the war as confusion, chaos and violence replaced them.

Through sexual rape and general acts of brutality associated with the war, the boys also lose their faith and innocence. As seen in the novel, whenever Agu thinks of the evil he has done, or, entertains fears of not realizing his dream of becoming an engineer or doctor, he becomes very sad. He laments thus after one of his homosexual encounters with the Commandant: 'It is making me to angry and it is making me to sad...' (84). Similarly, his rape of a woman keeps haunting him and he continually wrestles with the thought as to whether or not he is a devil. Ishmael in *A Long Way Gone* also tells us that at the Rehabilitation Centre, memories of the people he had killed caused him migraine, sleeplessness and sadness, especially when he remembered the first time he slit a man's throat and the day they buried alive all the prisoners of a particular village they attacked because the lieutenant said: 'it will be a waste of bullets to shoot them' (63). Also, each time Ishmael went to fetch water, he saw instead blood, and if he stood near a tree, he remembered how they used to tie people to trees, kill them and allow them to rot there.

Such experiences lead to severe emotional disturbances in the boys. Sigmund Freud observed that major personality traits are established in early childhood and that any subsequent traits are a mere elaboration of the earlier ones (1933: 19). O'Hagan (1993) has observed that often children are emotionally disturbed as a result of neglect in their early years. Thus, excessive neglect in infancy can lead to dysfunctional behaviour later in life. Also, over-indulgence can affect a child's personality to some degree. Thus, if a child's needs are frustrated or indulged too much, a particular aspect of the child's personality can become stunted. And so, it can be said that child-soldiering is a negative child-rearing pattern and therefore causes frustration which negatively affects the child's personality, feelings and needs for which the child and the society stand to suffer. This view is corroborated by Garbarino and Garbarino (1994) when they observe that emotionally disturbed children usually display anti-social behaviour such as anger, hostility, tension and short temper. All these are noticeable in the children who have become disheartened, disoriented, exhausted and bewildered.

In his research which identifies post-traumatic stress in children, Afua-Iwum Danso (2003) observes that the psychological effect of war on children can be described in terms of psychological reaction patterns ranging from aggression and revenge to anxiety, fear, grief and depression. Psychologically, a boy's potential is also thwarted. Danso further notes that the use and abuse of drugs by armed groups can result in low self-esteem, feelings of guilt, violent behaviour, shame and lack of trust and self-confidence. This is evident in *Beasts of No Nation* and Agu wishes that: 'One day there will be no more war and we can be living together in a house and eating all the food we are wanting to eat' (87).

In the camp, Agu experiences relative peace because according to him, he is tired of being in the midst of people who are screaming when they are killed. He expresses the hope of going back to school to study to become an engineer or medical doctor but he also fears that his present sadness might make him mad and possibly lead to his death if he cannot fight again, thereby missing the chance of being reunited with his mother and sister. He is also not spared memories of his father 'dancing the dance of death' in a hail of the enemies' bullets.

Other negative psychological consequences seen in the boys include, sleeplessness, nightmares, flashbacks, inability to go on with life, suicidal tendencies, sensitivity to strange or loud noises, feelings of shame and guilt about past actions, especially of having survived while others died, feelings of loneliness as a result of separation from once-loving family members, and a general fear of the unknown. These feelings become so acute at times that Agu feels like committing suicide so that he may be reunited with his war friends, especially Strika.

It is noteworthy that the story of *Beasts of No Nation* is told in Agu's voice in the first person singular. Here, one observes that Agu seems to have been so traumatized by the war that he can hardly articulate what he is witnessing. The voice creates a sense of chaos and strangeness of the world of war and of the confusion of being a child-soldier. Agu probably would have recovered much faster if he had returned to his family, but his continued separation from his family compounds his problems and prolongs his post-war period of rehabilitation and reintegration.

Socially, the children are also rendered misfits. We see in Ishmael Beah's *A Long Way Gone* the enormous challenges faced by the Rehabilitation Centre at the initial stage of the rehabilitation exercise. The boys' exposure to hard drugs like cocaine and to marijuana has had a devastating effect on them. For instance, the boys rush over food, a practice peculiar only to military training and to the effects of drugs. Ishmael tells us the military training concerning meals in the soldiers' camp thus:

> After we had done the running, crawling and crouching many times, we were allowed to have some bread and custard. The corporal gave us one minute to get the food and eat it. Whatever we hadn't eaten was taken away at the end of sixty seconds. None of us was able to finish eating on the first day, but within a week we could eat any food in a minute. (111)

The boys thus carried over this negative attitude to food when they came to the Rehabilitation Centre.

Ishmael also tells us that at the Rehabilitation Centre, ordinary advice and instructions irritated them since they believed the staff of the Centre to be 'civilians' who should respect them as soldiers who were capable of severely harming them. With this notion, the boys unleashed blows on any member of staff at the slightest provocation. Poppay for instance, was beaten into a state of coma for instructing them to dry their mattresses left by them in the rain the previous day. Also, since the boys had become addicted to drugs, at the Centre, Ishmael would roll sheets of paper to smoke when he craved for cocaine and marijuana and was not given any. However, when the paper failed to have the desired effect on him, he would resort to more violence, beating everybody in the vicinity. Alhaji on the other hand (another child-soldier), would punch the cement pillars of the building 'until his knuckles bled and his bones began to show' (140). On such occasions, he would be taken to the Centre's clinic and put to sleep so that he would not be able to hurt himself.

In order to occupy the boys' minds, to make them forget their involvement in the war and prepare them for life after rehabilitation, the Centre organized classes. But the boys would not accept this immediately and instead turned to make a camp fire of the school supplies, the books, pens and pencils given to them. As a result, attendance at classes had to be made a requirement to earn week-end trips to the city. The boys also find it difficult to trust anybody again. Even though the staff at the Centre, especially Esther, try their best to be friendly with them and encourage them to forget their past involvement in the war, Ishmael confesses:

> I... didn't trust anyone at this point in my life. I had learned to survive and take care of myself. I had done just that for most of my short life, with no one to trust, and frankly, I like being alone since it made surviving easier. (153)

After his rehabilitation, Ishmael is taken to a dance party by his cousin. However, Ishmael would not dance with any girl because the party triggered off the memory of a massacre at a school where he and his co-soldiers had killed several people. According to him, he 'could hear the terrified cries of teachers and students, could see the blood cover the dance floor' (184).

The boys also become so used to war and forest life that after Ishmael returned to Sierra Leone and war broke out again in Freetown, some of the boys with whom he had undergone rehabilitation rejoined the army. Such is the damage done to these young lives that they are unable to live normal lives again or reintegrate into the society even after they have been rehabilitated.

It becomes evident, from this description, children's literature in Africa has moved from this need to shield the young from the harsh realities of life to the depiction of grittier realities like war, sex and crime.

WORKS CITED

Beah, Ishmael. *A Long Way Gone: Memoirs of a Boy Soldier.* New York: Sarah Crichton Books, 2007.

Brassard, Maria and Steven Hart. 'Emotional Abuse: Words Can Hurt', National Committee to Prevent Child Abuse, Chicago: 1987, 91-103.

Doek, Jaap. 'Child Soldiers',. UN Report. Coalition to Stop the Use of Child Soldiers. London: 2001. http:i//www.child-soldiers.org. Retrieved on February 20, 2014.

'Children's Literature', unpublished lecture notes of the National Open University. Abuja, Nigeria, 2010.

Clark, John Pepper. 'The Casualties', in *A Selection of African Poetry.* K. E. Senanu and T. Vincent eds. London: Longman, 1976, 136-9.

Danso, Afua-Iwum. *Africa's Young Soldiers.* Institute for Security Studies (ISS) Pretoria, South Africa, 2003. www.issafrica.org/pgcontent.php. Retrieved on April 12, 2013.

Freud, Sigmund. *New Introductory Lecture on Psychoanalysis.* Norton: New York, 1933.

Garbarino, James and A. C. Garbarino. 'Emotional Maltreatment of Children', National Committee for Prevention of Child Abuse. Chicago: 1994.

Habila, Helon. *Measuring Time.* New York: Cassava Republic Press, 2007.

Indian Express. Mumbai: Indian Express Group, 10 February 2014, 7.

Iweala, Uzodinma. *Beasts of No Nation.* New York: Harper Collins Publishers, 2005.

Jarrett, Macaulay, Delia. *Moses, Citizen and Me.* London: Granta Books, 2005.

Makinde, M. T. 'Children's Literature' in *Aspects of Language and Literature: A Text for Tertiary Institutions,* eds. S. O. Ayodele, G. A. Osoba and Ola Mabekoje, Ibadan: Olu-Akin Printing Press, 2006, 361-74.

Ngugi wa Thiong'o. 'George Lamming's *In the Castle of my Skin', Critics on Caribbean Literature,* ed. Edward Baugh, London: George Allen and Unwin, 1978, 45-57.

Ofeimun, Odia. *The Poet Lied.* London: Longman, 1980.

O'Hagan, K. *Emotional and Psychological Abuse of Children.* Buckingham: Open University Press, 1993.

Onwuhanze, Jude. *The Genesis of Nigerian Biafran Civil War (1861-1970).* Enugu: Fourth Dimension Press, 2008.

Saro-Wiwa, Ken. *Soza Boy.* Port Harcourt: Saros International publishers, 1986.

Sherman, John. *War Stories: A Memory of Nigeria and Biafra.* Indianapolis: Mesa Verde Press, 2002.

Uko, Iniobong. 'Of War and Madness: A Symbolic Transmutation of the Nigerian. Biafran War in Select Stories from *The Insider: Stories of War and Peace from Nigeria'. African Literature Today.* Vol. 26, ed. Ernest Emenyonu, Ibadan: Heinemann, 2008, 49-58.

'Young Victims of War', *Awake Magazine.* New York: Watchtower Bible and Tract Society, 22 April 2005.

WEBSITE SOURCES: GOOGLE

http://www.britannica.com.EBchekked/topic/111289/childrens-literature
http://www.victerianweb.org/genre/childlit/definitions1 .html
http://www.ibby.org/index.php?id=718
http://www.partnersaginsthate.org.educators/books.html
http://www.breithinks.com/my-ibmedia/literature.htm
http://www.prisceten. edu-achaney/tmve/wiki100k/docs/Children_S_Literature

http://www.en.wikibooks.org/wiki/Choosing_High_Quality_Children's_Literature
http://www.slideshare.net/joh5700/defining-childrens-literature
http://www.jstor.org/discover/10.2307/2019821?uid=3738720 & uid = 2
http://www.ajol.info.index.php.udslj/article/view/26593
http://www.studymode.com/essays.The-Importance-Of-Teaching-Literature
http://www.childliterature.net/childlit/
http://www.oneotareadingjournal.com/2012/value-of-childrens-litrerature
http://www.comminfo.rutgers.edu/professional-development/childlit/ChildrenLit/
http://www.en.wikipedia.org/wikw/children's_literature
    (ALL RETRIEVED IN APRIL, 2014).

The Expatriated African Folktale

Exploring Adaptation in Juliana Makuchi's
The Sacred Door & Other Stories

EVE EISENBERG

This essay examines the multiple but interconnected textual, metafictional, and paratextual aspects of Makuchi's 2008 collection *The Sacred Door and Other Stories: Cameroon Folktales of the Beba.* The aim is to reveal the complexity of the contemporary status of the 'African folktale' as both text and concept in a global literary context, in relation to the concept of children's literature, and as part of a discourse of the African diasporic experience. *The Sacred Door* consists of a Foreword by Isidore Okpewho, a Preface by Makuchi, 34 tales, and an Afterword by Makuchi. The paratextual elements of *The Sacred Door* – Okpewho's Foreword, and Makuchi's Preface and Afterword, as well as the book's front and back covers – attempt to supply contextual components necessary for understanding the tales as print versions of oral literature.

Even as *The Sacred Door*'s paratextual elements depict the tales' contexts through a series of discursive tensions that Okpewho and Makuchi inaugurate (an attempt at contextualization taken up by other paratextual components such as the image on the book's front cover) the metafictional and paratextual elements of *The Sacred Door* ultimately point to the impossibility of re-creating the oral experience on the printed page. In her study of many aspects of the relationships between African oral arts and the African novel), Eileen Julien notes that oral tales cannot be understood in isolation from their contexts:

> There are, first of all, those written narratives that retell narratives of the oral tradition (A. Tutuola's *Palm-Wine Drinkard*, D. T. Niane's *Sundiata*). Because the new context of enunciation implies shifts in audience and message, such written texts are, of course, never transparent or equivalent copies of oral stories… (Julien 1992: 26)

The Sacred Door perfectly fits this definition as a 'written narrative that retells narratives of an oral tradition'. Julien's attention to 'the new context of enunciation' and 'shifts in audience and message'– from the scene of the performance of the oral tale to the printed page and a text published for an audience of readers instead of listeners/watchers/co-participants – points to her recognition 'that speech and oral traditions cannot be grasped adequately from paper representations', and that the study of orality 'is not simply a matter of "collecting stories" but, ideally, of understanding performances as do their participants' (Julien: 27). In other words, according to Julien, transmitting oral tales and their meanings requires interaction with more than a printed transcription of the tales. The performance of the tale, the setting of the performance – its social, historical, and political contexts, as understood by performer and audience – and the tale itself inextricably interweave within the performative moment to make meaning.

In her *Theory of Adaptation*, Linda Hutcheon comments that '[just] as there is no such thing as a literal translation, there can be no literal adaptation', and, indeed, moving an oral tale to a printed medium constitutes an act of adaptation (Hutcheon: 16). In the same vein, when Julien notes that 'written narratives that retell narratives of the oral tradition' are 'never transparent or equivalent copies of oral stories', she imbricates several concepts important to understanding oral literary arts. First, the dynamism of the setting of the live tale – the interactions between teller, audience, and world – can be described but not truly captured by simply moving an oral tale from its performed medium to a written one (Julien: 26). Important components of the oral tale's meaning, as its performer, audience, and context all together create it, come from the performative moment. Second, Julien's claim also recognizes the fundamental impossibility of a 'transparent' window from the printed word to the oral tale – the impossibility of producing a perfectly faithful version of the oral tale as a written one. Finally, her claim points to the problem of presupposing such transparency, for to presume it is to misunderstand, at an elementary level, that an oral tale's meaning and life spring from its moment of performance.

As Julien puts it, following Mikhail Bakhtin, 'Semiotically speaking, repeating an utterance is not, in fact, to repeat it but is, rather, to speak in a new context and thus create a new utterance. So the elements of traditional oral genres repeated, as it were, in new forms mean something new, accomplish something different' (47). *The Sacred Door*, rather than submitting – or submitting to – such a presupposition of transparency, ultimately calls attention in numerous ways to the impossibility of 'transparency,' to its own status as a 'new utterance,' and, eventually, to the liminal – and vexed – position of African authorship and African stories in a global diaspora.

Makuchi, the author of *The Sacred Door*, unarguably possesses capacious knowledge of African literature generally and Cameroonian oral folk traditions specifically, knowledge she earned for herself through the arduous upward climb through academe's various stages and ranks. Her studies and fieldwork amply qualify her to provide information about such topics. Although she published *The Sacred Door* simply under the name Makuchi, in academe she is Professor Juliana Makuchi Nfah-Abbenyi. She holds degrees from the University of Yaoundé in Cameroon as well as from McGill University, Canada, and has been working in the academy as a literature professor and literary scholar and critic since the 1980s. In addition to *The Sacred Door* and a lengthy list of critical studies, she previously published a collection of fiction short stories (*Your Madness, Not Mine: Stories of Cameroon*, 1999) As this summary of her accomplishments suggests while remaining involved with African literary arts no matter where she is located Makuchi has lived the transnational life of the African diasporic artist-academic, a familiar figure in the pantheon of late 20th and early 21st century African artists.

In *The Sacred Door*, Makuchi recounts the folktales (*ble*) *of* her youth in Beba, a village in the North West Province of Cameroon ('Afterword': 177). In her Preface to *The Sacred Door*, Makuchi explains her own history with the tales in the collection, describing how she grew up listening to the tales her mother and other relatives told, and she also did extensive graduate work from 1979 to 1987 on Beba oral literature. Her graduate work included laboriously collecting and transcribing her family's folktales, translating them, and then, as she puts it '[providing]…a final literary translation' for her dissertation (xxi). The stories in *The Sacred Door* represent what she can recall of the fruits of her doctoral research, and as such they cross disciplinary boundaries: if they are literary, because they are both stories and stories that were translated and re-crafted from a more raw form into a more polished one, the text also poses them as ethnographic artefacts of their place, community, and time, and thus as bearers of 'culture'.

While Makuchi authenticates the tales in *The Sacred Door* by presenting them as having been gathered as part of her doctoral work, thus grounding them qualitatively in the realm of academic rigour and methodologically in the Social Sciences, in the next breath she destabilizes any such grounding. Not incidentally, this destabilization of textual 'authenticity' and 'originality' coincides with the author's experience of intra-national movement and, eventually, international expatriation:

> Between 1981 and 1988 I moved five times within Cameroon…; then on to Montreal, Canada, in 1988 and the United States in 1994. In the process of packing, moving, and unpacking in Cameroon, property (including tape recordings, films of photographs and exercise books with handwritten notes) was damaged, lost, sometimes even destroyed by relatives in whose homes it had been stored over the years. The oral narratives of my graduate work have therefore never been published. The folktales presented in this book are my recreation of some of those stories we shared as a family – before and after I did graduate work – while we ate food, drank mostly palm wine and sometimes beer, socialized, and told *ble*. (Makuchi: 'Preface' xxi-xxii)

Because these are the tales as best she can remember them, 'recreated' and not recorded, some recounted to her as part of her graduate fieldwork and some from before that period, their actual sources obfuscated by Makuchi's inability to connect any tale in a direct line from the page to a prior storyteller other than herself; indeed, the stories become more literary – artefacts of memory and imagination – at the precise moment in which they become less ethnographic.

However, because some of them were, once, recorded, with all the rigour of scholarly discipline, the status of Makuchi's recollection achieves an enhanced authorization, which in turn casts the tales into, and reveals the existence of, a strangely liminal narrative space in which the intertextuality of texts is always being acknowledged at the same time as the contribution of individual storyteller-authors is also always foregrounded. This metafictional framing of the tales (metafictional because this is a story Makuchi is telling *about* the stories in her collection) reinforces an acknowledgement of their intertextuality because it renders each story in *The Sacred Door* a bricolage of multiple potential texts: a tale Makuchi heard at some time in her past, prior to her doctoral work, narrated by someone in her family; a tale Makuchi made the focus of her doctoral work by recording, transcribing, and translating it (and likely such a tale was *also* one she would have heard as a child); and a tale Makuchi has 'recreated' through the process of remembering both its oral echoes and, potentially, the literary form into which she rendered it as part of her scholarly work. Thus Makuchi's metafictional narrative positions the tales in *The Sacred Door* as already made up of multiple texts, all of them the products of memory, authorship, and selection.

This textual multiplicity also emphasizes the multitude of voices potentially involved in each tale, paradoxically both mystifying – and communalizing – the subject position of their authorship(s) while simultaneously insisting on viewing the tales as products of specific storytellers in specific moments. Simply by recounting the history of the tales and of her relationship to them, Makuchi invokes and sustains a tension that blurs the tales' origins; this blurring, in turn, brings to the surface the reality that authors – whether of oral tales or printed texts – always exist, even if we cannot precisely name or locate them, and even if no one can or will name them for us.

Thus, no matter the extent to which tales seem to be bearers of communal 'culture', individual subjects – with their own agendas, ideas, and prejudices – make, write, and tell all tales. Of course, Makuchi undermines this acknowledgment of the author-as-individual by blurring the actual identities of these individuals, and by framing the tales as profoundly intertextual artefacts of her own memory, each one the product of decades of her life experience. This blurring therefore contributes to *The Sacred Door*'s narrative liminality because of the text's refusal to either fully mystify or fully trace the author-/ownership of the tales. The tension produced by this blurring also renders visible another reality: despite the fact that, as noted via Julien and Hutcheon, it is impossible to reproduce perfectly the experience of an oral tale on the printed page, the communal life of each *tale* inseparably intertwines with each individual *storyteller.* The tales themselves become artefacts of the liminal space between subject and community. As Julien might put it, they derive meaning from neither speaker, audience, nor context, but rather from the interactions between all three.

Ironically, part of the tales' narrative liminality stems from the manner in which these 'Cameroon folktales of the Beba' were in fact remembered from the metropole, not pulled up directly by their roots from African soil. But while this irony is important – and is discussed further in this essay in relation to Akin Adesokan's theorization of postcolonial artistic 'expatriation' – this narrative liminality also descends, in an irony parallel to the previous one. The 'family' from whom the stories come is the same one that 'damaged, lost, sometimes even destroyed' the physical records of the stories themselves.

By metafictionally narrativizing her collection in this manner, Makuchi creates a literary ouroboros: the 'family,' sometimes metonymized by Makuchi's mother, and also always a metonym for the entire Beba community, both makes and unmakes its own tales. Or, rather, the family made the tales in a specific moment, and what it has consumed are only the static records of that moment, records in which the stories have become frozen in time, half-way between oral and printed media.

Makuchi's metafictional account of the tales thus positions them as liminal in several different registers: they are neither the faithful products of scientifically precise fieldwork, nor are they simply the mistily-remembered tales of a distant childhood. They are not localized to specific tellers and moments in history, or vaguely attributable to some unknown storyteller-speakers of a communal Beba history. They are neither fully oral nor fully printed. Other versions of them live and breathe in the same moment as *The Sacred Door*, making *The Sacred Door* a kind of literary doppleganger, a collection of versions of stories whose indeterminacy always points to the co-existence of other versions, other storytellers, and other story-telling moments.

As these metafictional examples indicate, *The Sacred Door* subverts the very impulses it seems to answer by creating, and then periodically re-introducing, various tensions, especially tensions of authorship. These may be between individual and communal authorship, and of disciplines: between the literary and the ethnographic, the Humanities and the Social Sciences. *The Sacred Door* could be said to inaugurate a kind of category crisis, precisely in the way it both embodies and subverts the authorial and interdisciplinary cross-purposes of the individual and the communal, the literary and the ethnographic.

While all of Makuchi's degrees are in 'Literature' in one form or another, the methodology she employed , and which she describes in her Preface, comes from the Social Sciences, especially from ethnography. In his Foreword to *The Sacred Door*, Isidore Okpewho reinforces this idea when he discusses one of the challenges confronting scholars seeking to provide English translations of oral narratives.

...the ethnopoetic revolution of the 1970s, which has demanded of scholars a considerable faith in their representation of texts they collect from informants and artists, in such a way as to respect the orality of the enterprise and thus the accuracy of the material. (ix)

Okpewho's description of the 'demand' for scholars like Makuchi to produce written texts which 'faithfully' and 'accurately' represent oral literature received from 'informants' demonstrates how such scholars straddle disciplinary boundaries. If her study of Beba tales as oral literature places her in Literature and the Humanities, the ethnographic demands of good fieldwork also situate her, and *The Sacred Door*, in the Social Sciences.

In order for Makuchi's collection of textually 'reproduced' oral tales to meet the academically rigorous 'demands' Okpewho mentions (and to which Julien alludes), she must deliver, alongside the tales, an exacting and detailed picture of their contexts. As part of the process of 'creating a new utterance' of her collection of Beba folktales, Makuchi is also creating a new utterance about African literary arts. Clearly well-versed in these theories of orality – no doubt due to her extensive scholarship in the field – Makuchi presents her reader not only with contextual information about the stories and the community from which they were gathered, but also about orality itself. The author of the collection's Foreword, Isidore Okpewho, remains one of the most prominent authorities on and proponents of African oral literature. In something of a violation of the conventions of children's literature, *The Sacred Door* introduces itself to its readership with a scholarly, though very readable, commentary on the state of African oral literature in translation.

Yet, similar to the way Makuchi's Preface creates and maintains tensions between different registers of authorship, Okpewho's Foreword counterposes the scholarly, academic pursuit of the gathering of oral tales against a concern for 'African youths in the mother continent' as well as 'those in the new African diaspora in the Anglophone Western world' (x). After lamenting the fact that Makuchi has been unable to return to Cameroon 'to revisit the sources of her material to re-cognize the context that enabled the tales and to check them with the relevant personnel, many of whom may have passed away,' Okpewho goes on to commend 'the spirit behind the effort' of *The Sacred Door*, because while it fails to meet academic standards for scholarly study, the tales it contains may serve another important function:

Because the tales are presented in a language and a format that appeals more directly to a younger readership than in a frame specifically geared toward more scholarly study, they would be particularly useful for bringing the lessons of the old traditions home to the appreciation of these youths. (Okpewho: 'Foreword' x)

Okpewho in his Foreword and Makuchi in her Preface construct a dialectical relationship between academic scholarship of African oral arts and children's literature, a dialectic that has the ultimate effect of simultaneously emphasizing and blurring methodological, qualitative, aesthetic, and utilitarian differences between the two. It is precisely because the tales in the collection 'are presented in a language and a format' that are *not* scholarly that they can 'appeal more directly to a younger readership'. The discourses of children's literature and upper-level academic scholarship thus appear both mutually exclusive and paradoxically always linked by the necessity of their co-defining one another; the academic is that which children would not understand and/or be interested in, and that which is for children lacks the rigour which would authenticate it to the academic.

Okpewho further imbricates these discourses as he interweaves fundamental information about African oral arts with an evaluation of the didactic properties of the tales, which, he claims, 'reveal a characteristically tropical African environment and outlook' (x). While he undermines the academic rigour of the collection due to its methodological shortcomings, Okpewho simultaneously authenticates the tales as accurate reflections of the culture from which they come. Even if, for Okpewho, they fail to meet the standards necessary for the academy, their didactic value persists

…because the lessons they yield belong not merely to a long-forgotten historical or so-called primitive past but very much to the present times in which we live. […] I particularly applaud Makuchi's restating the mores of African societies in the present tense, as a way of stressing that in whatever conditions we live today, the ideas that have guided our lives continue to be valid. (xi)

Okpewho thus contributes to the narrative liminality of the collection by framing it as a conveyor of 'the mores of African societies in the present tense'. In this metafictional construction, tales that Makuchi began gathering nearly thirty years prior to the publication of *The Sacred Door* contain universal truths that are, paradoxically, characteristic of 'a tropical African environment'.

Their fitness as didactic tools for children persists both because and in spite of the accuracy with which they reflect the specific, local culture from which they come.

The narrative liminality into which Okpewho casts *The Sacred Door* causes the text to throw into sharp relief the very rhetoric about orality which might otherwise go unremarked in both academic and children's literature discourses. By invoking the seemingly paradoxical tensions between textual accuracy and inaccuracy, and between rigour and appeal, Okpewho's Foreword emphasizes rather than occludes these discursive relationships.

This seems all the more remarkable in light of the resistance it offers to longstanding stereotypes about African oral arts. Eileen Julien crystallizes an essentialized – and essentializing – viewpoint both inside and outside of academe when she investigates the 'unspoken belief that novels were not for Africans (because oral forms were)'. The corollary of this statement is that 'the novel is not natural in Africa' (9). As a result of her analysis of multiple examples of rhetoric linking African orality to the production of a characteristically *African* novel, Julien finds that,

> Paradoxically, the assumption of the profoundly oral nature of African life and art is expressed more subtly in the expectation or requirement that novels be leavened with the appropriate African yeast of orality. [...] The implication is that the novel is European until it inscribes orality and thereby becomes African.
>
> It is this bias, it seems to me, which reveals our thinking that an African essence can be found in, and indeed is bound to, orality. (10)

Julien's discursive analysis unveils the manner in which critics isolate the form of orality itself, or the genre of the oral tale, from written story-telling, and make it the bearer of a racially essentialized version of Africanness.

Okpewho's Foreword, far from subscribing to such an essentializing view of orality, and as a result of the tensions it teases out between discourses, spotlights the fraught and tenuous position of the tales as bearers of 'culture'. No matter the extent to which they may convey 'a characteristically tropical African environment and outlook', the international, diasporic, hybrid world they enter, as Okpweho and Makuchi both describe it, is fundamentally incommensurate with such essentialized identities, an incommensurability which is, paradoxically, the very reason why the tales retain their relevance as didactic tools. Moreover, the work Okpewho has also done to destabilize *The Sacred Door*'s status as a transparent conveyance of oral tales renders his comments about the tales' capacity to teach youth the world over about 'the mores of African societies in the present tense' highly vexed, in turn emphasizing the problematic aspects of a presupposition of oral tales' relationships to 'culture' and 'authenticity'.

The discursively *African* identity that both Makuchi and Okpewho construct, within and as part of a description of the liminal position of the Beba tales, roots itself not in the African past, nor truly on the continent itself; rather, this identity derives, in part, from the experiences of transnational expatriation and global diaspora. Both Makuchi and Okpewho frame Makuchi's drive to write *The Sacred Door* as emerging from her desire to convey the tales of her youth to her children:

> Although story-telling was a family affair back then, I owe a particular debt and tribute to my mother, who played the pivotal role of getting things started and keeping them going. Ever since her death in 1984, I can hardly remember us, her children, duplicating as a group the family tradition [of story-telling] she started, nor have we done so with my stepmother (who is not Beba). Complicating this situation is the fact that as we got older and more Western-educated we moved away to other parts of the country, and even abroad, where we are raising our own families. Over the years our family visits to Beba have been infrequent. [...] I see my retelling of these folktales as another link in the chain of that creative spirit and legacy and also as a mea culpa to my own children who, I might add, speak very little Beba. (Makuchi 'Preface' xxii)

The emphasis Makuchi places on the subjective agency of the storyteller denaturalizes the notion that orality and Africanness simply go hand in hand; instead, story-telling represents a conscious choice to retain, imaginatively, 'links in the chain of that creative spirit and legacy' to connect the diaspora to the homeland and vice versa.

Along with this acknowledgment of the effort and volition involved in story-telling, the far-flung, international, multilingual, and metropolitan African family takes up and complicates the roles of storyteller and audience, writer and reader. In *Postcolonial Artists and Global Aesthetics*, Akin Adesokan is

> interested in the institutional and aesthetic context in which artists – writers, filmmakers, essayists – work, and how those contexts shape and are shaped by their works in relation to questions of cultural mobility, expatriation, and commodification... (14)

He pursues these interests, in part, via an inquiry into 'the phenomenon of expatriation and metropolitan location and its impact on genre in a global context' (19). As part of his historical materialist examination of these issues, Adesokan discusses 'a complex social formation, the *crossroads of capital*', his term for the polyvalent socioeconomic, cultural, and historical forces at work on African and other postcolonial artists over the past few decades (xii, emphasis orig.). Specifically in the context of his discussion of African artists' choices to employ new technologies such as video, and in the case of Ousmane Sembene to choose filmmaking over or alongside the genre of the novel, Adesokan remarks that, at this 'crossroads of capital', '[the] artists, like their audiences, are open to different formats, to using whatever works, given the socioeconomic structure' that influences what kinds of formats and, indeed, genres are possible at a given moment and in a particular location (22).

The Sacred Door demonstrates that, when 'the phenomenon of expatriation and metropolitan location' produces an 'impact on genre,' artists such as Makuchi respond by 'being open to new formats, to using whatever works'. In Makuchi's case, reproducing the setting and experience of oral story-telling can only take place as a result of a generic transition, from oral tales to written collection. Therefore when she describes *The Sacred Door* as her 'retelling of these folktales', Makuchi self-consciously draws attention to the generic refiguring she has enacted. As part of her larger project, in the text's Preface, of recounting the complex story of her relationship to the tales, and of her own experience of expatriation, her use of the word 'retelling' metaphorizes what is, in truth, a complicated endeavour of generic adaptation.

Makuchi's 'retelling' metaphor parallels oral story-telling with written story-telling and in doing so draws attention to their differences, especially to that which the written can never (re) produce: the aural experience of the sound of the storyteller's voice as she 'tells' it. At the same time, *The Sacred Door*'s significant paratextual apparatus – which includes, in addition to its Foreword and Preface, a lengthy Afterword which contains a great deal of contextual information – already attempts to supplement the gap to which the 'retelling' metaphor alludes. What *The Sacred Door* attempts to provide is some semblance of the 'heterocosm' of the village setting in which Makuchi originally experienced the tales. Linda Hutcheon, in *A Theory of Adaptation*, describes an adaptational heterocosm:

...Disney World visitors who go on the Aladdin ride can enter and physically navigate a universe originally presented as a linear experience through film.

What gets adapted here is a heterocosm, literally an 'other world' or cosmos, complete, of course, with the stuff of a story – settings, characters, events, and situations. To be more precise, it is the '*res extensa*' – to use Descartes' terminology – of that world, its material, physical dimension, which is transposed and then experienced through multisensory interactivity (Grau 2003: 3, quoted in Hutcheon: 14).

Unlike the Disney World 'Aladdin' ride Hutcheon describes, *The Sacred Door* lacks the capacity to provoke a truly 'multisensory interactive' experience. At the same time, the text delivers more than the tales; the paratextual elements include important visual components. A richly multi-hued photograph of the rolling green peaks and valleys of 'Mbama, Beba,' the mountains overlain by heavy grey rainclouds, spans the front and back covers of the book; a note on the back cover indicates that Makuchi took the photograph herself 'in June 1999'. The book also includes a photo of Makuchi on the back cover, and several maps, of Cameroon and of the Beba homeland, in the Afterword.

As part of the attempt to adapt into textual form the 'heterocosm' of the tales, the visual images play several roles. The landscape photo and maps aid the reader in picturing the geographical and political boundaries, as well as the natural surroundings, of the location in which Makuchi heard the tales. The photo of Makuchi herself helps the reader to imagine the person whose voice 'tells' the tales. If, as Okpewho notes in his Foreword to *The Sacred Door*, 'the collapse of structures sustaining honest endeavor in academic and other areas of life in African societies' has led to 'many of these African scholars [emigrating] to Western nations where their labors have found support', the circumstances of what Adesokan would call this 'crossroads of capital' (Okpewho: ix) force the storyteller to adapt oral tales into new, and decidedly vexed, formats. However, they fail to sever completely the African oral tale's connection to African expatriates and their descendants in diaspora.

In conclusion, it is noteworthy that several of the tales in the collection strongly recall other narratives. Okpewho notes the strong similarity between 'The Girl Who Refused Suitors' and a passage ('The Complete Gentleman') in Amos Tutuola's *Palm-Wine*

Drinkard, a parallel that begs interesting questions about how the story circulated amongst different West African regions, as well as why that particular theme resonated powerfully in different communities. Even more strikingly, 'The Unhappy Stepson' relates what will be, to many readers, the instantly recognizable 'Cinderella' narrative. Makuchi's version differs from Disney's in that it has a male protagonist and a much more rational figure in the 'fairy godmother' role; in Makuchi's version, Disney's cosmologically inexplicable fairy godmother is simply the spirit of the suffering stepson's deceased mother, lingering from beyond the grave out of concern for her child.

Even as the metafictional and paratextual elements of *The Sacred Door* emphasize the vexed, incommensurable, and liminal experience of the expatriated African artist and the expatriated African artwork, the text itself harmonizes to a different key of the same melody. '[We] experience adaptations', claims Hutcheon, 'as palimpsests through our memory of other works that resonate through repetition with variation' (8). 'The Unhappy Stepson', as it turns out, resonates with much more than the global commodity that is the Disney *Cinderella* film and all its permutations of 'princess culture'.

A version of this 'Cinderella narrative' is found in the 'Smeda Rmeda' tale of the Atlas Mountains of Morocco, from whence it then travelled, in 1955, to Israel, along with Moroccan Jews (Bar-Itzhak: 93-4). In Hausaland, 'The Maiden, the Frog and the Chief's Son,' despite coming from a region relatively close to Cameroon, has a female protagonist, as does 'Smeda Rmeda' and, of course, Disney's *Cinderella* (Bascom: 56-9). A very old Tibetan version, it turns out, possibly 'has an early source in Indian Buddhism' (Schlepp: 33). And the ninth-century Chinese tale of Yexian comes from the Zhuang people who 'lived at a crossroads in the ninth century, absorbing and resisting Hindu and Buddhist influences from South and Southeast Asia, and Han Chinese political and cultural dominance from the north and east' (Beauchamp: par. 2).

'The Unhappy Stepson' thus demonstrates that when people have travelled or become expatriated, so too have stories, and that even when the stories themselves change in small or large ways, often something recognizable remains, although it is not always the *same* recognizable thing as in other permutations. The tale thus indicates that Makuchi stands near the front of a very long line of storytellers, stretching back through time and crisscrossing every inhabited corner of the globe, making her part of a narrative continuity that is itself constructed, paradoxically, out of many experiences of discontinuity, of expatriation, of long journeys, and of diasporas.

WORKS CITED

Adesokan, Akin. (2011) *Postcolonial Artists and Global Aesthetics* Bloomington IN: Indiana University Press.

Bar-Itzhak, Haya (1993), '"Smeda Rmeda Who Destroys Her Luck with Her Own Hands": A Jewish Moroccan Cinderella Tale in an Israeli Context', *Journal of Folklore Research* 30, 2/3, May-Dec.: 93-125. www.jstor/stable/3814312. Accessed 5 February 2015.

Bascom, William (1972). 'Cinderella in Africa', *Journal of the Folklore Institute* 9,1: 54-70.

Beauchamp, Fay E. (1993) 'Asian Origins of Cinderella: The Zhuang Storyteller of Guangxi', *Oral Tradition*, 30, 2: 92-125.

Hutcheon, Linda (2006). *A Theory of Adaptation*. New York: Routledge.

Julien, Eileen M. (1992). *African Novels and The Question of Orality*. Bloomington IN: Indiana University Press.

Makuchi [Nfah-Abbenyi, Juliana Makuchi]. (2008). *The Sacred Door and Other Stories: Cameroon Folktales of the Beba*. Athens OH: Ohio University Press.

Nfah-Abbenyi, Juliana Makuchi. 'Curricilum Vitae.' Department of English faculty profile. North Carolina State University website. Accessed 27 February 2015.

Okpewho, Isidore (2008). 'Foreword', in Makuchi, (2008), ix-xv.

Schlepp, Wayne (2002). 'Cinderella in Tibet', *Asian Folklore Studies* 61: 123-47.

The Pedagogy
of Urban Children's Game Songs

Ageism, as a field of discourse, seeks to deconstruct and break barriers that are constructed because of age, and to open up interest in the understanding of the different ages. Although in ageist discourse no age is free from prejudice, the interest of this chapter is to find out whether the composition of game songs by children supports the argument that the children are innocent and naïve. The aim of the paper is to underscore the fact that children's game songs reveal who the children are and how well equipped they are to face the challenges that await them as they grow into adulthood in the African postcolonial society. The intention is to explore whether children's game songs generate a pedagogy that interprets and defines children from their own view point, which in adult discourse may just be considered meaningless. An analysis follows of songs by children collected in an informal play setting. This research is significant as it shifts from much of the professional critique to date on children's literature, as most critics interpret works written by adults for, not by, children.

Spontaneity is a central tool in oral composition and perform-ance, but the songs in this study were collected after children were organized to perform them in primary schools in the urban city of Buea in Cameroon. Buea is a cosmopolitan city, as it is the headquarters of the region. Children in postcolonial society have been introduced to television and computer activities more than to outdoor games and plays. Parents' diverse interests have also limited children's play times. The period that most children have for play is during lunch break in schools, lasting about 30 to 50 minutes. The organized performances took their steam as the children on stage put in their best in terms of singing and performance.

As a theoretical and conceptual consideration, the views of Paulo Freire in *Pedagogy of the Oppressed* ([1970] 2000) have been valuable. This book, which Donaldo Macedo, citing Stanley Aronowitz (2000, 11) describes as meeting 'the single criterion of a "classic" sets out Friere's ideology of deconstructing hegemonies even in the way education is conceived and transmitted. Freire argues that education 'must begin with the solution of the teacher-student contradiction, by reconciling the poles of the contradiction so that both are simultaneously teachers and students' (72). This argument is central to this discussion: the child is teacher and pupil at the same time; it deconstructs the concept of an adult teacher who assumes the all-knowing position and begins to 'deposit' information, values, or beliefs on a child, so that he or she has no possibility to create himself or herself.

To understand children's game songs, it is important to understand the performance context. To perform means to bring something to effect; be it a story, an identity, or a historical memory. Performance brings elements of beauty, mannerism, speech and body gestures. Helen Chukwuma (2002: 203) suggests that 'Performance is the life of oral literature and involves the totality of artist, audience and context. It is the main distinguishing feature between oral and written literature. An oral composition does not rest on a page.' For orature to exist, there must be performance. It is in this light that Ruth Finnegan (1970) agrees that 'the significance of performance in oral literature goes beyond a mere matter of definition: for the nature of performance itself can make an important contribution to the impact of a particular literary form being exhibited' (2). Thus, game songs can be better appreciated by observing how the children performed the different songs. The context of a performance enables us to examine the nature of the performance, the voice modulation of the performer, the costumes, props, and audience reaction. This approach seeks to establish that the compositions by the children are not entirely nonsensical as Nol Alembong (2011) suggests, but that their performances reveal not only the literariness of the text but actually interpret the context to the children, as Finnegan (1970) suggests.

Frequently, a performance is a stylish display of hands and legs movements. In most cases, there is a child who leads in the game and whose goal is to remain a leader as long as she can trick her friends. If her hands or legs move in the same direction as those of any of her playmates, the playmate 'wins' and takes her place. The games include 'My grandmother' and 'Awoum mbele'. Performance does not require a specific setting or arena, as the children just need a space at home, on the farm or during lunch-break in school. In this performance, two children can play the role of performer and audience and they swap places depending on whether the performer fails to trick the audience. When there are more children, the game becomes more competitive. The major 'stage props' for this performance are the legs and hands. Children clap to a specific rhythm that is very pleasing and entertaining even to adults. The hands are waved backwards and forwards with sporadic clapping, and various messages are conveyed by precise leg movements.

The lead performer has to be so smart that no other performer takes up the same steps or movements as hers, for that will bring her to the position of the secondary performer or into the audience. Children do not need any costumes or props to play the game.

A variation on this theme is 'swing' performance, a game with two competing teams. One team swings the rope, (the main prop, usually made of rubber), while the other team jumps to the rhythm of the song that the audience sings for them. At the same time, this second team has to avoid being tripped up in the rope. The context for this kind of game is school, home or farm. It has no special costume. The children just need some reasonable space to organize themselves for the performance.

Some children's games have dance as the principal act of performance, usually forming into circles. As far as children's games are concerned, these too are well organized. Such games have a lead performer who, for the most part, plays the role of the artistic director. The games often begin with a call and response, between the leader and players.

Lead: Form a circle,
Chorus: A circle
Lead: Wider wider,
Chorus: Wider

This rhyme goes on until the required size of circle is attained, as determined by the lead performer. The children hold their hands and hitch up their skirts or dresses for the game. In some cases, very little girls tug up their clothes into their pants. When the circle is formed, the lead singer pitches the song and the children dance in a circle. One popular song is 'You don marry'. The outer circle is the audience, and those dancing in the inner circle are the performers. Each dancer in the middle is expected to perform her best style. The game is not competitive, but any girl who cannot dance well is often mocked and laughed at; it is usual that a girl may end up crying or that a very courageous one ends up fighting to re-impose her dignity.

> The stage and context for this performance also vary as the children can play anywhere during any free time, however short that time is. Discussions with children on the performance context reveal that their songs produce some kind of creative ingenuity and sense of order among them. The children's songs show that children are capable of building communities whose wholeness rests on certain values that of 'belonging'. . . . It should be noted that in most team games, the children freely choose which team to join, and in some cases, when choosing is done by selection, some children refuse to adhere to fixed or set groups. In that case, they choose another group or are not part of the game. Thus, these games and their songs signify a strong force for community education that counters the individualistic Western life style that is eroding the African community with the introduction of television, internet, and other ICT gadgets. (Smith, 1998)

Children's game songs can also serve to liberate the mind. Paulo Freire's main concern in *Pedagogy of the Oppressed* is the liberation of those he describes as 'dehumanized'. He defines this as a condition 'which marks not only those whose humanity has been stolen, but also ... those who have stolen it' (2000: 44). This representation holds true in the binary of adult/children since adults define children to a large degree. Any consideration of the child is only interpreted by what Freire calls 'the form of false generosity' which is 'nourished by death, despair, and poverty'. He argues that children need to develop strategies of liberation. Frantz Fanon (1968) argues that such awareness must come through violence: in his view, if dehumanization comes through violence, re-humanization should come by violence. Fanon's notion of liberation is not different from Freire's who states that 'Liberation is thus a child birth, and a painful one' (2000: 49). The image of childbirth shows that liberation is urgent in human society and the child is not to be left out. The child's existence is relevant and it needs its own space. This liberation becomes even more urgent as children have never been given the opportunity to define themselves and are all the time seen as naïve persons who need adults in charge, in order to exist and to think.

Listening to and studying the lyrics of the children's songs during their games show that children are very creative, and that their songs contribute significantly to their education. Thus, children's songs become what bell hooks (2000) has described as a teaching whose pedagogy is that of liberation. Thomas Tenjoh-Okwen states that 'children's literature in Cameroon [and the world at large] … is perhaps, the most logical approach capable of providing, in the long run, a solution to the greater bigger problem…' (1996: 304). It is true that Tenjoh-Okwen's approach is focused on the fact that adults should produce for children, but children also often create their own literature.

Considering the phraseology of children's game songs, Nol Alembong (2011) suggests that 'Children's songs are songs sung either by those who have charge of the children as they grow up or by the children themselves' (91). Alembong's recognition of children's creative ability and the fact that children's creativity can inspire scholastic discourses is significant. They constitute an originality that is rare among literary professionals, especially in the area of postcolonial studies and postcolonial urban orature. The characteristics of simple language and structure of these songs is common in children's literature. Alembong writes that 'They are characterized by simplicity of diction, onomatopoeic words, striking tonal and phonological patterns, rhythm and cadence.' Alembong's focus is on 'songs sung by those who have charge of the children as they grow up and then on songs sung by the children themselves' (91). The characteristics of songs composed by children are the focus of analysis in the following section.

The songs are generally characterized by simple line structures with mostly monosyllabic words, and hardly use more than six words on a line. The simple diction and syntactic structure are built on heavy repetition, enhancing the musicality of the songs. They are usually in the the call and response style, shifting from 'Abstract Expressionism' to 'a new kind of realism' (Machlis & Forney, 1995: 559), an attempt to work 'in the gap between life and art' (Raushenberg 1995: 560). In the first song in the Appendix of Alembong (2011), the wording is:

Mini mini mini mini
Oh mini mini (2x)
Pick'am no fear
Oh mini mini
If you fear you go die
You go die oh mini mini

It is usually performed as children go about picking up litter in an effort to clean the school campus. The call and response nature of the songs shows that all the children are active as they sing and clean simultaneously. The simplicity of the lines and choice of words makes the song easy to repeat. Such simple structure and diction are also visible in the fourth song, 'Zuza zuza', in which the children's poetic imagery as well as their diction are direct and understandable. There is no space to construct a style or diction that will obscure the meaning of any of these songs: the children reveal their simple and plain minds, and their mode of interpreting and responding to issues in their world.

The lyrics of the songs also reveal that post-independence Africa and Cameroon have become multilingual. Children are able to use languages that they find in their communities and oftentimes, their songs are a blend of languages. Among the songs that were collected, there were hardly any entirely in one language. Some songs are rendered exclusively in Pidgin, such as 'Which Kind Soup?' (14), others entirely in English such as 'My Grandmother' (6). There are songs in a blend of mother tongue and Pidgin and/ or English and French : 'Awoum mbele' (3). Usually the words are mispronounced as the children in their performance may be more concerned with the tone and the sounds of the words and less with the semantics of the sounds they produce. Alembong (2011) refers to the meaningless sounds of many such songs. It is worth appreciating that children's ability to create texts and perform them as song helps them to sharpen their creative skills, hopefully to become credible poets and musicians in their adulthood.

Children's game songs can also be considered as dialogical educational tools. Freire's preference for dialogue in education as opposed to the 'banking' or storing up of information shows that children can teach themselves with their songs. Notions of classroom curricula shift as children are teaching and learning at the same time. Freire questioned that same notion of the teacher and student relationship:

> A careful analysis of the teacher-student relationship at any level, inside or outside the school, reveals its fundamentally *narrative* character. This relationship involves a narrating subject (the teacher) and patient, listening object (the student). The contents, whether values or empirical dimension[s] of reality, tend in [the] process of being narrated to become lifeless and petrified. Education is suffering from narration sickness. (2000: 71)

The all-powerful subject (the teacher) becomes an oppressor to the voiceless object (the student) and therefore, refuses him/her the mind to think since the 'teacher issues communiqués and makes deposits which the student patiently receives, memorize[s] and repeats (72). This is clearly what Freire identifies as the process of dehumanization. To 're-humanize', he advocates a dialogical approach to education which has two dimensions – reflection and action. When these two dimensions are met, Freire suggests, 'to speak a true word is to transform the world' (87). The concept of the 'true word' is important here. It has to do with words that come from conviction, that are freely expressed without any censor, or tele-guidance. Children's ability to interpret their own space through songs is already that effort to change the world around them as they do so in their own words and from their own perceptions. Through their songs, children are collectively educated, as in song 4, for instance:

> Zuza zuza on her
> Way to school
> Kaka Beri
> If you wish
> Names of
> Names of (food for boys, girls, animals)
> For example
> John. Be quick

Here the performers are very attentive so that they may hear the name called and respond promptly. Such songs sharpen hearing capacity. The performers must also respect speed and accuracy. That is why 'Be quick' is central in the song and game because slow and sluggish minds are not accepted. Usually the singers ask themselves for names of flowers, trees, animals (wild and domestic) and many other things in their environment.

The song starts with Zuza on her 'way to school', demonstrating that the children are conscious of the importance of attending it. However, it is interesting that there is a shift from Zuza to 'Kaka Beri' which helps a mature reader to decipher the origin of the song. Kaka is a derogatory name given to the Yamba ethnic group in Cameroon. Just like Mbum and Nso ethnic groups in Cameroon, Yamba people refer to their women as Beri. The performers are not interested in where Beri comes from, or how derogatory the expression 'Kaka' may be. Their task is the brain game of naming things and being quick. Here, we find children not only educating themselves but also being able to accommodate and respect one another.

Personal hygiene is very important in the lives of children and their environment and the song 'Mini Min'i' is a composition to remind the children. It is performed as a call for cleanliness. In the line 'Pick'am no fear' the lead voice is telling the other performers and singers that dirtiness needs to be eliminated without fear. In the next line, the lead voice sings 'you fear you go die' to show that if the children do not fight to keep their environment clean, dirtiness will kill them.

As far as personal hygiene is concerned, the children learn through their songs how to take care of themselves. In song 6:

My grandmother is
sitting on the waist.
She doesn't hear what
The doctor has said.
woupi a whoop. 3x

Now the time is six o'clock
We are going to brush our teeth.
woupi a whoop. 3x

The song in two stanzas has as a principal theme caring for oneself. The image of the grandmother in stanza one is very important because it represents the care, wisdom and protection that only grandmothers are widely known to give. However, the setting of this song is in the hospital and the grandmother seems to be very stubborn, as she does not listen to her doctor.

In the second stanza, the focus is on personal hygiene. The image used is cleaning the teeth. In terms of pedagogy, the word teeth is a metonymic as it represents the whole body and even the child's environment. The song's refrain, 'woupi a woup', is not obvious in meaning but a very melodious line beautifully structured in intervals of thirds. In its structure, this song represents the playful mind of the child, with no flow of thematic order. It symbolizes the excitement of the child composer at the game, so that any idea that comes to mind fits with the melodic line and it is rendered freely. If this is indeed a process of ideological construction, then children's creative activities should be taken seriously and they should be encouraged to create and recreate at will.

In these songs, the child is also seen as a satirical artist in the community, a kind of 'self-appointed guardian of standards, ideals and truth; of moral as well as aesthetic values' (Cuddon, 1999: 780). This suggests that children are not naïve and passive members of the society. Even a child can serve as a reformer. In song 13, for example

Je t'avais dit depuis hier,	I told you yesterday
Que ma mère est malade.	That my mother is sick
Tu étais à la maison,	You were at home
Maintenant elle est morte.	Now she is dead
Eh ya eh ya eh ya (3x)	
Maintenant elle est morte.	

The song was composed in the French-speaking section of Cameroon. It should be noted that Cameroon is a bicultural country with a legacy of both English and French colonialist practices. It is inaccurate to see Cameroon as a francophone country just because of its large French-speaking population and the fact that succeeding governments since 'independence' in 1961, have been predominantly francophone. English-speaking Cameroonian children performed it, indicating that such songs help to improve French and English/French bilingualism at a young age, a fulfilment of national policy. The song also shows the child responding to his/her multicultural and multilingual context by grasping different languages and recreating them artistically. This is also demonstrated in song 9, 'Mbolo mbolo', in which English, French and the mother-tongue are blended.

Song 13, 'Je t'avais dit' above shows that there is an active observer who may be regarded as a reformist. In this case, the child is 'self-appointed guardian of standards, ideals and truth; of moral as well as aesthetic values' (Cuddon, 1999). This means that the child becomes a satirist and a protest singer even in his/her game songs. The song is an open attack on irresponsibility and the song largely reminds the singers to be responsible in life and to learn to look after others. The tone of the song is not like a dirge, and the interjection 'Eh ya' is one of the most melodious lines of the piece and the dancing that accompanies it is most aesthetically performed.

Generally, the children's songs promote values of moral rectitude in children as the songs also attack vices in the society. In song 8

'I Love Mama' the children celebrate and honour the mother. In song 7 'Amina', the child learns the days of the week and how to count. In song 5 'This Girl has no Eyes' the stupidity of children is attacked and even discouraged. In song 10:

Toumbu toumbu
Bos calaba
Sika bele bos
Abele bele kang kang
Toumbu don bos
Bos bos bos bos

The first shall
be the last
And the last shall
be the first.

This song is more easily understood in its context: children sing it to settle a conflict. The song is also used when children may want to catch a thief among them: they point fingers at all the suspects and the person who gets the finger on the last note of the song is the culprit. Most children think that the verdict is always true. It is another example of how children are in the process of creating their own world and learning how to handle their difficulties.

In large part, adults are the creators of children's literature, imposing ther values and views. Children remain silent and suffer from the epistemic violence that every subaltern group experiences (Spivak, 1994). Children's creativity and literature should be given a place in the educational and formational stages of their lives. Paulo Freire proposed that education through dialogue, rather than the 'banking' of information is the most democratic form of re-humanizing an already dehumanized people, of whom children are a part. Therefore, in as much as the digital world of today makes its consumers feel sophisticated, children need their games to enrich and complete their emotional growth. With these informal outdoor activities, they learn to love, to care, to rebuke and even to punish, building humanitarian values in these times when technology and money have supplanted our innate dignity.

WORKS CITED

Alembong, N. (2011). *Standpoints on African Orature*. Yaounde: Les Presses Universitaires de Yaounde.

Chukwuma, H. (2002). *Igbo Oral Literature: Theory and Tradition*. Port Harcourt: Pearl.

Cuddon, J. A. (1999). *The Penguin Dictionary of Literary Terms and Literary Theory*. New York: Penguin Books.

Fanon, F. (1968). *The Wretched of the Earth*. New York: Grove.

Ferris, J. (2008). *Music: The Art of Listening*. New York: Mc Graw-Hill & Co.

Finnegan, R. (1970). *Oral Literature in Africa*. Oxford and London: Oxford University Press.

Freire, P. (2000). *Pedagogy of the Oppressed*. New York and London: Continuum.

hooks, b. (2000). 'Toward a Revolutionary Feminist Pedagogy', in D. H. Richter (ed.), *Falling into Theory: Conflicting Views on Reading Literature*. Boston: Bedford/St. Martins, 78-84.

Macedo, D. (2000). 'Introduction'. In P. Freire, *Pedagogy of the Oppressed*. New York: The Continuum International Group Inc., 11-27.

Machlis, J., & Forney, K. (1995). *The Enjoyment of Music*. New York and London: W.W. Norton and Company.

Smith, K. P. (1998). 'Beyond Illusion: Lessons of Morality in the Children's Narratives of Chinua Achebe'. In M. Khorana, ed., *Critical Perspectives on Postcolonial African Children's and Young Adult Literature*. Westport CT: Greenwood Press, 101-16.

Spivak, G. C. (1994). 'Can the Subaltern Speak?' In P. Williams & L. Charisma, eds, *Colonial Discourse and Post-Colonial Theory*. New York: Columbia University Press, 66-11.

Tenjoh-Okwen, T. (1996). 'Children's Literature in Cameroon: A Partnership Model for its Development and Promotion'. *Epasa Moto: A Bilingual Journal of Language, Letters and Culture,* 1: 304-9.

The Trickster Tale in Botswana
Does Gender Determine Levels of Violence?

WAZHA LOPANG

This article examines the figure of the androgynous trickster and how this concept can help empower both the male and female listener of oral narratives. It focuses on various scenarios in which the trickster is presented, to suggest that it is the androgynous nature, for example, of Hare that makes the character avoid abuse or violence. Tales that have the trickster as male, with a wife, are examined to show how it is the androgyny rather than the outward appearance that guarantees success. Seeing the trickster as male is misleading. This analysis considers issues such as how characters and storytellers use language, power, size and space to present a convenient image of the trickster as male when indeed this should not be the case.

Michael Carroll (1984) states that 'The term trickster was *first* introduced in connection with the study of North American Indian mythology and the North American trickster is not at all a clever hero' (106). Carroll's observation is that this trickster was obsessed with a need to indulge in food and sex and its attempts to satisfy its cravings tended to backfire spectacularly. This image of the trickster is very different from that found in Botswana. Mischief and buffoonery define the character of *Mmutla* (in Setswana) or *Shulo* (in Ikalanga). The humour in these tales are more pronounced. It is this laughter that numbs or distracts the child listener from the manner in which the characters interact, albeit at times violently. Carroll acknowledges that the definition of the trickster is broad, primarily because the androgynous trickster does not only appear in one particular place or in certain situations. This is quite a dynamic character, so that categorizing it simply as an object of buffoonery is inadequate and misleading.

Equally inadequate and misleading is to conclude that because the trickster is dynamic it is therefore male. Such gendering of the trickster needs to be explained because it has ramifications on how gender-based violence is viewed and interpreted by the listener. If the trickster tale promotes such violence, then the sex of the animals needs to be catalogued and analysed, because such narratives, though humorous, reflect real-life interactions and situations. The difference lies in the manner of the telling, using animals in place of humans and relying on humour to comment on norms and expectations.

The definition of trickster tales seems pretty straightforward. Okpewho (1992) defines them as '...involving trickery and deceit, a breach of faith leading perhaps to the end of a relationship between the parties involved, mostly animals' (182). This relationship could be one where an animal acts selfishly, refusing to share the proceeds of a raid in which a number of parties were involved. The trickster resolves the tension, yet at times also instigates it, bringing a sense of duality to a tale. However, Okpewho's definition does not touch on the violence in this genre. It is an important omission, for there is usually some element of violence directed either towards the trickster or some other animal character. How the relationship 'ends', as Okpewho puts it, is most likely due to some injury, harm or punishment inflicted. A crucial understanding lies in whether the animal characters are male or female and more importantly, what gender the trickster is, as the main player in the tale. Okpewho does not refer to the figure's gender although he does mention how trickster tales have a particular structure. Ruth Finnegan's seminal work, *Oral Literature in Africa* (1970) preceded Okpewho's studies by almost two decades but even then she was aware that the oral tale has a particular effect on the audience, and is sometimes adjusted: for instance 'the artist may tend to omit obscenities, certain types of jokes...in the presence of, say, children or missionaries' (10-11).

Trickster tales are not noted for their didactic function in that they seem not to have a prescriptive element about them. However, it is often overlooked that the characters are defined as either masculine or feminine depending on two important aspects, size and space. An understanding of these aspects shows how gender-based violence presents itself as well as revealing the gender of the trickster who is at the centre of the story. It is not the story that is important so much as where the action takes place and the representation of the characters. These two features of trickster tales are crucial to reinforcing patriarchal ideology in terms of gender roles and expectations. The storyteller consciously or unconsciously ensures that the narrative echoes patriarchal expectations of power and submission. Vladimir Propp (1968) asserted that the function of the characters remains the same although other elements such as setting may change. His argument on variable and invariable elements of a tale is influenced by Joseph Bedier's work, *Les Fabliaux* (1893). Propp also maintained that the function of a tale remains the same irrespective of whether the characters in tale A are humans while those in tale B are animals. In one tale, the trickster Hare locks up his beautiful wife in a hut but a man tricks her through song and kidnaps her. In another version of this tale among the Tswana, a daughter is locked up in a hut by her mother after she refuses to join her family in moving to a new home. A man tricks the girl through song and kidnaps her. According to Propp, the function of the tale does not alter despite a change in the dramatis personae. His argument may be used to ascertain that even in trickster tales known for their humour, episodes of abuse can and do occur. It is incorrect to pigeonhole abuse as belonging only to one type of narrative.

Dundes (1965) differs from Propp in stating that context is key. One cannot understand why, for instance, in Tswana folktales only households headed by women are visited by ogres unless the cultural politics are addressed. Dundes discusses etic and emic units which are not to be confused with Kottak's emic and etic approaches. For Dundes the terms etic and emic are fashioned from the linguistic terms Phonemic and Phonetic respectively. Nyaungwa (2008) states that an etic unit is of content while an emic unit is structural in a folktale (12). Interestingly, Dundes' concept of motifeme stems from the emic unit and is comparable to Propp's term, function. Dundes and his motifeme concept is discussed again, later in this chapter, since he addresses issues relevant to the analysis of abuse in folktales.

Harold Scheub's views on the oral narrative are relevant, offering fresh insight on the work of Dundes and Propp. Makgamatha (1991) states that Scheub's theory runs beyond a narrative's function and structure to focus on 'the performer and the performance occasion, regarding the folktale as a dramatic oral art' (22). Scheub (1975) realized the importance of the oral performer in bringing out the complete story, breaking down the folktale into two characteristics, a core-image and a core-cliché. The core image adds detail and depth to the narrative structure while the core-cliché may be a song or chant (which is a common feature of Tswana folktales). It is possible during a performance for the performer/oral artist to manipulate the core image for dramatic effect while also bringing in the audience to contribute to the core-cliché. This adds to the general atmosphere and enjoyment of the tale. Scheub acknowledges that the folktale cannot be studied in isolation which is contrary to Propp's view. Also, Dundes states that the narrative is based on reality, that is, a social context. His work is highly interesting on the relationship between the content of the tale and the cultural expectations of the society within which it occurs.

Adler et al. (2007) maintain that 'people typically use stories to explain how the *human* world works – how and why, that is, human beings do what they do' (97). Thus, how the storyteller portrays space is important: how the characters in the story manipulate this space that defines them as masculine or feminine. To control space is to control identity. Rush (2012) shows how classic gender roles have created two mutually exclusive spheres which can be said to dominate trickster tales even today. Rush mentions 'the domestic/feminine and the public/masculine' (4). Trickster tales tend to show particular animals in particular locations, and this use of space by the storyteller underlines expectations of patriarchy regarding how males and females relate to their environment. This relates to Julia Wood's definition of a role as a set of expected behaviours and the values associated with them (1994: 49). Using this as a point of departure, if trickster tales continuously depict certain animals in certain areas, the listener consequently infers that only a certain sex should rightly be in a certain area. Nkomazana states that

> ...the traditional Tswana status quo clearly demarcates the proper roles of men and women. There are cultural limitations to ensure that sexes do not trespass each other's role boundaries. If a man performs duties perceived as feminine it would be said *o jisitswe* – he has been bewitched. In most cases, this is assumed to be by the wife'. (2008: 8)

Mahadi et al. (2012) state that one's culture is a result of knowledge that has been socially obtained, highlighting how oral narratives may have an impact on socialization.

Trickster tales provide an important reference point through which children relate to the world around them. Lico (2001) states that 'Space is an instrument of thought and action, which enacts the struggle over power between genders' (30). If, for instance, children are made to believe by the storyteller that space is determined by one's sex and that how you behave is directly influenced by where you are as a male or female, then it becomes 'natural' to associate females with domestic space and males with economic space. Asher and Lascarides (2003) observe that 'If readers are carried beyond the textual bounds of the fictional world it is firstly, then, because texts are themselves worldly in the sense that they are already involved with and constituted through extra-literary discourse' (139). Although the authors are using the written text as a point of departure, the same holds true for the oral text. The medium may be different but the impact is similar. The oral tale comments on social dynamics just as the written tale does, but the oral tale is more immediate in that the storyteller's presence adds a dramatic appeal that the written text can never attain.

Parkin (1984) explains that oratory can be influential through its use of rhetoric, so that the line between fantasy and reality can be negotiated and successfully blurred for the audience, stating that, 'Persuasion, to which rhetoric is devoted, is arrived at by a speaker through experimentation and exchanges with his audience' (353). As the oral performer has honed his skill over time and performed his/her texts to different audience groups, he/she develops the experience necessary to coerce the mind and massage the emotions of the listener in a way that suits the purpose. Children laugh at the antics of the animals in trickster tales yet through this laughter they unconsciously learn that there are clearly defined boundaries that dictate movement of characters by sex. Asher and Lascarides (2003) underline the point by quoting the French philosopher Derrida, '...literature...always is, it says, it does something else, something other than itself, and it itself moreover is only that, something other than itself' (139). So, there is more to the story than the discourse and the antics of the trickster and the visual interpretations of the storyteller.

Stories symbolize a particular characteristic of the society in which they are from. They cannot be experienced in isolation. So, the representation of gender in the trickster tale, for instance, can be made in a humorous manner but an important observation is that: gender identity is not the same as gender stereotypes. The latter relates to a consensus that men (*and* women) may have personality characteristics that are attributed to one's gender. For instance, this can be seen in Tswana culture when storytellers associate decision-making with men and care-giving with women. In trickster tales the animals reflect this stereotyped image both in terms of the space they occupy and the manner in which they are presented. In Tswana culture men are stereotyped as being aggressive, temperamental and opinionated whereas women are seen as passive, helpful and accommodating. This portrayal of men and women is meted in the belief that such characteristics are innate and not a result of socialization. The anthropologist Margaret Mead in her book, *Sex and Temperament in Three Primitive Societies* (1935) concluded that the differences between men and women were not biological or natural but due to a process of socialization. Trickster tales depict these stereotypes but the psychological blow is softened by the manner in which the tales are packaged as humour and entertainment, such that analysis of these roles that buttress the patriarchal institution is muted if not ignored entirely.

Most written collections tend to present the trickster as male. Andrew Wiget (2000) states that the Native American Trickster is male. Though he does not account for why this is so, an explanation can be offered in terms of how the trickster functions. Space and language are attributes and manipulators of masculinity in patriarchy. The control of space (read country) goes hand in hand with the control of belonging (read citizenship). Similarly, the manipulation of language goes hand in hand with the definition and naming of who belongs where in the stratified social system, and why, how, if and when. In Wiget's analysis (2000), the trickster is male both in terms of how the trickster addresses other creatures and because the trickster is a hunter. The tricksters is not male but androgynous.

Consider the scenario where the trickster is by all intents and purposes presented as male. There is a particular tale titled 'Hare and his Wife', that my father once narrated to us children many years ago. The tale is about Hare's wife who is abducted by Hyena for the Chief's pleasure. When Hare discovers his wife's absence he sets out in search of her, following a trail of ash she left behind her. As Hare follows the trail of ash he sings a beautiful song that results in his being invited to sing for the Chief. The song however, carries a message of destruction that the other characters are not aware of. Consequently, Hare destroys his wife, who is not what she seems to be. She is made of sticks and is destroyed when Hare plucks the topmost stick from her head, causing her to scatter in all directions. Before offering an analysis of this tale, some thoughts on ownership in general follow, because it is important in making a case for how Hare the man treats his wife and how Hare the trickster treats the stick woman. In the larger context of gender-based violence the impact of the trickster in this regard will come to light.

> 'Hare and his Wife' (translated by Wazha Lopang)
>
> A long time ago there lived Hare with his wife in their house. Every day when Hare went to hunt, his wife locked herself in the house. This was because when he returned he would sing a secret song to his wife in order for her to recognize him and open the door. This ritual was important because there were certain men who wanted to steal Hare's wife. So, whenever Hare returned, he would sing the following song with his wife,
>
> *'janga janga kunda undi zhulile.'*
>
> The wife would reply as follows, asking him what he had brought from the hunt.
>
> *'janga kuli janga kunja waka senka ini?'*
>
> And Hare would say
>
> *'Hanga ne Shulo (a guinea fowl and a rabbit), janga kulinja ja kunja.'*
>
> His wife would know that her husband had returned. She would then open the door.

Ownership is a fundamental part of a patriarchal society. It delineates those who command influence and power from those who do not. For instance, in 'Hare and his Wife', Hare the man shows that it is the men who exercise power in traditional society because they treat women like commodities or property, as something that can be possessed. But before this power can be assessed it needs to be mentioned that in this particular tale power can be divided into two basic categories: perceived power and real power.

In terms of sex roles, perceived power is the power which the listener of the oral tale is likely to identify with the female character. This form of power is an illusion because it does not really empower the female character at all. It is a form of power that is commensurate with the position of women in traditional society, who are owned by their husbands such as we see in 'Hare and his Wife'. In this tale the wife's power is represented by her ability to control movement into the hut she shares with her husband. She holds the key to the hut and is seemingly a barrier to those who harbour sinister designs. Her power, however, is limited since although she holds the key to the hut she cannot leave it. Thus,

Hare the man owns her. Being beautiful, Hare the man locks her up for her own sake. Essentially, holding the key to her hut is a form of power that enslaves her. It is paradoxical that she is in control only as long as she serves the interests of her husband who owns her. She depends on Hare the man to complete a song that determines if she can exercise her authority and open the door. Her power is regulated. A listener might have the perception that the female character has some form of power when in fact this power is non-existent. Hare's wife is the ideal traditional female who defers to her husband. She also understands that her place is in the home and that it is in her best interests to remain there. As a kept woman, she is so used to her domestic environment that even when Hyena tricks her into opening the door she uses resources familiar to her as a woman, a gourd, to leave a trail of ash for her husband to follow. The female character mirrors the expectations of the society and as such there is a culturally defined code of conduct created by men for women which is not seen as female subjugation or moral debasement but as an ideal and standard of femininity. In this tale, sex roles mirror real life cultural expectations.

Among the Bakgatla for instance, this tale would be easy to relate to. Mosothwane (2001) states that the burial practices of the Bakgatla in pre-Christian times mimicked the spaces that the sexes had occupied while still alive. As such, women were buried in the houses while men were buried in the kraals. Mosothwane (2001) comments that the Bakgatla believed that a woman would continue guarding and working in the house in her afterlife and likewise a man was to continue taking care of his animals or crops (156). Such rituals made it extremely difficult for one to manoeuvre around because essentially to challenge them was to challenge the ways of the ancestors. The listener to the tale is able to identify with the characterization of the woman as she appears in this tale using his/her own perception of female relations as a point of reference. Thus the storyteller 'educates' the listener about the dangers of feminine beauty: that is a source of actual or potential conflict and why, being the property of a man, a woman must be symbolically locked up to keep her away from male suitors. Hare's wife precipitates the conflict, and, it is Hare the trickster, who resolves the conflict. Hare's wife occupies a feminine space that restricts her movement based on her gender, which is why hers is only 'perceived power'. It is a form of power that keeps her in her place, not one that expands her choices or equips her with so-called masculine tools of conflict such as a knobkerrie. This is why she does not openly confront Hyena. So, in this particular tale, the wife's power is only power in name. Hare's power in contrast is real. Hare is presented as male and therefore he has physical as well as mental options to deal with the wife's abduction by Hyena for the Chief to win and convert into a concubine. It is these options that will differentiate Hare the man from Hare the trickster.

Hare's physical option is violence. He arms himself with a knobkerrie before following the trail of ash left by his wife. The mental option, and the one that Hare the trickster prefers, is to use intelligence to resolve the conflict, a characteristic of androgyny. The intelligence is revealed in the song Hare sings. It is a beautiful melody but the lyrics are sinister.

The song warns that 'whoever has taken my wife, if I find her I will remove the stick at the top of her head causing all the sticks to scatter.' The onomatopoeia at the end of his words emphasizes the destruction that is going to occur. Through this song, Hare the trickster becomes distinguishable from Hare the conventional, patriarchal male who is the protagonist of this story. The song mesmerizes everybody and Hare is able to pluck the topmost stick and the wife goes 'scatter'. This song is what Harold Scheub terms the core-image and it helps to increase the tension in the tale leading up to its resolution. The core image, and its repetitive nature assures that the audience remembers it and also understands the power relations in the song. Hare the trickster destroys his wife and brings an end to the conflict. He does not directly go into conflict with the Chief or Hyena as Hare the man would have done. Instead, the androgynous Hare targets that which it believes to be the source of the problem, the wife.

The storyteller who argues that Hare is a male figure and not an androgynous being views the destruction of the woman by the trickster as connoting the male as creator and the woman as servant. This analogy is an example of real power as it is shown in the tale because husbands own their wives and do with them as they please. It is the male figure who holds in his hands the life of the female figure – and he is in effect depicted as a demigod. Even when she is deceived by Hyena and taken away against her will, she cannot destroy herself. She cannot choose when to die; that is a choice that is made for her by the husband who owns her. It is not clear from the narration whether the woman is aware of her mortality. However, she does seem to be aware of her limitations compared to the agency of males such as the Chief, Hare the man and even Hyena. So here the storyteller strengthens in the listener conditioned male-female power relations. The male's power is real; and members of the audience might opt for power of this kind in resolving their own conflicts.

If the storyteller presents the trickster as male, this conditions our subsequent opinions of the trickster. A male trickster echoes the community's own conception of maleness. However, the presentation of the trickster as male does not detract from my comments on androgyny. For instance, an idea of what constitutes maleness can be affected in cases where a male character responds unexpectedly to a situation that calls for a certain socially conditioned response. In 'Hare and his Wife' Hare's character responds unexpectedly in a crisis situation. This character does not fight for his wife's honour, which would be a typical male response in this particular situation. Fighting is not an option for this male character. The masculine paradigm does not manifest itself in Hare's character to the extent that warrants physical aggression.

Hare's action shows that the masculine paradigm (with its obsession to possess beauty) is preoccupied with a fruitless endeavour. Beauty is fickle and Hare's character is intended to prick the conscience of men and their traditional conception of beauty based on their understanding of maleness. At the end of the tale it does not really matter that the Wife has been destroyed. She is not real to begin with but a mere representation of a female person. Hare successfully challenges the Chief's dictatorial power, which has led him to abduct Hare's wife. The male characters have gone to great trouble to acquire something that is ultimately worthless. The woman's personality as defined by others is real but the form is not. It is because Hare's character does not operate within the confines of a masculine or feminine paradigm that this lesson can be imparted. The listener may not pick up this lesson if the tale is looked at solely as entertainment. We can thus conclude that ownership can be presented a positive thing for a woman to be a part of. As this tale shows, abduction can be a negative aspect of marriage, yet patriarchal ideology can make abduction seem like a step towards a more fulfilling social position – more so when the abductor is a man of power and influence. However, an androgynous trickster makes it clear that the ornamental value that most communities accord women is wrong and is yet another example of how patriarchy continues to impose conditions on women. So androgyny can be considered in a domestic setting and manifests itself in the reactions of an individual regardless of sex, to expose the negative actions that one gender commits on another. In this tale, androgyny is the state of a mind that has not been indoctrinated with the ideology of patriarchy.

As the above analysis shows, issues of space and gender-based violence tend to complement one another.

In Botswana, Ikalanga, and other languages of the Southern African region are such that the trickster is referred to with pronouns that are gender neutral. For instance, Ikalanga does not have specific referents of 'he' or 'she' though it does have referents for 'male' and 'female', which are exactly the same as for 'man' and 'woman'. The Ikalanga word *nlume* has multiple referents: male, husband, or man. It can also be used to praise one's manhood. The word *nkadzi* can refer to female, wife or woman depending on the context. Translation of the trickster tale in English changes this 'neutrality'. In English the pronoun 'he' genders the trickster. Sithole Zodwa (1997) observes that

> The character of the oral 'word' can change when transformed into another form, like the written for instance. Because of this reality, those involved in the exercise of transmitting the oral word from its primary and pure form of composition to another, such as the written, are often faced with the arduous task of capturing this oral text in its totality. (35)

The rendering of the Ikalanga third person pronoun in English is a case in point. Translating indigenous oral texts into English brings its own peculiarities. If one considers, for instance, that Ikalanga and Setswana have gender neutral pronouns, translating a text into English creates linguistic interferences. This is more so when the tale itself does not identify the gender of the trickster or that of the other animals. Faced with this problem, a translator could do one of three things. The first option would be to consider the context of the tale and make a decision based on the roles the animals portray, whether one is 'acting' masculine or feminine. In other words, if the trickster is portrayed as cooking or weeding a field the translator can assume that the trickster is female. Likewise, if the trickster is depicted as a hunter then an assumption can be made of the trickster being male. This method of gendering becomes problematic when the translator brings in his or her own cultural experience to the oral tale which may be at variance with what is in the fieldwork. This brings us to the second possible option – that of relying on the storyteller to gender the characters in the story for the translator. However, if the storyteller genders the trickster as male, can this be taken as an accurate representation of the character? It has to be questioned if the storyteller's assertion is reliable and what informs him or her of this. When the storyteller identifies the trickster as male this is a one-size fits all approach to trickster tales and creates problems when there is nothing in the plot that justifies labelling the trickster as male. Shole (2004) states that in a literal translation the translator is preoccupied more with the form of the original than meaning (52). This becomes problematic where pronouns are involved. Sol Plaatje's translation of Shakespeare's *A Comedy of Errors* into Setswana provides insight into how at times literal translation can affect the poetic elements of a language not to mention meaning. His translation was entitled *Diphosophoso* (1930) and the name itself avoids reference to the word comedy as it appears in Shakespeare's original. Instead what is implied in his Tswana word is that there are errors upon errors. The farce is implicit in the title and it shows he did not insist on mirroring Shakespeare's style to the cost of meaning. Gavin (1964) states that the translator feels the need to translate all the details as faithfully as possible, preferably word for word, without regard to their function which is different in terms of structural differences between the two languages and their place in the structure of the work. In any case, there are instances where the trickster contradicts the male tag and behaves in an obviously feminine manner. How can this situation be explained without compromising the 'maleness' of the trickster?

The third option a translator could consider could be to identify the trickster as a 'thing'. The translator would use the pronoun 'it' in place of the personal pronoun 'he' or 'she'. The major problem with this consideration is that the pronoun 'it' misrepresents the oral text. To do this is to alter the original and effectively that changes the sense. This form of translation thus becomes a rewriting. For instance, in Ikalanga the gender neutral pronoun 'wa' as it is used in the sentence '*Wa gina mu ngumba*' can be translated into '(he/she) entered the house'. In Setswana as well the pronoun 'O' as in '*O tsene mo ntung*' can be translated with little fuss into '(he/she) entered the house.' However, if a third option is adopted, referring to the trickster as an animal, the translations becomes unworkable. Consider again, '*Wa ngina mu ngumba.*' Although the pronoun is gender neutral it identifies the subject as human. Translated into

English, but this time identifying the trickster as an animal, the result is 'It went into the house,' which would mean that the original text in Ikalanga would be, *'Ya ngina mu ngumba'* whereby the pronoun 'Wa' has been substituted by another one, 'Ya'. So, the translator has changed the dialogue to suit his/her purposes and this distorts the story and exposes the translator's inaccuracies. Although Wittig (1986) states that 'English does not apply the mark of gender to inanimate objects, to things or non-human beings' (63) gendering the trickster offers challenges, given the peculiarities of the Ikalanga or Setswana language when it comes to translation and even interpretation.

One should note that even in tales where the trickster has no wife or where the role of the trickster cannot be said to be exclusively feminine or masculine, the storyteller stills identifies the character as male. In 'Lion and Hare' as well as in 'Tug of War,' the trickster is presented as male despite there being nothing that biologically defines the gender of the trickster in the story. The success of the trickster then is seen as an inevitable consequence of being 'male': a conclusion to refute. Ngugi in *Decolonising the Mind* (1994) shows that language is identity when he states that, 'the choice of language and the use to which language is put is central to a people's definition of themselves in relation to the natural and social environment, indeed in relation to the entire universe' (4-5). Thus, in instances where the trickster is not verbally identified as male in the story there is great psychological currency to ensure that 'he' is labelled as male. This could be by the storyteller emphasizing the roles of the trickster or by reinforcing tacitly the assumption that the audience has towards the trickster being male.

Sapir (1956) makes a point that shows how language is important to the Self and the awareness of one's position in the world. Sapir notes that, 'the "real world" is to a large extent built on the language habits of the group...The worlds in which different societies live are distinct worlds, not merely the same world with different labels attached' (56). If one society presents the trickster as male and another presents the same character as androgynous, the reception and the impact will not be the same. To label the trickster as male is to give the character exclusive qualities that cannot be found in female characters. However, to judge the trickster as androgynous is to entertain the view that the trickster does not belong to any one gender but is a hybrid of the two. The strength of either position will be tested in the actual analysis of the tales.

However, Sapir's statement shows that if a storyteller promotes the trickster as male this can lead to listeners seeing the male character as witty and decisive and the female characters as inadequate and dependent. Although scholars like Finnegan and Scheub comment on the 'male' trickster, one needs to ensure if this observation is appropriate given that the trickster is not always presented as a figure that is masculine in the way that other characters like Lion or Elephant are. As one listens to trickster tales, one realizes that the trickster is successful because it is androgynous. This is a fundamental characteristic. Harold Scheub (2012) states that the trickster 'is an ambiguous character: usually male, he is often androgynous' (34). Scheub's definition, just like Okpewho's earlier, is not a straightforward one which further emphasizes how complex this character is. Although Scheub acknowledges that the trickster is androgynous, Scheub believes that the primary gender of the trickster is male. This is at odds with the premise stated here that the trickster cannot be pinned down to a particular gender. The trickster, as already mentioned, does not work within the parameters of masculinity and femininity, and is not marginalized in any way, as this would imply that not being male or female is a disadvantage.

In his definition of the Tswana trickster, Matiakgole (2000) asserts that 'the trickster is entirely callous and greedy. He outsmarts the respected and stands half inside and half outside society' (74). This definition echoes in some way the one given by Carroll earlier. There is also the acknowledgement that the trickster is male and that of the trickster being preoccupied with the self. This definition needs to be analysed in relation to the one given by Solomon Ratt (1996), who states that 'Trickster is neither human nor entirely animal. He exists between animal and human societies, on the edge of each: he is a marginal figure' (6). What this implies is that the trickster is a character that a member of the audience cannot relate to since there is nothing 'tangible' in it. It implies that whatever antics the trickster gets into these cannot be used to inform behaviour in real life because there is no referent in reality to someone who exists between animal and human societies. So, where there are instances of violence or wit or foolishness involving the trickster, these can be analysed with a lesser degree of seriousness. As Ratt suggests, the focus should be on those characters who are distinctly male or female, whether animal or human. This puts the trickster in a very unfortunate position in that when it comes to dissecting elements of the plot, for instance, the input of the trickster will be watered down in that the audience may not be able to relate to the symbolic actions of this character.

A pivotal ingredient in understanding the impact of the trickster is the storyteller. The storyteller uses the trickster as a tool to criticize as well as reinforce societal norms. The storyteller is a critic of society in that the trickster figure in the story is a vehicle for highlighting such patriarchal flaws as domineering leadership. The importance of the storyteller in shaping perceptions is best acknowledged through a brief observation of how early scholars viewed them. Vladimir Propp, in his ground-breaking book *The Morphology of the Folktale* (1958) helped us to characterize tales and also trace their origins but it had one crucial shortcoming – it dismissed the input of the storyteller to the tale. Propp viewed the issue of artistic impact as inconsequential and it can be argued that this position made formalism unpopular. Dundes (1964) modified Propp's approach since it did not make allowance for the context in which it appeared. Context, taken into account with the input of the oral artist can enable one to appreciate why a tale is told the way it is.

Thus, Dundes in a way accommodated the storyteller. As Finnegan (1970) puts it, 'The performer of oral pieces could thus be said to be more involved in actual social situations than the writer in more familiar literate traditions.' (12). Propp's point regarding the stylistic quality of the tale is thus woefully inaccurate – in African oral literature at least. To dismiss the storyteller's impact is to undermine his influence on the audience and his/her ability to mould the listener's way of thinking. Tonal variations, inflections, stress and other vocalizations that are part of the narrative experience are thus not captured by the old formalist approach. Song, which is also an important feature of African narratives, would thus not be appreciated in terms of how it influences the reception of a tale. Psychoanalysis demands that we keep questioning ourselves; story-telling is a way towards understanding the self and one cannot avoid the themes inherent in oral narratives as part of this process towards finding meaning and purpose. Through subtle and explicit use of language the storyteller can be adequately resourced, especially when it comes to issues of gender politics. For instance, in trickster tales this character is pitted against male figures of authority such as the lion and elephant and is thus itself conceived of as male. In patriarchal discourse the understanding is that only male figures have the courage and intelligence to challenge other male figures successfully, especially those in positions of power. So, in denying the trickster androgyny, the storyteller reinforces the norms and values of the patriarchal society by passing off qualities that are essentially human as male. This should be understood in light of Baxter's (2003: 5) statement that gender is something that people enact or do, not something they are, own, or characterize. So, although one is born as either male or female that should not define what one becomes nor should it justify aspects of gender-based violence that a person experiences based on sex.

The trickster tale is unique in that most of the victims of gender-based violence are the masculine characters. This is different from the other narratives; the occupation of space and the size of the characters that are fooled incline them towards being male. The violence towards these animals is essentially because they occupy a space they deem exclusive. By encroaching on this space the trickster not only asserts himself but metes out violence as a means of controlling this space as well as ridiculing its occupants.

Female characters do not lend themselves to violence by the trickster because of the domestic space they occupy which is non-threatening: it is when these female characters encroach into the male space that they become victims of violence. What is clear is that trickster tales are set up such that the domineering character (which is male) is usually alone and instances of violence where they occur involve this male character attacking or abusing the other characters – invariably female. The trickster enters the male-dominated space on the side of the oppressed (read feminine characters) in order to deny the masculine character ownership or control of space. The storyteller of 'Hare and Lion', Tukulu Akanyang, in an interview maintained that the hare was male and she used its intelligence to justify her position. In this instance we have a storyteller using her own cultural upbringing to gender the trickster and doing so without feeling inferior. Similarly, the storyteller of 'How Lion got his Roar', Mpolokang Thangwane, believes that the hare is male simply because of the trickster's intelligence. Although the storyteller seemed surprised by the question, she was adamant that the trickster can only be male as the character is able to negotiate its way out of difficult and dangerous situations. It appears that for these storytellers, women can never attain the same attributes that men possess or at the very least that whatever qualities women have, these will never equate to those of men. The concept of an androgynous trickster is very difficult for the storyteller to adopt given that this gender is not 'visible' in African traditional culture. Being androgynous, the trickster's violence cannot be said to be because it is displaying masculine characteristics on another male, neither can we state that it is a feminine character seeking retribution for the mistreatment of its feminine counterparts. The violence that the trickster commits should not be confused with the violence that the masculine character displays, although both occupy, for a while, the same space. The motivations that drive the larger characters are not the same as those that determine the actions of the androgynous trickster. The lion, hippo and any of the larger animals are driven by a need to reaffirm their status as symbols of masculinity. It is a constant struggle to ensure the hierarchy of patriarchy is maintained with the male at the top and the female at the bottom. Because the trickster functions outside the parameters of patriarchy it has no need to conform to hierarchies. The violence that the trickster displays on these larger animals is not a struggle for power or to assert its dominance. Rather, it is merely to ridicule the patriarchal structure and expose how it can be taken apart by playing on the masculine insecurities of some characters.

Gender-based violence in trickster tales is thus presented on two levels: the masculine characters abusing the feminine characters while on another level, the androgynous character is abusing the male characters. So, in the trickster tale there is a pyramidal structure that sees the androgynous at the top, followed by the masculine character. Before the appearance of the androgynous character, the pyramid still retains this two-tier shape with the masculine character at the top followed by the feminine character at the bottom. The two-tier pyramid retains its form throughout the narrative. In one instance, the masculine character is abusing the feminine ones while the trickster is absent/ passive. In the other scenario, the androgynous character is abusing the masculine character while the feminine characters are absent or passive. It can be argued that violence in trickster tales is never multifaceted at any one time. The violence involves an instigator and a recipient, for instance, Lion devouring Zebra. There is never a situation whereby the violence spirals concurrently such as where the trickster mocks the lion who continues to be violent towards the other feminine characters. The violence in trickster tales is both linear and top down. What this implies is that the animal that is on top of the two-tier pyramid at any given time is the dominant animal. The reality is that it is only the trickster that never relinquishes its position in this pyramid, remaining at its apex. Being androgynous is the reason why this is possible. The trickster embodies both the qualities of the masculine and the feminine ideal. Being androgynous means it is not modelled as an exclusive facet of a dichotomized patriarchy, that is, being either male or female. The storyteller has been unable to account for this androgyny since for the storyteller the world exists in black and white where one is either male or female. There can be no compromise given that the trickster is an animal that outwits the larger characters and hence intelligence can be seen as a mark of masculinity. Androgyny strengthens rather than weakens it in the sense that what makes the trickster successful is not the quality of brute force or power displayed by the masculine characters. It does not define itself to physical attributes such as size: given its small stature this would logically label it as feminine. The androgynous trickster is not a victim of violence because the stereotypes of gender such as those pertaining to size do not apply to it. It functions outside the parameters of masculinity and femininity and emerges stronger as a result. Violence in trickster tales shows its brutality only towards those animals that subscribe to the male female dichotomy. Since the trickster is androgynous it exposes the limitations of gender-based violence – it can be overcome if one functions outside the dichotomy in the way that the androgynous trickster does. The implication is that androgyny is the key in dealing with gender-based violence. In simple terms, one's sex should not define how one reacts to situations. Like the androgynous trickster, one avoids being a victim of violence by working outside stereotypes of patriarchy such as those that pertain to space and size.

The trickster tale helps one to understand that in traditional patriarchy language is also important in determining how one becomes an aggressor or a victim of based violence. For instance, in trickster tales the characters that are generally perceived as male are essentially the ones who have a voice. They have vocalizations as well as dialogue. Language elevates the character above the other feminine characters in that it legitimizes or gives identity. By controlling the speech of these characters the storyteller is able to manipulate thought, to regulate in the audience things to think about. Ong (1982) states that 'in keeping with the agonistic mentality of oral cultures, Plato's Socrates also holds it against writing that the written word cannot defend itself as the natural spoken word can: real speech and thought always exist essentially in a context of give-and-take between real persons' (79). By being the link between the story and the audience the storyteller becomes quite influential and this can affect the tale's reception. Therefore, there are instances where the lion talks, the elephant talks and the hippo talks. The antelopes by and large listen and comply with these vocal characters. Where the storyteller mentions these antelopes it is usually through reported speech. In denying them a voice, the storyteller denies them positions of authority. They are emasculated and occupy the periphery of power. The storyteller should never be underestimated. Okpewho (1992) states that the oral artist 'has a more than average sense of what is beautiful and exciting, a high capacity for expressing oneself with effective idioms and images, and a deep interest in practising a particular type of art' (20). Discourse is a powerful tool. To avoid being too general, not all storytellers vocalize their characters in a manner that will identify them as male or female. The reason for this could be simply out of personal choice rather than due to any shortcomings in their delivery. In any case, in trickster tales the masculine animals speak and project their authority through language. Thomas and Wareing (1999) maintain that 'power is often demonstrated through language; it is also actually achieved or 'done' through language. For example […] through speeches, debates, through the rules of who may speak and how debates are to be conducted' (11).

With this in mind it is understandable why some storytellers would label the trickster as male. This is the only character that speaks besides the larger more distinctly powerful animals. Speech groups the trickster with the male characters and in this case it can be argued that in an African context this is an indicator of masculinity. However, the trickster uses language not to emotionally abuse a character; it is not a sign of authority but a means with which to engage and turn the tables on these masculine characters. The language that the trickster makes use of is simply a tool. In speaking the trickster simply engages the masculine character on a level platform. Through speech the trickster enters the space of the masculine character, dominates that space and then abandons it when the trickery has been accomplished. The androgynous trickster does not replace the masculine character; in speaking, the trickster does not become masculine. This is why after the trickster has finished making fun of these masculine characters, it returns to its place, neither with the feminine characters nor with the masculine characters. Androgyny enables it to operate in both spheres at will but not to ultimately reside permanently in any particular one. The use of language is useful for the trickster but it does not compromise its fluidity, its ability to enter and leave a sphere at will. With gender-based violence, the masculine characters use language to complement their abusive relationship with the feminine characters. Language identifies these characters as dominant and the lack of language by the other characters identifies them as submissive. They do not challenge or question what they are told by these masculine characters. The same cannot be said of the trickster. This character enters the male space not only physically but also through language. The androgynous trickster questions, feigns ignorance, taunts, and so on all through the use of language. It displays in its speech none of the submissive qualities that the other animals display through body language. It approaches the masculine on equal terms but it does not substitute its space for that of the male. Once its job is done it leaves the masculine space. Trickster tales thus inform us that because the storyteller provides certain animals with speech, and because the same storyteller embellishes the speech with appropriate gestures and facial expressions, then it is these characters that dominate the attention of the listeners, and gain prominence in the their minds. As Finnegan states, (1970) 'There is no escape for the oral artist from a face-to-face confrontation with his audience, and this is something which he can exploit as well as be influenced by' (10). So, the influence of the storyteller is key to the way in which some animals (and by extension, gender roles and expectations) are given prominence over others.

Wanjiru Kabira's (1994) study of Kenyan folktales puts this into perspective. Kabira concerned herself with how women are controlled, especially in their representation in Gikuyu oral texts. She states that the female form is to a large extent vilified in narratives and the excuse is that women are controlled for their own well-being. This 'Big Brother' attitude towards women needs to be understood with the observations made by Senkoro (2005) earlier that women oral artists can also actively undermine patriarchy in the manner in which they perform a tale. Although these scholars seem to focus exclusively on how women are impacted in texts as opposed to men, they do show that there is a deep concern about how narratives can promote undesirable and stereotypical views of women. In trickster tales, for instance, when the other characters are denied a voice, they are seen by the audience as peripheral to the story, mere props to the depiction of a power struggle between the trickster and the male animals. Since the trickster has speech and engages these characters on their own turf, logic assumes that the trickster must be male. In other words since the trickster overcomes these larger animals then it implies that the trickster must be male. The listener concludes that one has to be male to challenge and overcome gender-based violence. This puts the girl child, a member of the audience, in a difficult and dangerous position. To believe that the trickster is male is to believe that gender abuse in all its forms can only be overcome if the affected seek assistance from another male. Just as the abused antelopes are assisted by the trickster in the story 'Hare and Lion', likewise in reality the battered female child can only be assisted by the intervention of a male figure. Of course the entertainment factor mutes the true impact of this tale but there is a real danger of trickster tales creating a dependency syndrome in the listener in future years. An insistence on the trickster being male on the basis of its ability to speak language and on the strengths that it occupies the masculine space when it confronts characters is wrong. The implications on the male listener are also significant. A male trickster puts undue pressure on the boy child to maintain a confrontational attitude towards life's challenges. Cobb (1993) has observed that through tales the young learn by mapping their own world view.

Trickster tales, it can be said, become building blocks through which children construct their understanding of the world and to some extent, their place in it. Since the 'male' trickster solves problems the male boy must step up and deal with his own problems regardless of the fact that a girl child could play a pivotal role in assisting him or even solving the problem altogether. There is not a single trickster tale in Botswana where the female characters overturn the dominance of the male characters. Only the trickster does this and to deny the trickster androgyny is to relegate the female child listener to the unenviable status of a spectator in a male dominated environment. Gender-based violence is complex yet there is no need to complicate it further by assuming that only one gender can deal with it. Using a male trickster as a symbol of males overcoming males is misguided. The trickster as already mentioned simply occupies space without becoming what that space demands of other characters. If the girl child learns that having an androgynous mind-set towards abuse is what is required, they can become their own role models and avoid turning to males to deal with such issues. Trickster tales then need to be carefully assessed in terms of how they create certain assumptions about patriarchy that the storyteller is only too keen to project through his/her performance. Future studies may reveal the link between African spiritual beliefs and prose narratives in terms of how the latter upholds the former.

WORKS CITED

Adler. J.M; McAdams D.P. (2007). 'Time, Culture and Stories of the Self', *Psychological Inquiry*, 18 (2): 97-128.

Asher, N. and A. Lascarides (2003). *Logics of Conversation. Studies in Natural Language Processing*. Cambridge: Cambridge University Press

Baxter (2003). *Positioning Gender in Discourse: A Feminist Methodology*. Basingstoke: Palgrave Macmillan.

Cobb. E. (1993). *Ecology of Imagination in Childhood*. Dallas: Spring Publications.

Dundes, Alan (1965) (ed.). *The Study of Folklore*. Eaglewood Cliffs: Prentice Hall.

Finnegan. R. (1970). *Oral Literature in Africa*. Nairobi: Oxford University Press.

Gavin. P.C. (1964). *A Prague School on Esthetics, Literary Structure and Style*. Washington DC: Georgetown University Press.

Kabira. W. (1994). 'Gender and Politics of Control', in A. Bukenya, O. Okombo, eds, *Understanding Oral Literature*. Nairobi: Nairobi University press.

Kottack. C.P. (2010). *On Humanity: A Concise Introduction to Anthropology*. New York: McGraw-Hill.

Lico. G.R. (2001). 'Architecture and Sexuality: The politics of gendered sexuality', *Humanities Diliman*, 2.1: 30-44

Mahadi T; Jafari. S. (2012). 'Language and Culture', *International Journal of Humanities and Social Science* 2 (17): 230-235.

Makgamatha. P.M. (1991). *Characteristics of the Northern Sotho Folktales: Their Form and Structure*. Johannesburg: Perskor.

Matiakgole. K. (2000). The Structure and Style of Oral Narratives. Master's thesis, Vista University. Accessed 22 July 2014.

Mead, M. (1935). *Sex and Temperament in the Primitive Societies*. New York: Dell.

Mosothwane. M.N. (2001). 'An Ethnographic Study of Initiation Schools among the Bakgatla Ba Ga Kgafela at Mochudi (1874-1988)', *Pula: Botswana Journal of African Studies*, 15 (1): 144-65.

Ngugi wa Thiong'o. (1994). *Decolonising the Mind, The politics of language in African literature*. Nairobi: East African Educational Publishers and Oxford: James Currey.

Nkomazana, F. (2008). 'The Experiences of Women within Tswana Cultural History and its Implications for the History of the Church in Botswana', *Studia Historiae Ecclesiasticae* 34 (2): 83-116.

Nyaungwa O. (2008). 'Folklore Influence on the Shona Novel', MA Thesis, University of South Africa.

Okpewho. I. (1992). *African Oral Literature: Backgrounds, Character and Continuity*. Indiana: Indiana University Press.

Parkin. D. (1984). 'Political Language', *Annual Review of Anthropology*. 13: 345-65.

Propp. V. (1968). *Morphology of the Folktale*. Trans. Laurence Scott. Austin: University of Texas Press.

Ratt. S. (1996). 'Continuing Trickster Story-telling: The Trickster Protagonists of Three Contemporary Indian Narratives', MA Thesis. University of Regina.

Rush. L.M. (2012). 'An Auto Ethnography of Fuencarral 43: Women in Masculine Public Space,' *The Journal for Undergraduate Ethnography*, 12, 1: 1-13

Sapir. E. (1956). *Selected Writings in Language, Culture and Personality*. Berkeley: University of California Press.

Scheub H. (1975) *The Xhosa Ntsomi*. London: Oxford University Press.

Scheub H. (2012). *Trickster and Hero, Two Characters in the Oral and Written Traditions of the World*. Wisconsin: University of Wisconsin Press

Senkoro. F.E. (2005) 'Understanding Gender through Genre: Oral Literature as a Vehicle for Gender Studies in East Africa', *Gender, Literature and Religion in Africa*. Dakar: CODESRIA Gender Series 4: 5-24.

Shole. S. (1990). 'Shakespeare in Setswana: An Evaluation of Raditladi's *Macbeth* and Plaatje's *Diphosophoso*', *Shakespeare in Southern Africa*, Vol 4: 53-64.

Wareing S., Thomas L. (1999) *Language, Society and Power: An Introduction*. New York: Routledge.

Wiget. A. (2000). 'Cycle Construction and Character Development in Central Algonkian Trickster Tales', *Oral Tradition*, 15 (1): 39-73.

Wood. J. T. (1994). *Gendered Lives: Communication Gender and Culture*. London: International Thompson.

Zodwa. S. 1997. 'The Dynamics of Oral and Written Transmission, Processes in Siswati Oral Poetry', *Research in African Literatures*: Special Issue; The Oral-Written Interface, 28 (1): 35-48.

Ifeoma Onyefulu

Author & Photographer
of Children's Books

PATRICIA T. EMENYONU

In mid-March 2014, the *New York Times* published two op-eds – 'Where Are the People of Colour in Children's Books?' and 'The Apartheid of Children's Literature'. Walter Dean Meyers and his son Christopher Myers (both prolific children's and young adult authors) were responding to a new study by the Cooperative Children's Book Center at the University of Wisconsin. Over the past 18 years, from 1994–2012, the Center found that only 10% of children's books contain multicultural content, whereas 37% of the US population are people of colour. The actual trend is slowly sliding down: in 2008/12% of children's books had multicultural content; in 2009, 11%; in 2010 and 2011, 10%; and in 2012, 9%. However, the projected US population for 2060 (50 years hence) will be 57% people of colour. What are the actual numbers of children's books published? In 2013, the Center looked at 3,200 children's books and only 93 of them were about black people. Most of those were about slavery, the Civil War and the Civil Rights Movement – all important times in US history, but almost none showed black kids having the kind of daring adventures or finding the love of princes (ccbc.education.wisc.edu/books/2014statistics). Ashley Samsa goes further to discuss the consequences for young minority children:

> This is a problem for young children of colour, to be sure. Instead of seeing images of themselves on the pages, they are forced to split their consciousness and filter their dreams and ambitions through white protagonists while understanding that their underrepresentation holds certain messages for them – namely that it's the white kids that get to have all the fun. However, this is a problem for white children, as well; by not seeing diversity among children's books, they learn other unconscious messages; for example, that black kids are only interested

in slavery and civil rights. Just like feminism is important for young boys, diversity is important for white kids, too. (care2.com/causes/children-of-color-need-to-see-themselves-in-books retrieved March 2014)

Over a decade earlier a young African photographer raising two sons in London realized the gap in multicultural books for her children growing up in UK:

> I began writing for children because I wanted to show [my son] the Africa I grew up in, and its culture. (http:biography accessed March 2014)

Thus motivated, Ifeoma Onyefulu, Igbo photographer and writer who grew up in Onitsha, Eastern Nigeria, and moved to London to study and work, wrote her first picture book *A is for Africa* (1993) which won an NCSS-CBC Notable Children's Trade Book in the field of Social Studies award. More than a decade ago she grabbed the attention of teachers and educators by depicting her homeland's rich heritage in incisive and authentic pictures. For the next dozen years, she continued to produce concept books about numbers, colours, and shapes as well as stories about family and community that are beautifully presented and positive messages about village life in Nigeria and other parts of Africa. From marriage (*Here Comes the Bride,* 2004) to naming the new baby (*Welcome Dede,* 2003) to age-grade membership (*One Big Family,* 1996) to death and burial (*Saying Goodbye,* 2001), the global community soon embraces this growing extended family she writes about. What makes her picture books so remarkable is, first, the simplicity and universality of the concepts represented which allow young children and young adults alike to see themselves in the games that are played (*Ebele's Favorite: A Book of African Games,* 1999), the jobs in their neighbourhoods that are similar or different (*My Grandfather is a Magician: Work and Wisdom in an African Village,* 1998) and the journeys or trips undertaken (*Ikenna Goes to Nigeria,* 2007) In all these, however, family relationships and community togetherness are emphasized.

The second aspect of her glowing picture books is the artistic presentation. Living and working in London has meant that the technical side of her publications is outstanding – the quality of the paper and clarity of the photographic production, for example. As Cullinan et al., have said, 'In picture books, principles of design relate to the overall design of a book as well as to individual pictures, and are integrated with the content (2002: 183) These elements of total design include the cover design, end papers, text placement, illustrations, use of white space, and typography. The arrangement and sequencing of design elements 'lead the eye effectively through the book' (183). Onyefulu's seventh book, *Saying Goodbye: A Special Farewell to Mama Nkwelle* (2007), is a great example of her work which demonstrates the success of her structure and design layout in all her picture books. Effective layout means that illustrations appear in close proximity to the text they illuminate, and the amount of text and illustrations on a page does not make the page appear crowded or overwhelming (Cullinan et al. 256).

Starting with the cover, the choice of colour – bright gold with subtle butterfly prints surrounding a large picture of a group of women dancing toward us – creates a welcoming feeling rather than a sad funeral sombreness. The women are led by a small girl who is smiling broadly as are many of the women also caught in motion, arms swinging, feet stepping down the ochre earth path with tropical green vegetation behind them. They are all wearing bright white blouses and wax print double wrappers with red and gold head ties (the traditional attire of married women in Igbo land). The title is in bold black letters that convey a hand-written quality. There is nothing to indicate the serious side of death.

On opening the book, there is a double spread tie-dye design in light indigo blue and white in diagonal stripes with the woven design of the fabric showing through – a fabric of life statement. The title page includes a colour portrait of Mama Nkwelle (3 inches by 6 inches) with a light orange border. She is looking elegant with her red, full head-tie, necklace, and embroidered red dress. She is looking straight into the camera with confidence and dignity. This is the only portrait of the subject of the book and it illustrates the title of the story.

The story begins on the next page and is viewed through the eyes of the author's young son, Ikenna, whose portrait fills half the page with the text beside it. 'My great-grandmother gave me some *akwu* (palm kernels). Now that she is gone, I am going to grow them,' (3) announced this young boy holding a plate of red palm fruits/kernels. He, too, is looking straight into the camera as if he is speaking to the reader. Pictures and text continue to tell the story of how everyone prepared to say goodbye to Mama Nkwelle. Since Mama Nkwelle had died when she was very old (100 years plus) and had lived a remarkable life, preparations took on a special note. From the sewing of the white clothes that all her descendants would wear for the burial, to the cleaning of the compound where she had lived, to the cooking of the food for the *Umuada* (female descendants in her lineage), the illustrations catch the women and men in action, in candid shots that show the reader the actual village, not some cleaned-up and romanticized version for foreigners. The compound, for example, is bare earth and erosion has undermined the cement block foundation and steps of the windowless home. The cooking is done over an open fire with large cast iron pots steaming in the yard, an old, rusted car in the background. Those women and men in the photos are not posing; they are caught in action and seemingly unaware that they are being photographed. Pictures and text tell the story in a balanced way. Those in the pictures are aunts and uncles of the young voice recounting the story of his great-grandmother's funeral ceremony.

The story in a nutshell: Ikenna starts to feel different as soon as he puts on his new white clothes. His grown-up relatives keep an all-night wake, dancing and singing for Mama Nkwelle. On the big day a 21-gun salute is fired to begin the celebration. In Mama Nkwelle's now empty house, her decorated bed is brought into the sitting-room, adorned with her picture. The priest says prayers, then kola nuts are offered and dancing begins to the sound of drums. *Ikpuawa* (gifts) of cloth are brought, and Ikenna is asked to offer a gift too. Seven days later Ikenna watches as people gather to remember Mama Nkwelle. Finally, he plants his own special memorial, knowing that he will never forget her. From beginning to end the words and art are interwoven and inseparable. Together they create a meaning that neither could achieve alone. The illustrations extend the text, adding visual information or meaning not presented in language (Nodeiman, 1988 as cited in Cullinan et al. 88) All elements of line, shape, texture, colour and space provide the expressive qualities that help the reader feel the story.

As an insider, Ifeoma Onyefulu is able to capture the essence of village life in Igboland, having grown up in that cultural setting. She writes with understanding and knowledge of her subject, setting, characters, and themes. For young Nigerian and African children reading or being read to, her picture books enable them to learn about themselves. They are discovering who they are and what they can do. They are watching others to compare with themselves and in the process their self-understanding develops as a direct result of their interaction with the environment at home, at school, and vicariously in the illustrated stories featuring children in situations resembling their own where a problem is resolved or skills are learned. Imagine the excitement of a child who finds a character who has the same name as himself or herself and/or who looks like himself or herself. 'My name is Ebele and I live in Nigeria' (4) is the first line of the book about African games – *Ebele's Favourite: A Book of African Games* (1999). Ebele has a cousin from Senegal, Ngony, who will be visiting and she wants to know Ebele's favourite game. Because Ebele plays many games, she is having a hard time deciding on which game is the one she likes best, so she asks her friends which one they like the most (problem solving). Their names are Amaechi, Chima, Okey, Chi-Chi, Ify, Amaka, and they all have different games as favourites.

Most of Onyefulu's stories have child narrators. In *Emeka's Gift: An African Counting Story* (1995), the narrator, Emeka, is on his way to visit his grandmother and wants to take something specially for her. Walking towards her home he sees many items that would make a perfect gift, but he cannot buy four brooms, five big hats, six necklaces, seven musical instruments, and so forth, so he arrives empty-handed to be welcomed with open arms by his grandmother who tells him, 'Child, you're the best present of all' (18).

In her story set in Ghana, *Welcome Dede: An African Naming Ceremony* (2003), the focus is on the naming of a newborn child. The narrative begins with the young cousin of the infant addressing us, 'I have a new cousin. At the moment everyone calls her "Baby". I can't wait for her to have a name. My name is Amarlai, which means I am the fifth son, and my uncle's name, Amarkai, means he is the third so' (3). In the course of the tale, we learn that his mother's name is Ayeley, meaning first daughter; his father's, Amartai, 'second son', and his aunt's name, Ayikai, 'third daughter'. But the young baby will have to wait eight days before she will be given a name in a special ceremony. After days of preparation including cooking their favourite food, *kenke* (a savoury bun made with corn), the family and friends gathered. The grandfather said a prayer and poured a libation, then other uncles prayed and poured wine on the floor before drinking. The grandfather then dipped his finger in the wine, placing a drop on the baby's tongue and said, 'Your name is Dede, which means first daughter.' Then the baby was carried home and the music and dancing in celebration began (15). Many of her books include a name in the title. *Chidi Only Likes Blue: An African Book of Colours* (1997) or *A Triangle for Adaora: An African Book of Shapes* (2001). The book about colours begins, 'My name is Nneka, (pronounced n-EK-a). My little brother's name is Chidi (CHEE-dee). Whenever we play the game Colours, Chidi says, 'Nneka, my favourite colour is blue...' (1).

A is for Africa, Onyefulu's first picture book, is especially appealing because she focuses on the human side of Africa. 'A' is for Africa, a great continent of many countries and peoples. 'B' is for beads that a girl might wear. 'C' is for canoe – people might visit their friends or take their children to school by canoe. 'D' is for drums. When a new-born baby is named, relatives and friends might welcome him or her into the world with the sound of drums. There is no 'E' is for elephant or 'Z' for zebra which are the commonly used animals for standard alphabet picture books and our stereotypical image of Africa We see the ordinary people and objects that are part of everyday contemporary Africa through the lives of the African people.

From the examples above, it is apparent the first person narrative is a favourite technique in Onyefulu's stories, to draw the reader into the tale. Ikenna's voice of innocence and naiveté endears him to the reader and helps readers to identify with his character. There is an exuberance and eagerness in many of Onyefulu's young narrators that makes for a positive impression and lasting vision of the customs and realities of ordinary lives in modern yet traditional Africa.

The language in picture books is one that adults can read and children can understand. This is true of Onyefulu's texts. Literature connects to life in three important ways: first, in the connection from text to self when the story reminds the reader of family (Cullinan et al. 110). After reading Onyefulu's picture books, readers might indicate they feel the same way that the character feels or have had the same or similar experiences as the character. Playing games is enjoyed world-wide. Learning the concepts of numbers, colours, shapes, and letters is part of early education in all societies. Marriage customs, the naming of children, experiencing death and burial are universal events although the specific way in which each of these benchmarks in life is practised varies from culture to culture.

Second, text can connect to life/world in which case readers may acknowledge that the same things have happened in their town or on television. (Cullinan et al. 111). They identify people in the story with people on the street in their neighbourhood. The young couple who are getting married in *Here Comes Our Bride* (2004) show a common practice but extend that ceremony to show that in many places in Africa marriage '...is not just about the union of two people, but of two families'. There is no Bridal Shower, but the groom's family is given a list of things to provide (such as gifts) and a time limit for completing it before the wedding takes place. Third, text-to-text connections can be made (Cullinan et al. 111) where Ikenna's story, for example from *Saying Goodbye*, may remind them of another book they have read or the character may seem similar to a person in another book. Children forge connections between the books they read and the life they live because literature reflects every aspect of their expanding world (110).

Ifeoma Onyefulu has written more than a dozen picture books set in Africa with authentic African characters, settings, and themes. She produced roughly a book a year for two decades. How prolific can one artist be to be able to bridge the enormous gap between what exists for mainstream American middle-class Caucasians and what exists for other children of colour? 'All children from all cultures and in all places need to see books that reflect themselves and their experiences as well as allow them the opportunity to discover the lives of others' (Cullinan et al. 275). If children never see themselves in books, that omission subtly tells these young people that they are not important enough to appear in books; that books are not for them (Cullinan et al. 277).

Further, when children of colour do see themselves in books, it may not be their reality. Cullinan et al. have noted that 20% of the total number of titles about persons of colour are folktales. This helps to perpetuate the stereotypical view that such people are quaint, different, or even primitive. Folktales reflect values, but not the lives of contemporary members of these cultures (Sims Bishop (1994), cited in Cullinan et al.).

Bishop's research in the nineties found that 3-4% of the children's books published in 1990, 1991, and 1992, related to people of colour. In *A Guide to New Multicultural Literature for Children and Young Adults* (2000), Helbig and Perkins listed only 541 books that related to experiences of parallel cultures published in the five-year period between 1994–1999, out of a total of about 25,000 children's and young adult books published over the same period. The field of children's literature changed considerably during the last half of the 20th century as it began to reflect the cultural diversity that marks North America, and to include literature from around the world (275).

The establishment of new awards such as the Coretta Scott King Award (founded in 1969) has helped promote a more diverse collection of children's books. The award has been given annually to outstanding African-American authors and illustrators of books for children and young adults that demonstrate an appreciation of African American culture and universal human values. Similarly, the Pura Belpre Award (established in 1996) is presented to a Latino/Latina writer and illustrator whose work best portrays, affirms, and celebrates the Latino cultural experience in an outstanding work of literature for children and youth. Others include awards for non-fiction, such as the Orbis Pictus Award (since 1990) of the National Council for Teachers of English; the Boston Globe Horn Book Award for nonfiction; and the American Library Association's Silbert Award for nonfiction (since 2001). Onyefulu has won a number of awards including Junior Education's Best Books of 1994 for *A is for Africa*. *One Big Family: Sharing Life in an African Village,* was chosen as a 1997 Notable Book for Children by the American Library Association and in the same year, as a Notable Children's Trade Book in the Field of Social Studies by the National Council for Social Studies and the Children's Book Council in America. In 1997, *Chidi Only Likes Blue: An African Book of Colours* won a Scientific American Young Readers Book Award. *Here Comes the Bride* won the Children's Africana Book Award in 2005 while *Ikenna Goes to Nigeria* won the same award in 2008.

Organizations such as the International Reading Association (IRA) and the International Board on Books for Young People (IBBY) have membership from around the world and help sustain a global perspective. Book Fairs such as Bologna, Frankfurt, London, Guadalajara, and Zimbabwe have also celebrated the diverse literature that is being published. In 2004, the Nigeria Liquefied Natural Gas (NLNG) Ltd instituted the Nigeria Prize for Literature. The overall objective of the prize is to encourage and stimulate authorship and develop a literary culture in Nigeria in terms of creative writing, production and reading. A particular genre is always selected for each year among prose, drama, children's literature, and poetry (Uko 2014: 2). In 2011, a total of 126 children's books were handed over by the Advisory Board to the judges for assessment. This number was reduced to 42 in the first stage and then a final three were selected from which the winner was chosen. The large cash prize makes this an attractive incentive for the production of excellent children's books in Nigeria. This is an example of the way individual countries can also promote children's literature within their borders.

In the USA, in the 1980s, an increasing demand for multicultural books developed as demographies and school populations began to change. However, a lack of cultural diversity persisted among editors and other publishing professionals who made decisions about what books would be published and how they would be marketed (Huck et al., 2001: 106). There are, of course, always exceptions, such as Hyperion's 'Jump at the Sun' imprint that is intended to spotlight African-American writers and illustrators under the leadership of people such as Andrea Davis Pinkney, a writer herself, married into the Pinkney family of writers and illustrators (Jerry, Gloria, Brian). Other small presses have also made commitments to multicultural publishing – Carolrhoda, Children's Book Press, and Lee and Low, for example.

Moll and Greenberg (1990, in Cullinan et al.) have pointed out that we all live in families and communities that draw on a wealth of knowledge and skills to help us function. Much more than race, ethnicity, gender, sexual preference, or special needs, culture involves values, attitudes, customs, beliefs, and ethics. (275). Onyefulu's books are culturally rich, depicting experiences embedded in a particular culture (Igbo), with settings, plots, and characters inextricably tied to culture. Her books allow readers to look through the window at characters just like or different from themselves; to recognize their own or learn about another culture. They offer the opportunity for a more than superficial experience with diverse characters.

Literature can act as both mirror and window for its readers (Cullinan et al. 276). Sims Bishop applied this metaphor to culturally diverse literature:

> ...the best books offer an experience that is more like looking through a window into another world – but gradually as the light fades, the image of oneself becomes reflected, too. Children's books at their best highlight the unique characteristics of the cultures represented by their characters but also speak to universal experiences. With them we can celebrate differences, call attention to commonly held values and experiences, and promote empathy and a sense of common humanity. (1985: 11-12)

Sims Bishop further tied in the reason to teach multicultural literature in the United States: '…the goal of creating a more equitable society requires that people from many backgrounds learn to live together peaceably' (1985: 9).

> The gratifying thing about good art is the longer one looks at it, the more one sees; the more one sees, the deeper one feels; and the deeper one feels, the more profoundly one thinks. Looking at art is everything. (Cianciolo 1997: 69)

Why is it that too few of us are even aware that Ifeoma Onyefulu has published such outstanding books for children? How can we help to promote the 10 per cent of children's books that do provide a true multicultural perspective?

WORKS CITED

Cullinan, Bernice, Lee Galda, and Lawrence R. Sipe (2002). *Literature and the Child.* Belmont CA: Wadsworth/Thompson Learning, 5th Edn.

Cianiolo, Patricia. (1997). *Picture Books for Children.* Chicago: American Library Association, 4th Edn.

Helbig, A. K. & Perkins, A.R. (2000). *Many Peoples, One Land: A Guide to Multicultural Literature for Children and Young Adults.* Westport CT: Greenwood. http://biography.jrank.org/pages/1257/Onyefulu-Ifeoma-1959.html#ixzz2htzR6I2T

Huck, Charlotte, Susan Hepler, Janet Hickman, and Barbara Z. Kiefer (2001). *Children's Literature in the Elementary School.* New York, NY: McGraw-Hill Higher Education, (7th Edn).

Meyers, Walter Dean. 'Where Are People of Color in Children's Books?' *New York Times,* 15 March 2014.

Meyers, Christopher. 'The Apartheid of Children's Literature', *New York Times,* 15 March 2014.

Nodelman, P. (1988). *Words about Pictures.* Athens GA: University of Georgia Press.

Onyefulu, Ifeoma (1993). *A is for Africa.* London: Frances Lincoln Ltd.

—— (1997). *Chidi Only Likes Blue: An African Book of Colours.* London: Frances Lincoln Ltd.

—— (1999). *Ebele's Favourite: A Book of African Games.* London: Frances Lincoln Ltd.

—— (1995). *Emeka's Gift: An African Counting Story.* London: Frances Lincoln Ltd.

—— (2004). *Here Comes the Bride.* London: Frances Lincoln Ltd.

—— (2007). *Ikenna Goes to Nigeria.* London: Frances Lincoln Ltd.

—— (1998). *My Grandfather is a Magician: Work and Wisdom in an African Village.* London: Frances Lincoln Ltd.

—— (1996). *One Big Family: Sharing Life in an African Village.* London: Frances Lincoln Ltd

—— (2001). *Saying Goodbye: A Special Farewell to Mama Nkwelle.* London: Frances Lincoln Ltd.

—— (2000). *A Triangle for Adaora: An African Book of Shapes.* London: Frances Lincoln Ltd.

—— (2003). *Welcome Dede! An African Naming Ceremony.* London: Frances Lincoln Ltd.

Samsa, Ashley Lauren (2014). 'Children of Colour Need to See Themselves in Books', 18 March 2014. Care2.com/causes/children-of-color-need-to-see-themselves-in-books. htmi

Sims Bishop, R. (1985). 'Children's Books about Blacks: A Mid-eighties Status Report', *Children's Literature Review,* 8: 9-14.

Uko, Ini. (2014). 'Judging Children's Literature Competitions: The Example of the Nigeria Liquefied Natural Gas (NLNG) Prize'. Paper presented at the 40th African Literature Association Conference, Johannesburg, South Africa, April 2014.

Re-Presenting Africa in Young Adult Speculative Fiction
The Ekpe Institution in Nnedi Okorafor's *Akata Witch*

LOUISA UCHUM EGBUNIKE

In expressing the 'unique set of imaginative possibilities' (Dubey 2010, 779) that speculative fiction presents to people of African descent, Walter Mosley identifies science fiction as a genre that offers 'an alternative where that which deviates from the norm is the norm' (Mosley 2000, location 6792). The exploration of divergent realities and the disruption of normative frameworks are central tenets of science fiction, establishing it as 'a literary genre made to rail against the status quo' (Mosley 2000, location 6800). It provides a platform through which global inequalities can be challenged and oppressive structures dismantled. Science fiction and other associated genres present a paradigm through which communities who have endured subjugation can reclaim their narrative. The historical ruptures experienced by African-Americans, born out of the forced removal and enslavement of African people in the New World, left a populace 'cut off from their African ancestry by the scythe of slavery and from an American heritage by being excluded from history' (Mosley 2000, location 6792). It is from the position of a historically displaced people that Mosley explores the transformative potential of science fiction in its ability to revise histories and rearticulate futures through 'changing the logic, empowering the disenfranchised, or simply by asking, What if?' (Mosley 2000, location 68187). In recognition of its suitability to the expression of alternative realities and possibilities for people of African descent, Mosley has proclaimed that 'science-fiction writers have become our most important writers' (Mosley 2015).

Walter Mosley's assessment of speculative fiction's capacity to confront and contest jaundiced images of people of African descent lies in its ability to subvert dominant narratives and recalibrate normative constructs. Mosley locates the black reader within the struggle for global transformation, describing the 'power to imagine' as 'the first step in changing the world'. In this way, the act of writing and reading science fiction is inherently political; undertaken 'every day by young, and not so young, black readers who crave a vision that will shout down the realism imprisoning us behind a wall of alienating culture' (Mosley 2000, location 6804). Mosley identifies science fiction as a genre through which African-Americans can engage in the discourse of historiography and representation and challenge Euro-American hegemony. For Mark Dery, the suitability of speculative fiction to the articulation of African-American history is evident. Writing in 1994, Dery describes the underrepresentation of African-American writers in speculative fiction as 'perplexing' considering that African-Americans, in a very real sense, are the descendants of alien abductees; they inhabit a sci-fi nightmare in which unseen but no less impassable force fields of intolerance frustrate their movements; official histories undo what has been done; and technology is too often brought to bear on black bodies (branding, forced sterilization, the Tuskegee experiment, and tasers come readily to mind) (Dery 1994, 180). Dery's identification of the African-American experience as convergent with the tenets of speculative fiction is reiterated by Kodwo Eshun who states

> Afrofuturism does not stop at correcting the history of the future. Nor is it a simple matter of inserting more black actors into science-fiction narratives. These methods are only baby steps towards the more totalizing realization that, in Greg Tate's formulation, Afrodiasporic subjects live the estrangement that science-fiction writers envision. Black existence and science fiction are one and the same. (Eshun 2003, 298)

Note that 'Afrofuturism' is a term coined by Mark Dery which refers to 'speculative fiction that treats African-American themes and addresses African-American concerns in the context of twentieth-century technoculture' (Dery 2008, 9).

Mark Dery and Kodwo Eshun both communicate the continuities between aspects of African-American history and the motifs of science fiction. The rudiments of this analytical position was articulated by Octavia Butler, a pioneer in African-American science fiction writing, who in her 1980 novel *Wild Seed* reframed the transatlantic slave trade within a science fiction paradigm. Butler provided an alternative lens through which to survey the experience of people of African descent in America and examine Europe's relationship with Africa. Nigerian-American author Nnedi Okorafor has built upon Butler's foundations in her exploration of colonialism and the postcolonial experience in Africa. Okorafor, who writes and interprets literature through the lens of speculative fiction, provides another mode through which to engage with African narratives. In a tweet, Okorafor offers an alternative reading of Chinua Achebe's *Things Fall Apart,* drawing on the thematic concerns of science fiction. Okorafor states, 'I have always read *Things Fall Apart* as an alien invasion novel' (Okorafor 2014a), locating Achebe's seminal text within a repertoire of speculative fiction. In positioning her narrative and analytical lens on Africa, Okorafor contributes to broadening the Afrofuturist literary paradigm which is rooted in African-American speculative fiction, bridging Afrofuturist narratives with African literature. The dearth of African science fiction and fantasy literature indicates that these genres are still emerging, which according to Okorafor has the following impact: '1. Africans are absent from the creative process of global imagining that advances technology through stories. 2. Africans are not yet capitalizing on this literary tool which is practically made to redress political and social issues' (Okorafor 2014b). Echoing the words of her fellow Afrofuturists, Okorafor expounds the aptness of speculative fiction in narrating Africa-centred stories and highlights the pertinence of African writers' contributions to the conceptualization of our collective futures.

In writing Africa-based narratives and privileging African world-views, Nnedi Okorafor's works contribute to the on-going process of decolonization, which in an age of neocolonialism remains an incomplete task. The identification of literature as an important site of decolonization is asserted by Chinweizu, Jemie and Madubuike in *Toward the Decolonization of African Literature,* where they state

> our culture has to destroy all encrustations of colonial mentality, and (…) map out new foundations for an African modernity. This cultural task demands a deliberate and calculated process of syncretism: one which, above all, emphasizes valuable continuities with our pre-colonial culture, welcomes vitalizing contributions from other cultures, and exercises inventive genius in making a healthy and distinguished synthesis from them all. (Chinweizu, Jemie, and Madubuike 1983, 239)

The syncretism which underlines the 'inventive genius' called for by the 'bolekaja' critics ('Bolekaja' is a Yoruba term which means

'Come down and fight!' It is used by the authors of *Toward the Decolonization of African Literature* to describe their critical approach) is apparent in the works of Okorafor as they utilize the medium of speculative fiction to disturb the binary opposition of 'tradition' and 'modernity'. In encouraging readers to transcend a polarized interpretation of these constructs, Okorafor creates new worlds that are both familiar and distinct, crafting a sphere of possibilities grounded in African realities. Nnedi Okorafor's youth novel, *Akata Witch,* presents Africa as the site of a global power base in which Africa occupies the position of a producer rather than consumer of knowledge. Okorafor's re-presentation of an indigenous institution forms the core to her 'end of world' narrative. The power invested in 'leopard people', a secret organization modelled on the Ekpe institution, enables its young members to save the world from its impending destruction. The reimagining of Ekpe and its central positioning in the text provide insight into Okorafor's stance on the continued importance of pre-colonial organizations in present-day Africa. The novel presents an institution that has adapted to suit and reflect contemporary realities so that within the context of postcolonial Nigeria, the nation's pre-existing culture and traditions are represented as a key source of identification and an important site of power.

In the field of African literary criticism, discourse on dismantling colonial constructions of Africa has concentrated almost exclusively on literature written for an adult readership. Writers such as Chinua Achebe, Ama Ata Aidoo and Ngũgĩ wa Thiong'o are credited with authoring texts which centre African experiences and expose the misrepresentations of the continent in the colonial canon. Their writings have contributed to shaping discourse on literature and the politics of decolonization; however, the works they have produced for children and young adults are often omitted from this analysis. In recognition of the impact literary texts have on shaping young people's image of Africa, the aforementioned authors have ensured that their bodies of writing are inclusive of a younger audience. The centring of African young adults in narratives written for this demographic serves as a source of validation whilst also creating sites of resistance to (neo)colonial constructions of Africa. The underrepresentation of children's literature in academic studies however, presents a clear disconnect between writers and literary critics. This has led Robert Muponde and Pippa Stein to declare that the study of children's literature in Africa is not 'considered a field worthy of intensive study in major African universities. It can best be described as an emerging field of study, with pockets of interest from scholars dispersed around the continent' (Muponde and Stein 2004, x). Ernest Emenyonu has also spoken of the 'abysmal neglect of children's literature in Africa where often it is mistaken as childish literature undeserving of serious attention even by publishers' (Emenyonu 2004, 430). African children's literature remains an under researched area of study, in spite of its consistent development alongside African literature written for an adult readership.

For writers who came of age in colonial Nigeria, children's books were unlikely to have featured in their childhoods. Chinua Achebe describes how he and other parents 'saw a chance to give to their children the blessings of modern civilization which they never had'. Under the semblance that these books would assist in their children's development, many parents utilized this resource. The European children's books that Achebe purchased for his first child however, demonstrated to him that the extension of Eurocentric representations of the world were not solely located in anthropological and historical texts, but were also reproduced in children's literature. Achebe quickly learnt that parents must not assume that all they had to do for books was to find the smartest department store and pick up the most attractive-looking book in stock: 'Our complacency was well and truly rebuked by the poison we now saw wrapped and taken home to our little girl. I learned that if I wanted a safe book for my child I should at least read it through and at best write it myself' (Achebe 2010, 69–70).

Chinua Achebe speaks of the situation in the 1960s when African children's literature was still an emerging genre. The condescending images of Africa presented in Eurocentric children's books negatively impacted upon the way in which both children of African descent and children of other backgrounds understood the world in which they lived and their space within it. Achebe's impetus to write children's literature was brought about by the need to create literature in which African children could see positive images of themselves and their environment. In centring the African child's narrative, Achebe sought to validate the experiences of the continent's children. In recognition of the changing dynamics within family life and the wider Nigerian society, Flora Nwapa articulated the increasing importance of children's books as a means of imparting social and cultural knowledge to young people. Nwapa, who was both a writer and publisher of children's books, stated

> We have our own myths, folktales and all. We want them to know about these things. This is the era of television. Children no longer have the time to sit around the fireside and listen to stories. If the writer can capture all these things in books then children will read them and know about their own culture.(Olayebi 1986, cited in Ezenwa-Ohaeto 1998, 193)

Nwapa identifies the importance of engaging with children through mediums that are both accessible and of interest to them. African children's literature continues to reflect the changing realities and influences of its readership, with writers such as Nnedi Okorafor taking the genre in new directions.

In the field of contemporary young adult literature, Nnedi Okorafor faces a new frontier as she writes children of African descent into spaces they have previously been peripheral to or absent from. The underrepresentation of children of Africa descent in popular young adult science fiction and fantasy series such as *Harry Potter* by J. K. Rowling and *Twilight* by Stephenie Meyer, renders black children invisible in these worlds. Okorafor explains that

> There continues to be a dearth of young adult fantasy novels featuring main characters of African descent. In my experience visiting high schools and grade schools, black children very much want to see themselves reflected in these types of books. They want to go on adventures and perform the magic, too. They want to imagine. Non-black readers also enjoy the ride and new setting. (…) I also hope that as children (and adults) read my works, they will eventually follow the roots that extend deep and firmly into the rich African soil and sand and learn a thing or two about this potent part of earth.(Okorafor 2009)

In her writing, Okorafor moves the centre from Europe or America, locating her works in Africa. Her layered narratives provide specific cultural and historical contexts, engaging the reader with Okorafor's own image of Africa. Writing speculative fiction which focuses on children of African descent, Okorafor encourages her young readership to rethink notions of normativity with regards to race, gender, culture and characterization in science fiction and fantasy literature. The exploration of diasporic and continental African realities through the eyes of young characters within speculative fiction provides new ways for young people to engage with traditions, cultures and histories of Africa. In recognition of the social and educational role that fantasy literature can play for children of African descent, Nana Wilson-Tagoe states that 'for fantasy to be culturally relevant it must by contrast or comparison, provide useful insights into a child's real life and culture' (Wilson-Tagoe 1992, 22). The 'insight' called for by Nana Wilson-Tagoe forms the ideological foundations for Okorafor's young adult fantasy literature as African cultural institutions and traditions form the framework of Okorafor's writing.

Akata Witch explores contemporary issues of migration, diaspora and the politics of 'home', whilst grounding the narrative within a particular Nigerian milieu. In articulating the conceptual basis for her writing, Okorafor states 'the fantasy that I write is far more than what is on the surface. I am not just 'making stuff up'. She explains, there 'is a method, purpose and realness to my madness. It is not fantasy for fantasy's sake, as so many reviewers have speculated' (Okorafor 2009, 277). In this novel, Nigeria is constructed as a space of possibilities, adventure and new realities for both its people at home and in the diaspora. In presenting a spectrum of young people of African descent, Okorafor's young black readership engages with characters who not only look and sound like them, but who also are cast into heroic roles. The novel depicts Nigeria as a site of cultural, historical and spiritual richness, challenging the dominant portrayals of the continent in the global north.

Sunny, the protagonist in *Akata Witch*, is a young girl who is born in America to Igbo parents and returns to Nigeria at the age of nine. Representative of Nigeria's recent diasporic community, Sunny must negotiate the multiple intersections of her identity and positionalities as she explains

> I have two older brothers. Like my parents, my brothers were born here in Nigeria. Then my family moved to America, where I was born in the city of New York. When I was nine, we returned to Nigeria, near the town of Aba. (…) We're Igbo – that's an ethnic group from Nigeria – so I'm American Igbo, I guess. You see why I confuse people? I'm Nigerian by blood, American by birth and Nigerian again because I live here. I have West African features, like my mother, but while the rest of my family is dark brown. I've got light yellow hair, skin color the color of "sour milk" (or so stupid people like to tell me), and hazel eyes that look like God ran out of the right color. I'm albino. (Okorafor 2011, 3)

Okorafor constructs and centralizes a character that is marked by difference both physically and culturally. These differences initially influence Sunny's interactions with children from her community. Her socialization in America creates a barrier between Sunny and her peers, whilst her albinism impacts upon her capacity to engage in outdoor social activities. Sunny experiences isolation due to her socio-cultural and physical limitations. In contemplating the intersection of her gender and albinism, she decides that this combination has rendered her less favourable to her father. Their turbulent relationship is articulated by Sunny who reflects, 'Sometimes I hated my father. Sometimes I felt he hated me, too. I couldn't help it that I wasn't the son he wanted or the pretty daughter he'd have accepted instead' (5). In this statement, Sunny discloses her feeling of being 'othered' by her father, both in relation to her biological sex as well as her albinism. The narrative of Sunny's marginalization is foregrounded in the novel's opening to provide a wider context for the metamorphosis she undergoes during the course of the narrative. Ekpe proves to be a transformative force in Sunny's life and her coming of age narrative is told in relation to her engagement with Ekpe.

Okorafor's reimagining of Ekpe as a site of resistance to global destruction stems from her recognition of its historical importance in regions of southeastern Nigeria and southwestern Cameroon:

> Ékpè had four major roles in pre-colonial life: first, the conferment of full citizenship holding a title in Ékpè accorded one the status of full citizen with rights to make decisions having implications for the entire community (...). Ékpè was also the no-nonsense community police, with the power to discipline and, as a measure of punishment, to confiscate the property of a community member who disobeyed the law. And Ékpè provided entertainment, with dances, music and body-mask performance, for members. Finally, Ékpè was a school for esoteric teachings regarding the human life as a cyclic process of regeneration, with the eventual reincarnation of that being. (Miller and Ojong 2013, 266–7)

In acknowledgement of Ekpe's vast geographical influence and its imprint on multiple facets of life, Okorafor locates her narrative of resistance within this institution. In *Akata Witch* we learn of the character Black Hat, whose wave of assaults on society begins with the murdering of local children. When it is later revealed that Black Hat is in fact a leopard person, his capacity for destruction is fully realized. The world is faced within impending doom due to Black

Hat's summoning of Ekwensu, an evil, powerful and destructive masquerade. In employing the powers of Ekpe to fight Black Hat, an initiated member of the institution, Okorafor's narrative subtly asserts that Africa holds the solutions to its own problems. The novel's resolution depicts Sunny leading her fellow leopard people in a successful battle with Ekwensu in which Aba, Nigeria is centred in a narrative of heroic resistance to global destruction.

The Ekpe society is used to re-present African traditional institutions, characterizing Ekpe as a global transcultural network whilst locating its spiritual centre in Nigeria. Its inclusion in *Akata Witch* establishes a historical realist source for the novel which is then reinterpreted through the lens of fantasy. As Ekpe traverses Nigeria's contemporary ethnonational constructions, the reader is presented with the interactions of its members across linguistic and cultural lines. In representing the Igbo-Efik-Ejagham axis in *Akata Witch*, Okorafor subverts the fixedness of national borders erected during the colonial era. The multicultural and transnational dimensions of Ekpe, which span West and Central Africa, serve as a point of reference to a history of migration and exchange. According to Simon Ottenberg and Linda Knudsen,

> The widespread diffusion of this form of society and its masqueraders helped to create greater cultural unity in the region despite differences in language and some cultural features; it did so without political centralization of the area. Certain aspects of this form of secret society spread together: the skin-covered carvings, body masks, nsibidi signs, mysterious sounds, music, lodge with shrine, the wealth and rank reflected in the hierarchical organization, the usage of particular costumes by particular grades, and the emphasis on secrecy for social control. The Ejagham area, Calabar, and Arochukwu were the focal points of power and distribution. (Ottenberg and Knudsen 1985, 94)

Akata Witch draws on aspects of Ekpe such as masquerade and nsibidi, whilst utilizing the framework of a secret society to provide the basis for an exploration of esoteric knowledge and power. Through the creation of imagined epistemologies of Ekpe, Okorafor portrays an institution that is home to restricted knowledge of global significance and consequence. Ekpe's reach is presented as extending beyond Africa. The historical basis for this assertion is identifiable in the cultural retention of enslaved Africans in the New World in the form of Abakuá in Cuba. Abakuá is 'generally understood as a diasporic reinvention of the ubiquitous Leopard Societies of historical peoples from present-day eastern Nigeria and coastal Cameroon, a diasporic derivation of the men's title societies of Biafran Africa' (Chambers 2010, 110–111).

As a feature of her writing, Nnedi Okorafor explores the connections between Africa and its older diaspora, so that her narratives are informed by the connectivity that has survived enslavement, colonization and neocolonialism. In this sense, Africa is constructed as a homeland, to which her children can return, whether they are part of a recent or older diaspora. In *Akata Witch* we see the return of young people from Nigeria's diaspora who then participate in issues of national and international importance. Ekpe provides a framework through which to engage with discourse on locations and origin, the past and present, cultural memory and the bridging of time. The novel's rootedness in social structures which predate colonial contact, re-presents Africa as the birth place and home to a powerful global institution. The narrative is located within the Aba area of Igboland, but extends its cartographies beyond Nigeria and continental Africa, seeking to disrupt the binary of 'local' and 'global' through the examination of and engagement with this transnational secret society. In *Akata Witch* the centrality of Ekpe and its spiritual basis extends beyond Africa, as it forms the foundations for discussions on global spiritual networks.

Nnedi Okorafor's interest in cultural intersections is further engaged with through the incorporation of the African-American experience into the novel. In addition to Sunny who is born in the USA, Okorafor constructs the young African-American character Sasha, who is also a 'leopard person' but whose rebelliousness brings about his relocation. Sasha's journey to Nigeria can be read in terms of a 'homecoming', as he is liberated from the institutionally racist society in which he has been raised. Sasha makes frequent reference to his life in the USA vis-à-vis its racial politics, stating that his 'parents were stupid enough to move into a neighbourhood that was not only all white but all Lambs' (Okorafor 2011, 59). ('Lambs' is a term used in the novel for those who aren't 'Leopard People'). The racism ingrained in American society is explored in Sasha's narration of an encounter with the police in which he recalls that the police 'were harassing me and my friends, (…) They were pushing around this girl I know. And they were just … they were abusing the power they were given!' concluding 'Y'all don't know what it's like for a black man in the U.S. And y'all certainly don't know Chicago cops on the South Side. Here everyone's black' (Okorafor 2011, 60). In the globalized spiritual network Okorafor constructs, members are not free from prejudice or marginalization. Sasha asserts that the New York headquarters of the Leopard People in the United States 'doesn't represent black folks. We *are* a minority, I guess. As a matter of fact – everything's biased towards European juju' (Okorafor 2011, 79). Nigeria allows Sasha to escape the racial prejudice of his birthplace, providing a space of affirmation for his blackness. Sasha's relocation to Nigeria reiterates the African-American connection to Africa. Africa is presented as providing a secure and empowering environment for its children, whether like Sunny they are from a recently established diaspora, or like Sasha, a longer standing one. The trans-Atlantic voyage that Sasha embarked on depicts a realization of the Garveyite 'back to Africa' vision in which children of African descent can escape racial oppression in the New World through returning to the continent of their ancestors.

In Nnedi Okorafor's recasting of indigenous socio-political organizations, new gender dimensions emerge. In their original configuration, parallel and complementary gendered institutions were in existence. The reconfiguration of these institutions by Okorafor in which they now operate within the same sphere, is representative of wider social changes in which 'male' and 'female' spaces are no longer as clearly defined. The Ekpe society still remains a predominantly male society, however, there have been alterations made in other gendered spaces such as the home. Whereas in a precolonial Igbo household a husband and his wife or wives would have lived in separate structures within the same compound, now the marital home is a single structure that houses husband and wife. Although senior members of the Ekpe society can initiate their daughters into the institution, albeit in a largely titular capacity, the Ndem society amongst the Calabar and the Nimm amongst the Ejagham are important female orientated organizations whose complementarity to Ekpe is apparent in the totems of power associated with each institution. Ekpe's literal translation is 'leopard', a land animal whose strength, agility and energy were revered by those living in forest regions. The Nimm and Ndem are associated with the strength and power of the crocodile, a powerful aquatic reptile. Ekpe ruled the land whilst Ndem/Nimm ruled the water, but both institutions associated water with the realm of the ancestors. Ivor Miller explains that 'In many Cross River settlements, the Ékpè leopard society and the Ndèm mermaid society are separate but interconnected' (Miller 2009, 47). Miller further states that

During the Ékpè ceremonies, a portion of offerings are customarily reserved for Ndèm and taken to the river. Meanwhile Ndèm priestesses are ordinarily initiated into Ékpè in order to be "fully effective". (…) Ndèm is a source for Ékpè's authority, as well as for that of the paramount ruler of the community. (Miller 2009, 47)

The interconnectivity of Ekpe and Nimm is extended by Okorafor, who integrates the two institutions in her writing. The existing spaces within Igbo-Efik-Ejagham cultures for women's religious, political and economic expression forms the basis for the novel's womanist perspective. The female-centred narrative in *Akata Witch* draws on the existing institutions to provide the constructs for female achievement as Sunny's journey to self-discovery is interlinked with her realization that her grandmother, Ozoemena Nimm was of 'the warrior folk of the Nimm clan' (Okorafor 2011, 343). The revelation of Ozoemena Nimm's position within the leopard people made Sunny feel as though she 'had just gotten a glimpse of her own soul' (Okorafor 2011, 345). In linking Ozoemena and Sunny's narrative, Okorafor seeks to historicize women's contributions to the shaping and betterment of society, drawing a clear trajectory that spans three generations. Sunny is depicted as picking up the mantle left for her by her grandmother, asserting the continued importance of female participation in the multiple spheres of life.

Speculative fiction is used by Nnedi Okorafor as a medium through which to challenge societal norms as it 'triggers both a distancing and associating effect. This makes it an excellent vehicle for approaching taboo and socially-relevant yet overdone topics in new ways' (Okorafor 2014b). In her writing, Okorafor explores the position of women in contemporary Nigerian society. The advent of colonization witnessed the implementation of patriarchal institutions such as the government and the church, so that women who had previously held strong political, economic and religious positions were now marginalized from important power bases. Whilst patriarchy within the Nigerian nation space pre-dates colonial contact, the participation of women in important social spheres was greatly reduced with the implementation of Victorian notions of 'a woman's place'. In this sense, the feminist or womanist struggle in Africa is not distinct from the process of decolonization.

In *Akata Witch*, Okorafor's re-presentation of indigenous socio-cultural institutions and the position of the girl child within them present the interplay of two realities. Susana M. Morris has suggested that because 'much of Afrofuturism's transgressive politics align with the fundamental tenets of black feminist thought, (…) it is critical to understand these epistemologies not only as related but as, in fact, in conversation with one another and potentially even symbiotic' (Morris 2012, 153). In this way Afrofuturism presents a framework through which the various intersections of gender, race, culture and heritage are engaged with. Ytasha Womack suggests that Afrofuturist narratives centralize the female, as the 'subconscious and intuition, which metaphysical studies dub as the feminine side of us all, are prioritized in the genre' (Womack 2013, 104). Afrofuturism not only shifts the focus from Euro-American narratives to narratives of people of African descent, it also centralizes women and the female principle. For young female readers, Afrofuturist narratives can offer a liberating space in its capacity to subvert the male dominance existent in mainstream science fiction and fantasy literature.

The creative freedom that speculative fiction permits its writers enables them to present the world in new ways, in which normative racial, gendered or cultural constructs can be dismantled. Okorafor's writing of Africa-based speculative fiction challenges the absence of Africa and Africans in images of the future projected by mainstream science fiction and fantasy literature. In speaking of her need to 'see Africa in the future', Okorafor states 'I started writing science fiction set in Africa, based in specific African cultures, from an African perspective because I wanted to READ these stories' (Okorafor 2014b). The speculative fiction paradigm provides Okorafor the space in which to explore the cultural and spiritual beliefs of peoples in Africa vis-à-vis her literary constructions of African pasts, present and futures. In privileging the voice of people of African descent and locating her narratives in Africa, Okorafor centres Africa in the world of her writing, locating her projection of global futures within an African context. In this literature of decolonization, the marginalization of Europe or White America subverts what Teju Cole has termed 'the white saviour industrial complex' (Cole 2012) so that in *Akata Witch* the heroes of the world are young people of African descent, living on the continent. In challenging racial, cultural, spiritual, gendered and disability stereotypes, Okorafor encourages her young readership to reconceptualize the world in which they live, presenting the first step towards effecting and realizing change.

WORKS CITED

Achebe, Chinua (2010). *The Education of a British-Protected Child*. London: Allen Lane.

Chambers, Douglas B. (2010). '"Will You Join Me In El Monte?": A Kongo African Spirit in Modern Cuba (Regla, June 2000)', *Southern Quarterly* 47 (4): 110–19.

Chinweizu, Onwuchekwa Jemie, and Ihechukwu Madubuike (1983). *Toward the Decolonization of African Literature*. Washington DC: Howard University Press.

Cole, Teju (2012). 'The White-Savior Industrial Complex', *The Atlantic*. Accessed January 21 2015. <http://www.theatlantic.com/international/archive/2012/03/the-white-savior-industrial-complex/254843/>.

Dery, Mark (1994). 'Black to the Future: Interviews with Samuel R. Delany, Greg Tate, and Tricia Rose'. In Mark Dery, ed., *Flame Wars: The Discourse of Cyberculture*, Durham NC: Duke University Press, 179–222.

—— (2008). 'Black to the Future: Afro-Futurism 1.0.' In Marleen S. Barr, ed., *Afro-Future Females: Black Writers Chart Science Fiction's Newest New-Wave Trajectory*, Columbus: Ohio State University Press, 6–13.

Dubey, Madhu (2010). 'Speculative Fictions of Slavery', *American Literature* 82 (4): 779–805.

Emenyonu, Ernest (2004). 'Selection and Validation of Oral Materials for Children's Literature: Artistic Resources in Chinua Achebe's Fiction for Children'. In Ernest N. Emenyonu and Iniobong I. Uko, eds, *Emerging Perspectives on Chinua Achebe*, Trenton NJ: Africa World, 1: 427–40.

Eshun, Kodwo (2003). 'Further Considerations of Afrofuturism', *CR: The New Centennial Review* 3 (2): 287–302.

Ezenwa-Ohaeto (1998). 'Breaking Through: The Publishing Enterprise of Flora Nwapa'. In Marie Umeh, ed., *Emerging Perspectives on Flora Nwapa: Critical and Theoretical Essays*, Trenton NJ: Africa World Press, 189–99.

Miller, Ivor (2009). *Voice of the Leopard: African Secret Societies and Cuba*. Caribbean Studies Series. Jackson: University Press of Mississippi.

Miller, Ivor and Matthew Ojong (2013). 'Ékpè "Leopard" Society in Africa and the Americas: Influence and Values of an Ancient Tradition', *Ethnic & Racial Studies* 36 (2): 266–81.

Morris, Susana M. (2012). 'Black Girls Are from the Future: Afrofuturist Feminism in Octavia E. Butler's "Fledgling"', *Women's Studies Quarterly* 40 (3/4): 146–66.

Mosley, Walter (2000). 'Black to the Future'. In Sheree R. Thomas, ed., *Dark Matter: A Century of Speculative Fiction from the African Diaspora*, Kindle Edition. New York: Warner Books.

—— (2015). 'Novelist Walter Mosley Headlines FAMU Literary Series', *Walter Mosley*. Accessed February 02 2015. <http://www.waltermosley.com/novelist-walter-mosley-headlines-famu-literary-series/#more-710>.

Muponde, Robert, and Pippa Stein (2004). 'Mapping the Terrain: Introduction', *Journal of African Children's and Youth Literature* 15-16: x – xv.

Okorafor, Nnedi (2009). 'Organic Fantasy', *African Identities* 7 (2): 275–86.

—— (2011). *Akata Witch*. New York: Viking.

—— (2014a). ' "Have Always Read *Things Fall Apart* as an Alien Invasion Novel – Much Better than *War of the Worlds*" – @jacques_e_loupe.' Twitter. @Nnedi. Accessed 5 January 2015. <https://twitter.com/Nnedi/status/424356591878410240>.

—— (2014b). 'African Science Fiction Is Still Alien', *Nnedi's Wahala Zone Blog*. Accessed 15 January 2015. <http://nnedi.blogspot.co.uk/2014/01/african-science-fiction-is-still-alien.html>.

Ottenberg, Simon and Linda Knudsen (1985). 'Leopard Society Masquerades:

Symbolism and Diffusion', *African Arts* 18 (2): 37–104.

Wilson-Tagoe, Nana (1992). 'Children's Literature in Africa: Theoretical and Critical Issues'. In Chidi Ikonne, Emelia Oko, and Peter Onwudinjo, eds, *Children and Literature in Africa*, Ibadan: Heinemann Educational Books (Nigeria), 18–23.

Tomorrow's Kings & Queens

Gender Representation
in Ghanaian Children's Literature

JULIANA DANIELS

Gender inequality is a major issue all over the world. In Ghana, it ranks highest among the factors that militate against national development. Research has shown that many children acquire gender awareness before their teenage years yet most gender discussions in literature are focused on works for adults. This article examines how gender disparity against females in children's books sends children a message that women and girls occupy a less important role in society than men or boys. The discussion is projected through a textual analysis of gender representation in some randomly selected Ghanaian children's literature.

Books, whether electronic or in print, influence lives in one way or another. Through words and illustrations they are able to usher the reader into a world of unlimited adventure and discovery while tucked up in a quiet spot. Books facilitate seeing others and other things in relation to ourselves and our environment. Through books we get to know ourselves better in terms of who we are and what our values are. During the formative years of their lives, up to twelve, children build up theories about what it means to be male or female as they observe how society classifies people and how gender roles are applied in society. They also begin the development of attitudes about the gendered features of toys, activities and work related roles. Thus the study of the content of children's literature in Ghana is much needed. The rationale for this chapter is rooted in the fact that amongst other factors, gender stereotypic philosophies have the potential to limit children's choices, interests, and abilities. Ultimately, it can inhibit the maximization of their potential. The relevance of books to children is undoubtedly one, if not the most significant aspect of developing the younger generation for a better society tomorrow. For this reason it is not only important that we give children books to shape their lives but also consider carefully the kind of books we give them.

Theoretically, Bem (1983), and Martin and Halverson (1981) suggest that based on gender schema theory, children develop their attitudes to their society in the early years. In support of the feminist views on gender awareness in children, Sandra Bem, an American psychologist specializing in gender studies, has found that by the age of four or five, children have already formed sex typing documentations in their minds (1983: 598). Bussy and Bandura (1992), drawing on social cognitive theory, also suggest that gender development in such children involves their own perceptions and understanding of the differences between males and females. A prominent influence in this process is that books are a major vehicle for handing down norms and traditions (good or bad) from one generation to another, including the universal yoke of gender inequalities. Learning is easier than unlearning: it is better to expose children to appropriate knowledge in their early years, rather than waiting till they are older, when gender stereotypes and enveloping sex typing may have already been established and thus difficult to unlearn. Even in the simple storybooks for children, communication or reverence for both genders ought to be delicately conveyed. It is imperative to steer clear of books that have strident messages on gender even-handedness, for children have a propensity to avoid books that sermonize. As in the words of Mem Fox's article, entitled 'Men who weep, boys who dance', 'laboring the point kills the point of laboring' (1993: 85). According to Pressley et al. (2003) many research findings on motivation show that in order to get young readers to reconsider the existing gender trends, the use of books that spark some level of critical awareness can be explored. Although the very essence of literature is to entertain and for leisurely purposes, the element of didacticism, dissemination of information and development of ideas is often drawn from the message of a text: its implied meanings cannot be overlooked. In support of this view, Strickland, Gald & Cullinan (2004) comment that when children read engaging books, then think, write and talk about them, they are able to develop their higher order thinking skills. They suggest that this is the kind of skill required for success in the world of the 21st century. Indeed, cultural ideas and fundamental power relations are embedded in many objects (Grauerholz & Pescosolido, 1989). In Africa, literature is often an illusory visual rendition of a world in which traditional family roles prevail. Mothers undertake caring and fostering, whilst fathers are the suppliers of financial support. If social structures inculcate gender roles then there is every reason to look for analogous changes in media projections on the whole, and in the portrayal of gender in children's literature in particular. This suggests that the aim of creating gender role sensitization must begin with the youngest children.

Many critics have made remarkable efforts to prove the existing gender bias in children's books. Jett-Simpson & Masland (1993) assert that content, language and illustrations of many children's books are the means to challenge this. In an analysis of children's books, Ernst (1995) suggests that nearly twice as many titles of children's books contain a masculine word. She adds that often when the names were feminine or gender neutral, the story often had male central characters. Fox (1993) comments on the stereotypical representation of females in children's books, while both Simpson & Masland (1993) and Ernst (1995) have shown that in many instances, girls are depicted as sweet, naïve, conforming, and dependent whilst boys are represented as strong, adventurous, independent and capable. Temple (1993) adds that more often than not, roles such as fighters, adventurers and rescuers are ascribed to boys while girls are depicted as caretakers, mothers, princesses and other passive players. Rudman (1995) even believes that in many children's books, girls only achieve heroic feats because they are helped by males or older people. Rudman's finding reinforces the view that gender bias in children's literature is not just a matter of the predominance of male characters but also an issue of the stereotypical representation of female characters. The overall effect is the suppression of freedom of expression of both genders, of abilities and the capabilities of the 'small fry'. The long-term effect is the dwarfing of the subjugated gender and the construction of the suppressive 'glass ceiling'.

The relevance of literature to growth and development of the child and the daunting issue of gender sensitization brings up the subject of what kinds of books are on the Ghanaian market for the consumption of our children? How do these books reinforce or correct gender stereotypes? The following analysis offers a gender audit in an attempt to unearth the nuances that underlie gender representation in Ghanaian children's literature. The books analysed in this chapter are all written by Ghanaians. They have local settings, and the target audience is the ordinary Ghanaian child. The books were purchased at random on the open market without reference to data on what the ordinary Ghanaian child is likely to read. No specific credence was given to the educational level of the author's targeted readership: titles were broadly viewed as suitable for readers between six and twelve years of age. The end-date reflects the fact that this is the stage of development where children begin to understand and appreciate gender differentiation and expectations according to the norms in society. As indicated by Maccoby (1998), this change is visible in the choice of gendered behavioural patterns. It is appreciated that the sample size could be expanded to cover a larger number of texts; for the purpose of establishing a general picture of the situation, a modest number of books was selected.

Literature, whether oral or written, is an integral part of society as a mirror of life. Mainly, it serves the purpose of entertainment and education. It also serves the role of conveying social order from one generation to another. In many societies in Africa, it serves the important function of ensuring preservation of lineage and practice with the hope that the younger generation will take over from the older successfully. Aside from improving the linguistic competence of children, literature also serves as a manual for the maturing of the young into adulthood. Character and characterization in literature forms an important part of literature's ability to impact positively on its young readers. If the efforts to bring about equality and equity of gender for national development are anything to go by, then there is every need for caution as to how gender and gender roles are portrayed in children's literature. According to Fox, 'Everything we read ... constructs us, makes us who we are, by presenting our image of ourselves as girls and women, as boys and men' (1993: 84).

In Ghana, especially, attitudes that give concern about gender representation come in many forms. Today's culture is unremittingly drawing strength from the existing patriarchal traditions in Ghana. According to Kane (2006), by age two, most children would not only have been aware of the importance of gender but they also would have been active contributors to gender practices. Many children at that age are likely to differentiate between their clothes and that of the other sibling who is an opposite sex. They are also likely to say whether they like to play with dolls and flowers or toy cars and footballs. In a society where the upbringing of a child is a communal responsibility, as in

Ghana, society's assignments of tasks and expectations of children reinforce differential treatment of the sexes. For example, in *The Girl Who Lived in a Tree* (unknown author and date of publication), Amaka's dead father, Ogbo, empowers her through dreams with the skill of climbing trees. Ogbo believes that living on the tree is the only safe way for his daughter to escape the deadly disease that is killing every young person in the village. Thus Amaka decides to live on the tallest Odum tree in the village after her parents die of the strange disease, and her grandmother of old age. In this story, when Amaka first climbs the tree

> ...some of the elderly ones among them (villagers who came to see her) cautioned the little girl not to give the whole village such heartaches by climbing up tall trees like that again especially as she was a mere girl and girls were not naturally the type who took on such daring adventures. (15)

Amaka's grandmother also adds to the chorus saying to the little girl, "You know you are a girl and in our part of the world, it is a very unusual thing for a girl to climb trees especially trees as tall as that" (16). This assertion by Amaka's grandmother reflects how some elderly women are not only conditioned to accept gender stereotyping but also find themselves propagating such socialization consciously or unconsciously.

Like Amaka in *The Girl Who Lived in a Tree*, Joana in Yaw Ababio Boateng's *Miss John* (1991) is a masterpiece on gender balance. Mrs. Tetteh is a bank manageress and a single parent with three girls; Joana the oldest, followed by Fiona and then Martha the youngest. The story opens with Joana showing her disapproval of her mother always telling her that she was behaving too much like a boy and getting too friendly with boys (1). Joana does not see anything wrong with a fourteen-year-old girl playing football and having a bit of fun with the boys (1). Once again we see parents cultivating gender differentiation amongst their children. Here a mother tries to socialize her daughter by preventing her from freely mixing with the opposite sex. Through the character of Joana, Ababio criticizes society for inappropriately fostering the separation of sexes amongst children. Later on in the story, workplace gender struggle is criticized. Mrs Tetteh is a subordinate to a Mr. Pambour in a banking firm. According to Joana, the two do not get on. The result is that Mrs. Tetteh is transferred from the city to a village branch (3). Through Joana, Boateng (1991) interrogates such workplace power struggles. Joana therefore expresses her disapproval of her mother's intimidation when she exclaims: "Can't you do anything about it, mum? Mr. Pambour can't send you to some far away village because he doesn't like you." The helplessness of females in gender conflict is depicted in Mrs. Tetteh's sad tone: "I have to go. I have no choice" (3). Girls who read this book will surely be prepared to find placatory ways of pleasing their male bosses in order to be well treated. Boys who read the story will learn that they can make assertive women pay for disrupting the social order. Children will also learn from this text that women work under the supervision of men: thus they must be liked and happy. Joana does not give up in her battle against gender discrimination. George, Mr. Pambour's son begins to physically assault Joana for accidentally breaking his bowl of eggs. To his surprise, Joana defends herself by hitting and kicking him till he gives up fighting back:

> Suddenly, George grabbed Joana and started to hit her. Joana kicked George on his leg. Then she kept kicking him as hard as she could until he let go. George fell on the ground crying. (10)

Joana teaches her readers to take a second thought about the idea of females being the weaker sex. She therefore discourages violence against females by males. At her new school, Joana questions the existing arrangement of the separation of sexes common in some Ghanaian schools. For instance, the norm in her school is for girls not to run in races but to sing and cheer the boys who do so. This does not sit well with Joana who looks angrily at the excited boys who tell her the rules. Since nobody will allow her to register for the race she had to find an alternative means of breaking into the line-up which she does successfully, going on to win the race ahead of all the boys. Once again, Joana echoes the capabilities of the feminine gender when given equal opportunity with males. She tells Boamah, one of the boys who is all for the existing gender hierarchy, next time the boys will sing while she runs (30). This opportunity comes when Boamah, the epitome of masculinity, tells her about an excursion meant for the boys only. Boamah had teased Joana saying she would never have an opportunity to see what the inside of an airplane looks like. This is after making faces at her and calling her a 'tomboy' (31). The term 'tomboy' is derogatory and usually meant to intimidate assertive females. Joana, nonetheless, responds to the challenge, seeing to it that the girls in the school are allowed to take part in the trip. Supported by Serwaa, one of the students in her class, the two manage to convince the school administration to allow some female students to go along too. According to the story, of the 60 students, 45 were boys and 15 were girls. The issue of gender imbalance still applies here but credit will however be given to Joana for the effort of getting some girls to make the trip. Once again, Ababio reiterates his call for gender equity amongst children.

Joana's fight against gender inequality does not end with getting the girls on the trip. She seems not to be just interested in gender equity but also in proving that girls have the potential to outdo their male counterparts. Though she finds herself in some measure of trouble at the end, Joana certainly surpasses her male counterparts when she goes beyond just looking into an airplane to actually flying in one. At the airport, Joana hides in the toilet of the plane so that she can experience flying. She is caught, given a flight back and warned about her behaviour. Interestingly, just as her mother makes arrangements to send her to boarding school in Accra in order to keep her away from further mischief, Joana's school management board comes to plead on her behalf. The decision of the board is informed by Joana's ability to educate them on the need to give both genders equal opportunities, especially when girls are young. Through Joana's actions, the once gender-segregated, boys' and girl's sections are disbanded and the school reverts to a mixed gender policy. Joana succeeds in deconditioning the minds of the adults who have reinforced gender discrimination amongst children. . Boateng's story draws the attention of heads of schools, parents and the society in general to some of the decisions that heighten the problems of gender conflict in Ghana today. The most intriguing episode of the story is seen when Boamah, the epitome of masculinity, and Joana's sworn enemy, finally appreciates the potential of females, admires Joana's prowess, and falls in love with her. Joana herself, the quintessence of femininity, echoes the fundamental agenda of African feminism as a movement that does not seek to underrate masculinity but merely to make a case for the need for feminine spaces. Joana does not hate Boamah when he keeps emphasizing male superiority. She does not even hate him for calling her 'Tomboy'. Though Joana tells her younger sister, Fiona, that from the first day she met Boamah she did not like him, the actual truth is revealed when Joana, without hesitation accepts Boama's proposal to be special friends and to be her 'boyfriend' as understood in the Ghanaian context.

S.Y. Manu is another contemporary Ghanaian writer of children's literature. His story *Every Good Turn Deserves Another* (2001) tells of a chief who decides to kill any animal that offends him but each time he summons one, his son comes to plead on behalf of the offender. Such pardon is never granted. Whenever the offenders are bound to be executed the next day, the chief's son helps them escape. One day, the chief wakes up to find that not one of his own farm animals could be found, so his son sets out to look for them. With the aid of all the animals he has helped escape from his wicked father, the boy is able to return with all the lost farm stock: thus the title; *Every Good Turn Deserves Another*. Elements of gender imbalance are typified in this text in the sense that of the six characters in the story, not one of them is a female. Of the two humans and four animals none is given a feminine attribute. A gender stereotype is echoed here when the two male characters are described as cruel in one breath and generous, wise and forgiving in another. The question remains whether S. Y. Manu forgot about females because he himself is a male and imagines the world as one of males only.

In Manu's other story in the Ladybird Series entitled, *Ananse the Treacherous One* (2001), the story revolves around a spider (Ananse) and a pig who decide to team up in life. They set up a farm that is very successful but Ananse kills the pig and takes over the property. The pig's children are offended and attack the spider, who runs into the topmost corner of the room. The corner agrees to host the spider only if he promises to build a cobweb for it. To this the spider agrees. Ananse, the spider, is described as smart and greedy whiles the pig is portrayed as good and a caring father of many children. Once again, Manu presents Ghanaian children with a world where females are insignificant and non-existent.

The last story in this Ladybird Series of three stories is *How the Crow Got a White Collar* (2001), written by Jane Osafua Dankyi, a Ghanaian female author. A mother, Afua Ataa, and her daughter, Adwoa Mansa, go to get fish from a river. In the process, Afua Ataa falls into the water and her daughter is left alone crying for help. Three animals, the hawk, vulture and crow come to their aid but it is the crow that is able to save Afua Ataa. In return, the crow asks for a white collar to be sewn around his neck. The story is interesting in the way it projects gender. There are two females, mother and daughter, and three animals. All the animals are presented as males. The two females are presented as helpless and in need of rescue by males. The moral here is that females, regardless of their number, are weak and helpless without males who hold the keys to their salvation. For a female author to project gender in this light reflects perhaps the gendered socialization of the author which permeates her writing.

Williams Asamoah is another well-known name on the block of children's literature writers. *The Three Friends* (2006) is one of his most famous stories. Three young men agree to go into cooperative farming which turns out to be a successful venture. When one of the men finds a pot of gold hidden in the land, they decide at first to share it equally, but greed sets in. Tatahwe kills his friends, takes all the gold, marries the wives of his friends and also has children with them. Not long after, the ghosts of the two friends begin to haunt him until he finally goes mad.

In this story, gender imbalance is reflected in the three-to-one ratio of males to females. According to the story the men decided to work hard because they wanted to take care of their wives and children. Tatawhe's wife, the only female who is mentioned just once in the story, is even described as difficult to please. This is obviously not a pleasant or positive portrayal of a female character to share with children. The idea that the men go out to work in order to fend for their wives suggests that women are to be taken care of and that their role is to take care of the house and the children. In the story, Asamoah presents his male characters as hard-working and caring but by the end of the story, they are also greedy. Their attempt to eliminate one another because of money leaves their children likely not to trust their peers with such issues when they in turn grow up. At this early age, Asamoah's story also introduces his young readers to polygamy as an acceptable social practice in Africa that women accept as normal. Making the wives of the dead agree to marry Tatawhe implies that females cannot do without men. Children reading works such as this will only grow up erroneously thinking that men have absolute control over women.

In Derrick Anorvey's *Modern English Reader* (2008), for Primary One pupils, the male/female character ratio is equally unimpressive. There are eight males, compared to three females. Ama (a female character) is described as fat, and Kofi (a male character) as with a big head with a love of food. Meanwhile, whereas Mr Ibrahim is seen going to pray, Mrs Mensah is associated with dressing up and liking children. The other female in the story, an old woman, is tied to going to fetch water. For the other males, one plays football, the other has a mobile phone and another is a doctor whilst the other, an old man is going to meet his wife. Anorvey's *Reader* enforces the stereotype that a woman's interest must be in trivial things such as beautifying herself whilst that of men should be in education and technology.

In Williams Asamoah's other work, *Primary English Course Book* (2006), there is a more balanced representation of gender in terms of ratio and characterization. Both boys and girls play, and they play together so that no games are strictly applied to a particular gender. Although boys are not depicted playing with dolls, they do play with flowers and conversely, there are girls who ride bicycles. The only slight gender query identifiable in the text is that although Asamoah names two boys and two girls in his story, in one of the illustrations, there are three boys and only one girl. In relation to adults, he associates mothers with the kitchen when Adjo's mother is seen putting fish in the oven. Adult males are however portrayed as those who go out to work, travel the world over, and bring home gifts for children: for example Adjo's uncle returns from London with many gifts for them.

Gregory N. D. Ankrah's *Twelve Great Ananse Stories* (2007) includes the story of the spider (Ananse) known in the Ghanaian culture as cunning and untrustworthy. Many writers use Ananse to depict the essence of wisdom and sometimes the foolishness of characters. This collection of stories includes titles such as 'Ananse The Teacher', 'The Pot and Whip', 'Kweku Ananse and The Glue Statue', 'Ananse and The Rich Farmer', 'Ananse and The Crocodile' and 'Ananse and the Crocodile's Children'.

Throughout the book and in all the subtitles, Ananse has a wife and four children – all of whom are boys. There is a gender ratio imbalance: five males to one female. The stories mainly centre on Ananse and his children while his wife is rarely mentioned. From these stories, it could be deduced that the stereotype of women being relegated to the background and often regarded as second to men is pervasive. All the major decisions in the stories are made by the male characters. Although occasionally Ananse's wife proposes an alternative solution to a problem, Ananse always relegates that to the background and carries out his own plan. Indeed, the wife figure in the stories is one put in the caretaker role, a role termed 'house wife'. Hers is to always be with the children either on the farm or at home whilst her husband goes to town in search of other means of providing for the family. None of the stories portray the wife as a career woman who can fend for herself but rather as always dependent on the husband. The lesson children may learn here is that a man provides for the house, he makes all the decisions and a woman's duty is to take instructions from the man, obey him, and serve him and their children.

Drawing from the analysis thus far, it is obvious that that much of Ghanaian children's literature depicts gender stereotyping. Characters are predominantly males who are depicted as bread winners while female characters are limited to nurturing responsibilities. Remarkably, boys and girls play together in many of the books. Of major concern to this article is the extent to which parents, guardians and other members of the Ghanaian society reinforce patriarchal tendencies as in the case of Amaka, the girl who lived in a tree and as in Joana in the story *Miss John*. It is conclusive that Ghanaian children's literature presents a valuable resource for influencing children's gender attitudes, hence the need to pay attention to the content of books provided for them.

Since children start nurturing their gender schemas in their early stages, they could be tremendously influenced by their environment, including the books they are exposed to. Therefore it is recommended that preferably, all children's literature should depict deliberately constructed male and female characters whose characterization typifies gender equity and equality. Knowing that as early as age two, children are gender sensitive, books made available to them must depict appropriate gender colouring. In this way, children will grow up socialized in a culture of mutual gender respect in deeds and thoughts.

This appeal is made against the background that children have very little influence on the selection of books they read. The choice often rests with the teacher, parent or other adult members of society. As a result, further study must be undertaken to demonstrate the extent to which these important stakeholders in children's gender sensitization are aware of the role of gender representation in the literature they select for their children. There is also a need for all to make the conscious effort to ensure that books made available to our children promote gender equity. Literature selected for children's consumption should include those that depict individuals with idiosyncratic personalities, irrespective of their gender, also books in which accomplishments are not divided on the basis of gender and professions are not gender-ascribed, books in which femininities and masculinities are projected fairly, and where the language of the texts is not sexist in tone.

Finally, stakeholders in the development of children's literacy need consciously to find books that portray women and girls in a more affirmative light with self-motivated and dynamic roles. Essentially, efforts must be made to produce and provide children with books and stories that do not depict either masculinity or femininity in a banal or stereotypical manner. Perhaps further research should delve into how gender-sensitive the writers of children's literature actually are. The findings of such a study will provide essential data for developing strategies to make children's literature a vehicle for the promotion of the equality of the sexes.

WORKS CITED

Ankrah, G. N. D. (2007). *Twelve Great Ananse Stories*. Accra: GND Ltd.

Asamoah, W. (2006). *The Three Friends*. Accra: Knowledge Source Publications.

—— (2006). *Primary English Course Book*. Accra: Knowledge Source Publications, Bk 3.

Bem, S. L. (1983). *Gender Schema Theory and Its Implications for Child Development: Raising Gender-Aschematic Children in a Gender-Schematic Society*. The University of Chicago Press, 8:4, 598-616. http://www.jstor.org/stable/3173685.

Boateng. Y. A. (1991) *Miss John*. Essex UK: Heinemann Publications.

Dankyi. O. J. (2001) 'How the Crow Got A White Collar'. In *Tales of Ghana: Lady Bird Series*. London: Ladybird Books Ltd.

Ernst, S. B. (1995). 'Gender issues in books for children and young adults'. In S. Lehr (ed.), *Battling Dragons: Issues and Controversy in Children's Literature*, Portsmouth NH: Heinemann, 66-78. [ED 379 657]

Fox, M. (1993). 'Men who weep, boys who dance: The gender agenda between the lines in children's literature', *Language Arts*, 70 (2), 84-8. [EJ 457 107].

Jett-Simpson, M., & Masland, S. (1993). 'Girls are not dodo birds! Exploring gender equity issues in the language arts classrooms', *Language Arts*, 70 (2), 104-8. [EJ 457 110].

Manu. S. Y. (2001) 'Every Good Turn Deserves Another', *Tales of Ghana: Ladybird Series*, London: Ladybird Books Ltd.

—— (2001) 'Ananse the Treacherous One', *Tales of Ghana: Ladybird Series*, London: Ladybird Books Ltd.

Rudman, M. (1995). *Children's Literature: An Issues Approach*, White Plains NY: Longman. [ED 379 684] (3rd edition).

Temple, C. (1993). 'What if "Beauty" had been ugly? Reading against the grain of gender bias in children's books', *Language Arts*, 70 (2), 89-93. [EJ 457 108].

Unknown author & date of publication, *The Girl Who Lived in a Tree*. Accra: Masty Publications Ltd.

Sindiwe Magona

An Interview for ALT
by Ernest N. Emenyonu & Patricia T. Emenyonu

18 March 2015, University of Michigan, Flint

Ernest Emenyonu: With us here is Sindiwe Magona, an illustrious and versatile South African writer. Best described as novelist, activist, social worker, visionary, and so on and so forth. Two days ago I found out to my pleasant surprise that you've recently published about 130 children's books and still writing. But not much is talked about this as part of your creativity, so I'll start with that. Why is there this omission? Is it accidental or is it deliberate? Or do people just feel that books for children are not all that important?

Sindiwe Magona: No I think it's accidental, but it's also a reflection of how much attention we put on children's writing and children's books, and that's why children's books are seldom reviewed, especially those written in African indigenous languages – those are never reviewed – period! In South Africa you might get an odd review of a book written in English or even in Afrikaans, but never a book written in African languages; there are no reviews of these books and so critics who may want to include them in what they put on the internet have nothing to go by. And the publishers themselves who publish children's books in African indigenous languages, are themselves, I think neglectful, because they will not publish such books unless they are used in schools, otherwise they amount to nothing really much. There is no great push for children's books unless driven by commercial motives.

Ernest Emenyonu: Now that you've answered that, let's go to the journal, *African Literature Today*. The issue (*ALT 33*) that's just about to go to print is on children's literature and story-telling in Africa. And incidentally, the response to, the call for papers, for it, has been abysmally poor, to put it mildly. So what do you think accounts for this general neglect or disregard of children's literature, when Africans are traditionally a story-telling people and story-telling begins with children?

Sindiwe Magona: Well, speaking from a personal perspective when I hear or see 'Call for Papers', I say, 'that's academic' and so that excludes me, a writer. I don't regard myself as an academic, I'm just a writer. And I think unless people in academia, offer courses in children's literature, and critics and teachers at that level take up the writing of papers on the genre, it's not going to come from storytellers. I'm thinking here of a particular excellent storyteller in South Africa. This is a woman who has never been to school, she tells marvelous stories. She plays the traditional harp, you know, *uhadi*, but she is never going to write a paper, she can't even write her own name. It's for the academics to write about what the storytellers produce. And if they don't, it says a lot about the scholars and critics not the storytellers or writers of children's books.

Ernest Emenyonu: The call for papers is indeed for critics, teachers, and students who read the books. They're supposed to write about what they have actually read…

Sindiwe Magona: Generally, they don't read! If it doesn't concern their particular courses or fields of study, they do not care about storytellers and story-telling.

Ernest Emenyonu: Many, many years ago in my primary school in Nigeria, there was a subject called 'Story-telling'. I think it was once or twice a week and was known as the 'story-telling hour'. The teachers told stories in the local language and then later on children were encouraged to tell stories themselves. The stories told were folktales. So my question is, to keep story-telling alive, do you think we should go back and have Story-telling as a subject in our primary schools?

Sindiwe Magona: We should. It is important enough that it should be included in the curriculum. In South Africa, there is, at least on the syllabus, things like story-telling where Idioms and other special linguistic features are becoming lost in African languages (because people don't use them anymore). But how effective that is, I don't know. And occasionally a school would invite a storyteller, but this is maybe, during a book month, book week, or during heritage day, when there is something in the calendar that points to 'let's remember our history'. It's not something that is an integral part of the child's schooling anyway.

Patricia Emenyonu: We were unaware of your children's stories partly because, they're published in South Africa and somehow because they're published there, they are not accessed in the United States or there's no easy access to them. However, to say that you've published 130 children's stories means that your publisher believes that what you're writing is good and that it's worth putting out there. How do you see the role of your publishers in making the books available globally? And in South Africa do you have hopes that your children's books could be used in schools since the reading habit is not really prevalent among many South Africans, Africans and even Americans? We've often bemoaned that!

Sindiwe Magona: The books have been published by several publishers. What made my output jump was that I introduced in my language a series where you see the same characters in different situations and there is growth. So I talked to a publisher who asked for a proposal. I did the proposal, submitted it and I was thinking of something maybe like 6-12 books. To my utter surprise, the publisher came back saying okay, we bought the idea, now could you write the stories in sequence for all the grades in the school system? I went and bought a whiteboard, and mapped out the storylines I would do. And I did this for the 3 grades (16 EACH FOR 3 GRADES COMES TO 48 BOOKS), so that's what made it jump up a bit. So it's a series of books under the title 'SIGALELEKILE' which means 'WE'VE ARRIVED/HERE WE ARE!' I thought carefully about the themes I would include such as family values, things that are of historical importance. But most deal with present day issues and dilemmas facing families and the joys of family life.

Patricia Emenyonu: So, the stories focus on family life. Do you project particular family values?

Sindiwe Magona: It's the traditional family, and the stories revolve around the escapades of the children. The questions the children bring to the parents and the things they discover together, including the mishaps, wishes, joys and sorrows of a family, and family life in general.

Ernest Emenyonu: When you write children's books, who do you have in mind? Do you have in mind South African children or kids in all of Africa?

Sindiwe Magona: For the series, the immediate focus was on children in South Africa, specifically black children. But we have a divide between the rural child and the urban child. Even if they belong to one ethnic group, we have such a divide between the black child and the white child. To the black child, the white wealth is something beyond comprehension. So this is what I was trying to show the children in South Africa, that 'this is who you are'. The children in the townships, for instance, have no idea that there can be filth in white homes. But it is the management of that filth, of our garbage that makes the difference. The environment defines our actions and vice-versa. For instance, if you are visiting a school in the townships and it's after lunch, the teacher is standing at the stoop doing this to the table cloth (motion of shaking all the garbage throwing it out). Thus, garbage belongs to a garbage can or dump. There is the need to create an awareness of things today that are very important such as waste management and environmental issues.

Ernest Emenyonu: When you write for black South African children, do you anticipate that it could be read also by white South African children?

Sindiwe Magona: Yes! Because they depict life as it is for anybody who wants to know something about other lives whether it's within the boundaries of the country or outside. Anybody picking up these books sees they depict the lives of black kids of a particular, socio-economic class and how their lives are lived day to day. Both parents are there so this is not a poor, broken family. It's not a wealthy family, but the parents are caring and they are there. They take the kids up the mountain so that they see these are things that you can do with your kids.

Ernest Emenyonu: We have talked about the status of children's literature in Africa that it's not highly regarded, now how do we fix this? Do you think there's something government should do, or roles private sector organizations can play to effect change? How do we increase the awareness, importance, and significance of children's literature in Africa?

Sindiwe Magona: If it is something that we care enough about, we need to begin a concerted effort. One of the things that saddens me is that, take South Africa for instance, children who grow up with the folktales of the Xhosa have no access to the folktales of other ethnic groups within the country, and vice versa. I don't have the folktales, but I am friends with South African's premiere storyteller whose stories are in Zulu language. Now I have access to her stories. In fact, she paid me the huge honor of asking her publisher, she has published two volumes of folktales, to ask me to translate them into Xhosa. She writes in Zulu and her books are also in English. I don't know whether she did the English editions herself or with other translators, but she now has her stories in Zulu, Xhosa, and English. I did the Xhosa version of those stories. Then I got to know more of the Zulu. There are folktales in all the 11 languages of South Africa, but the children will only know those of their mother tongue, if they're exposed to them... It is ridiculous that I know more of English literature, American literature, than I know of literature within the African continent. Ridiculous. So we could begin by translating African children's stories into various African languages on the continent.

Patricia Emenyonu: In Nigeria, when we were there more than 20 years ago, Flora Nwapa, who was known because she published her novels *Efuru* and *Idu* in the Heinemann African Writer's Series, eventually founded her own printing press, (Tana Press) and began to write children's stories. Unfortunately, the quality of the production was poor, so that when you had a picture on one page it sort of bled into the next page and that sort of thing. But we also had Mabel Segun who wrote for children and who established a children's literature organization. But this was many years ago and there's been no real serious follow-up.

Sindiwe Magona: And what has happened to the initiative?

Patricia Emenyonu: It has just pretty much vanished. But now we have someone who is living abroad in England, a photographer (Ifeoma Onyefulu) who's doing wonderful work and her children's stories are appreciated in England as a way of educating children there about life in various situations in Africa, but not much about her books is known or read in Nigeria. Now some of her children's stories are set in Ghana, Ethiopia, etc., but she is read mostly outside the African continent.

Ernest Emenyonu: It is important that children's literature, just like adult African literature, should really be read all over the continent.

Sindiwe Magona: I totally agree.

Ernest Emenyonu: So how do we do that?

Sindiwe Magona: Well my dear, I wish I had the answer to that. But the first thing really is the recognition of the problem. And then looking at ways of promoting children's literature like literary competitions and prizes. Even the books published, I don't see a lot of circulation coming out of that. I may be wrong.

Ernest Emenyonu: So you're talking about establishing some literary competitions to promote children's literature in Africa?

Patricia Emenyonu: Like Coretta Scott King established an award for literature by African-American writers and illustrators. There are monetary awards, as well as recognition. But there's still a problem here in the United States, because those authors that are African-American are a tiny proportion of the total authors of children's literature.

Ernest Emenyonu: We have something of a history here to emulate. The early missionaries recognized the importance of literary contests for promoting literature. They established literary contests and then published winning entries in African languages. This gave rise to the publication of novels in African languages which predate the publication of African novels in European languages. That said, the question remains: what role do you think publishers can play in the promotion of children's literature in Africa? Do you get the feeling that they think that it really doesn't make as much money as adult literature and, therefore, not worth investing in?

Sindiwe Magona: You know, we have book fairs. There should be book fairs for children's literature. They may start off by being regional or country by country. But then there should be something that brings African children's writers or people writing for children in Africa together to exchange ideas among themselves and with publishers of children's books, exhibit children's books published in various parts of the continent and hold conversations with publishers who publish in African indigenous languages. The other thing is that as long as the writing and the production of children's books remain in the hands of people who do not speak the languages, these languages and writings in them will not thrive. This is the blight in South Africa. Most of the publishers don't speak African languages, even when they publish those languages. They will employ anybody who impresses them and it doesn't necessarily mean that the person has a great love or understanding of the language. You get books published in Xhosa; you get books winning prizes. And when you read the book, it may not be a bad book per se, but there are so many errors of spelling, never mind punctuation! And you think to yourself, wow!

Ernest Emenyonu: Do you see any link between having a reading culture and having viable children's literature?

Sindiwe Magona: Of course there is. If people don't read, you can't have a viable literature, because the end result of writing a book is to have a reader. If the reader isn't there, the publisher is not going to have any reason to publish a book.

Ernest Emenyonu: How would children's books assist or enhance the reading culture anywhere in Africa?

Sindiwe Magona: Books are there to be used. If we keep leaving the parent out of this and I don't understand why the parents and the home are left out in educational process. The education of a child cannot start at school, it's too late BY THEN! Inculcating a reading culture in a child is not something you can leave for 5 or 6 years and then think it can start and thrive. It's already too late. Pregnant mothers should be encouraged to go to prenatal clinics. At those clinics part of whatever they are getting there shouldn't only stop at the physiology, biology or whatever, it should also include the long-term development of the child, which implies that the child must read at every age and stage. Mothers at the clinic should be given books they can read and asked questions about. How did you enjoy it? What was it about? They should form clubs of pregnant mothers, so when they come to the clinic, they also share stories they will later on share with their children. The mother must start thinking along the terms of nurturing the child, including reading. If I were the government in South Africa, I wouldn't give any mother any grant, if I wasn't also monitoring the nurturing and development of that child.

Ernest Emenyonu: You anticipated my next question, because I was going to ask who would provide those books? So this is where the government can come in?

Sindiwe Magona: Yes! If government begins to take reading seriously and shows the parents that this is part of your duty, just as government has the duty and obligation of helping you raise the child. Part of raising that child is insuring that that child is armed to be able to negotiate education. No child is going to get an education when he or she can't read. Children love books and should be nurtured to have story-telling abilities in themselves.

Ernest Emenyonu: How can we harness technology towards the improvement of children's literature in Africa? It's so easy these days to find children playing games on gadgets and some people say well, this is one of the problems of children not reading. So how do you think we can use technology to enhance reading by children?

Sindiwe Magona: Right, I'll start with the end of what you're saying. Children were not reading long before technology, so this is nothing new. We neglect the children. We neglect to instill a reading culture in them. Technology aside, they don't read. But we can also become a little bit aggressive and get into technology, so that our books, include techno stuff. Or our reading material can get into technology so that we have games in our languages; we have quizzes in our languages, we have stories that we tell and can only be completed in our languages. We should stop at nothing in our bid to instill the reading culture in our kids. Technical skills can be worked into the reading process.

Ernest Emenyonu: It has been suggested that one way to use technology is to have film adaptations of children's books. They will watch the films, enjoy the visual qualities, but that will not enhance their reading abilities. How do you respond to that?

Sindiwe Magona: We have lots of picture books. Why can't these be adapted into animations where the child hears and sees the word at the same time as he or she follows the action or the storyline?

Patricia Emenyonu: We've just come back from a meeting at the Flint Public Library where you interacted with young kids who were brought to the public library to meet and talk with you. Are there libraries in South Africa that are community-based and open to the public?

Sindiwe Magona: There are. But again, there too, the challenge really is making them effective. Does the librarian see her job as somebody who can be a stimulus in the community? I come back to the roles of teachers, librarians, and parents. Unless the person is herself/himself in love with reading, he/she is not going to instill a reading culture in anybody. So, the majority of

African parents cannot perform this role because of who they are and what didn't happen in their own lives. It is up to the writer, the publishers, teachers, librarians and the few parents who can, to stand together and agitate on behalf of the children. To stand together and say, 'for our children's sake, this needs to happen. This needs to be in place'. In Cape Town, you can go to a place where the library is spic and span, but that's because nobody uses it really. And then you go to Sea Point, where there are Pram Jams. Do you know what a Pram jam is? You know who's in a pram? A baby! At Pram Jam, I think it's Friday's, the mamas bring the children there. But these are mamas who love books. Mamas who read. Mamas who went to universities. How do you get that same sense of responsibility to the mama who never went to a library?

Ernest Emenyonu: Let's talk specifically about your own writing, your own approach to children's books. I see that in some you go back to the oral tradition, to the folktales, and you recreate some of them.

Sindiwe Magona: Yes

Ernest Emenyonu: I even saw that you did something with the *Pied Piper of Hamelin*? Do you recommend to writers of children's books to recreate great fables, any famous fable from any tradition giving it African (local) images and settings?

Sindiwe Magona: Yes. You use anything and everything. What gave you joy as a child, surely might give joy to a child today. So you share your own experiences with today's child. I go back to my childhood, I remember the stories and the folktales I listened to, and I write them. I tell them to the children. But I also realize that the folktales that were available to us as children, most probably were written in past centuries, and address problems of that era. Why don't we take our problems and put them in a story like the Emperor's New Clothing? There must have been an emperor, there must have been this situation that gave rise to the story at the time. So that's how I got to write a children's story called, "The Cruel King Still Lives". But I also wrote another one, because after Mandela's passing, I, at my age, learned a new metaphor I had not realized existed in my language. We bury people, we use the word, *ngcwaba*; *ngcwaba* is to bury. But we don't *ngcwaba* our chiefs, we plant/*tyala*. That's a great metaphor, particularly for children. So one of the tales I wrote is "Today We Planted a Chief" or "*Namhlanje, Sityala Inkosi*".

Patricia Emenyonu: That's another aspect of nurturing. Children growing up need to have heroes, need to have mentors, need to see people who they can aspire after.

Sindiwe Magona: Yes. That's why we have *Today we Plant a Chief*.

Patricia Emenyonu: Yes, that was one of the things that happened in East Africa. The East African Publishing Company, had a series about well-known East Africans, you don't see that frequently in Africa for children.

Sindiwe Magona: No, no, no.

Patricia Emenyonu: That's important, and exciting.

Sindiwe Magona: I've just finished doing a children's edition of Eleanor Sisulu's biography of her parents-in-law, 'Walter and Albertina Sisulu'. First I was asked to split it, so I have Albertina Sisulu standing alone, Walter standing alone, and also to rewrite it in simpler English, so that it's for non-mother tongue speakers – that was one. And now I've been asked to do it in an edition for children, YA, a children's book. Less than 100 pages and it's about people they know in real life.

Ernest Emenyonu: Okay, let me just float an idea, some of the folktales were from centuries ago. Nobody knows how old these folktales are

Sindiwe Magona: They've been there forever.

Ernest Emenyonu: There are still some, many of them, that reflect values of all time.

Sindiwe Magona: Of course!

Ernest Emenyonu: Alright, so don't you think that this could be a starting point in terms of writing children's stories that could be read across the continent? Take a story, a folktale that has been recreated, a folktale that is known continent-wide, and then modernize it for contemporary values. What do you think about that?

Sindiwe Magona: It's an excellent idea, because the values that human beings subscribe to are for everybody. They are not confined to a specific group of people. If you take courage for instance, if you take honesty for instance, if you take hard work, even, that's for everybody. If you take dedication, if you take sacrifice, sacrificing oneself for a cause – those are values that are universal.

Ernest Emenyonu: Let's end by asking you: What's your message for people who want to write children's stories today? What's your message for parents who have children, but may not be aware of the importance of these stories? What's your message for the children, African Children, about these stories?

Sindiwe Magona: For the children, books and reading books are your best friends. They don't ask for anything in return from you. They will never be unfriendly to you. They're always there when you need them. With books you'll never be lonely. You can take a book anywhere, it's not too heavy. Books are your best friends, really. And they open your eyes to so many things. You can travel in books, meet friends you'd never meet physically. So books for children are things that every child needs in order to befriend a book. And I subscribe to the ABAB Principle: 'Always Bring A Book.' It doesn't matter where you go – always bring a book with you. On the bus, on the train, going on a trip, always bring a book. That's the idea I seek to plant in all children.

Ernest Emenyonu: And then for writers of children's books?

Sindiwe Magona: For writers, remember your own thrill at reading a new book. The stories that excited you, made you wonder, made you weep! Write such stories; they are even better for today's child.

Ernest Emenyonu: For parents?

Sindiwe Magona: For parents, it doesn't matter what the occasion is, birthday present, Christmas present, whatever, always include a book. We mustn't say to children, 'books are important, you must read', but in our own behavior, we don't display the importance of books. You go and say, 'books are expensive,' then you go and buy Nike shoes or whatever shoes that are even more expensive. What in the child's life determines the kind of a human we are growing? Is it expensive shoes or is it a book?

Ernest Emenyonu: What is your message for publishers?

Sindiwe Magona: Publishers. Make books accessible to everybody. Try to bring the price, the cost down. Fight the government's imposition of a sales tax on books. Be loud in your opposition to this. And also, grow writers. Grow writers!

Ernest Emenyonu: Government?

Sindiwe Magona: People in government should know, should care, that the rest of the nation really depends on them to become better people. So they should read, they should care, and especially those who are responsible for the welfare of children, they should make sure that reading and story-telling are part of the nurturing of the spirit of the child. In the support

they give parents, reading and writing should be included, to
encourage love of books.

Ernest Emenyonu: And then the last person, the teacher?

Sindiwe Magona: Teachers should really know an essential truism.
'Don't teach if you don't like reading.' Especially teachers of
children who come from the formerly disadvantaged group of
people in South Africa. Teachers are the first line of defence for
the children of South Africa. If the teacher cannot widen – push
the horizon of the child, who else will do that for the child? Most
of the children come from families that are absent as far as the
education of the child is concerned. So the teacher must take it,
just as it's been done before in South Africa. During Apartheid,
teachers used to teach the syllabus then they would say 'that's for
answering examination questions', but here is the truth! So you
would have juxtaposed the history as is taught in school with
the folk's history, what people believed happened, what is right.
If the teachers then knew that the political fight was their fight,
and they did that, you know risking being arrested, being made
jobless, being fired from the job, today's teacher has no excuse!

Ernest Emenyonu: And finally, your thoughts on the scope of
African children's literature: In this age of globalization, the
books you write in South Africa, children's books you write
there, and all the others that African writers write, should we
restrict them to the African continent or market them globally
and why?

Sindiwe Magona: Children's books are to travel, because if you
subscribe to the creation and work of organizations such as
the United Nations which promote understanding between
the peoples of the world, where best to start, if not with the
children? Understanding, and this happens with film, if you go
to South Africa, everybody's talking about 'Frozen'. We are all
Frozen the world over. If it can be done with film, why not with
books? Let's all get Frozen!

Ernest Emenyonu: Thank you very much for a most enlightening
interview!

Nadine Gordimer
A Tribute to Grace

IKEOGU OKE

The Tree[1]
For Nadine Gordimer

I came to you afraid and trembling,
And you stilled my nerves with your calming touch;
Now I shall chase you forever
With the ghost of my gratitude.
Mother of what I am and all that I may become,
Rooted like a sapling in the nursery of my art.
Great tree, feminine and resilient,
Veteran of many seasons marked by chills and windblasts,
You spread your oaken branches above the hapless weak,
And shed your thoughts like acorns to feed a famished world;
Your roots are sunk in virtue, your trunk stands firm on right;
Your leaves, green slates for justice, are always filled with light.
You shine with rainbow flowers, the type the world may see,
Only when, in aeons, your type returns to earth.

Even if I was born for a life destined to surprise the unworthy and
uplift the underserving, it would still be a rare good fortune that I
knew Nadine Gordimer closely, that she adopted me as her friend,
that I benefitted from her support as a writer. That I was not born
for such a life makes my privilege more special, my gratitude more
profound.

I was introduced to Nadine on 23 May 2008, by the South
African culture activist Raks Morakabe Seakhoa. He organized
the celebration of Chinua Achebe's *Things Fall Apart* at 50 in
Johannesburg and invited me to take part in a panel discussion
and as a performance poet and arranged my meeting Nadine on
the side.

With a manuscript of *The Heresiad*, my book-length, pro-pace and anti-censorship poem meant as a gift for Nadine, we arrived at her house in the company of Phakama Mbonambi, a close associate of Raks. (Incidentally, I call *The Heresiad* operatic poetry because it is also a musical work conceived for performance as an opera, with some of its lines having been set to music in the manuscript I presented to Nadine.)

For such a revered writer and global figure, I was surprised that she would keep me completely at ease for the nearly two hours' duration of our meeting. Not hers the airs I had sometimes noticed from some far less accomplished writers. I could hardly believe that such a great figure could embody such humility.

'Poetry is closer to the essence,' she said, comparing the purity of the literary genres after she offered me a seat on a settee and sat right next to me. Then she opened my manuscript and proposed a reading game. She requested that we took turns reading from the poem, a line at a time. She reciprocated to my gift of the manuscript after the reading with a gift of her collection of short stories, *Beethoven was One-sixteenth Black*, autographed 'For Ikeogu Oke – To mark the pleasure of our meeting...', a pleasure she made far more mine.

Before we left she told me how she cherished the memory of her visit to my country to take part in an event held in honour of Wole Soyinka. Then she took me to a secluded corner and showed me a handwritten birthday message Soyinka had sent her, her eyes radiant with pleasure, in which Soyinka apologized for his unavoidable physical absence to celebrate with her and added with touching humour that if she heard 'a glug' at the stroke of midnight it was him drinking to her health. For me it was an unforgettable initiation into literati privilege.

She was a gracious and an untiring mentor. When I called her after my return to Nigeria she would regularly ask me 'What are you writing now?' and say 'Send it to me!' after I have told her. Following the publication of my second book of poems, *Salutes without Guns*, I sent her a copy through Raks. I was surprised by her letter thanking me for the book and praising the poems. But a greater surprise from her awaited me: Later, the Nigerian journalist Tolu Ogunlesi notified me of her selection of the book as her Book of the Year (2010) for *The Times Literary Supplement* (*TLS*) – jointly with the novel *Point Omega* by the American writer Don DeLillo. Tolu then sent me a copy of the *TLS* in which the selection was published.

I couldn't believe that a writer of her galactic stature would remark of a struggling writer like me (and stake her reputation with the remark by having it published in the *TLS*): 'Here is a writer who finds the metaphor for what has happened and continues, evolves, not often the way we want in our lives in Africa and the world. He does so timelessly and tellingly, as perhaps only a poet can.' Her life, marked by such extraordinary gestures, was an eloquent testimony of grace.

'What are you writing now,' she asked me again during a telephone conversation about a year later. 'Send it to me,' she said enthusiastically after I told her that I had just finished work on a new collection of poems, *In the Wings of Waiting*. I sent her the manuscript with a letter requesting her to write a Foreword for the collection; and I would have understood if she ignored or turned down the request.

She called me a few weeks later. 'I have read your manuscript,' she said excitedly. 'I love the poems. I will write you the Foreword on one condition.'

'What condition?' I wondered, concerned that I may not be able to meet her condition. 'Remove the two poems you dedicated to me in the collection. I will not write a Foreword for a collection in which poems are dedicated to me. There is nothing wrong with your dedicating poems to me. I am grateful. But I do not want anyone to think that I wrote the Foreword in exchange for the dedication. Your works merit it. Your erotic poems are some of the best I have read. I do not say things I don't believe in. I will send you the Foreword in two weeks,' she said, riveting me to a spot as I marvelled at her unique way with integrity, evident in her insistence that I excised the poems dedicated to her in the collection as her condition for writing the Foreword.

I received the Foreword in the post with her handwritten note dated exactly two weeks from the date of that conversation. She kept her word with precision!

Unstinting in her appreciation of other writers regardless of stature, one phrase stuck out most memorably from the Foreword: 'No end to the wide illumination in the protean gifts of this man.'

I called to congratulate her on her ninetieth birthday. 'Thank you, Ikeogu... I can't believe I have got to ninety... I never wanted to... But you know we can't decide such things,' she said after my felicitation. And I wondered if she belonged to a different world from the rest of us who prized longevity beyond curtailment. She had apologized for cutting our conversation short to prepare for 'a precious visit' from her daughter, indicating that she put her children first as every good parent should.

Before leaving Nigeria for the 2014 African Literature Association (ALA) conference held at the University of Witwatersrand, Johannesburg, I called to let her know that I would be visiting her country once more. She wished me a safe trip and asked me to let her know as soon as I arrived Johannesburg.

I called her after I arrived Johannesburg on 4 April 2014. 'I want to invite you to my house for a drink. Come no later than 5.30. I want you to meet my friends,' she said, sounding persuasive rather than peremptory.

Long after 5.30 (in the evening) I was still locked in traffic with a cabby who didn't seem to know his way. I called to let her know, suspecting she would call off the appointment, the time having elapsed.

'Give the phone to the driver,' she requested.

I did. And she patiently gave directions to the driver and told me she would wait after he returned the phone to me.

It was a rare evening spent in the company of her friends: Maureen Isaacson, Mary Beth and David Goldblatt. I was meeting the last two for the first time. Holding court, she steered our conversation effortlessly from the Pistorius trial in her country to the Boko Haram insurgency in mine, from literature to religion. And poetry was not left out of the bounties we shared at that gathering: I performed 'The Tree', one of the poems I dedicated to her, the epigraph to this tribute, in which I acknowledge her as 'Mother of what I am and all that I may become'.

Before leaving I offered her an autographed copy of *The Lion and the Monkey*, my children's story first published in *Nal'ibali*, a South African journal based at the University of Cape Town, and *Song of Success*, my collection of poems for children published (with a sing-along CD) by HEBN, Ibadan.

'Do you have all my books?' she asked as she received the books from me, her eyes agleam. 'No,' I said.

'Which ones do you have?'

I mentioned those.

Then she asked for one of her books. With an autograph that read '...Ikeogu Oke. With much love and celebration of your work.' she handed me a copy of *My Son's Story*, her book brought by Maureen Isaacson.

Then she said: 'We must always give back', a remark for which I thought Mahatma Gandhi should have added 'Taking without Giving' to his famous list of deadly sins.

'When I return to Nigeria I will send you a copy of *The Second Genesis*. It is an anthology of contemporary world poetry published in India, in which the poem I have just performed for you is published,' I said as I gazed at the autograph in her now unsteady handwriting.

'That's if I'll still be around,' she replied, hinting at something for which everyone present, except her, glanced at the next person apprehensively.

'You're not going anywhere,' I said after a long frozen silence.

I received news of her death, on 13 July 2014, before I could send her the book with the poem. So, as she had hinted, she would not be around to receive the book if I sent it.

The most valued of the many precious things I got from her are the words: 'I do not say things I don't believe in' and 'We must always give back'. For with them came her most prized lessons of integrity and positive reciprocity, by subtly urging me never to say things I don't believe in and never to fail to give back. I have gratefully internalized both lessons.

I salute her life of courage, grace, integrity, sacrifice, service, and tireless giving. She was, beyond a great writer and humanist, a philanthropist of virtue.

REVIEWS

EDITED BY OBI NWAKANMA

Okey Ndibe. *Foreign Gods, Inc.*
New York: Soho Press, 2014, 335pp, $??
ISBN 9781616954581 paper

Novelist Okey Ndibe stands tall among a new breed of African diaspora writers who offer fresh perspectives on African identity in the 21st century. In *Foreign Gods, Inc.*, Ndibe succeeds in capturing perhaps the worst of both worlds of the African immigrant who navigates a marginalized existence in America. *Foreign Gods Inc.* is a bold and riveting story of Ike Uzondu, a Nigerian immigrant whose success is crushed against the dark underbelly of the American dream. Although he graduated with honors in Economics from Amherst College, no one will employ him because of his Nigerian accent. His spirit and determination are ravaged over time by a bleak and meager existence as a taxi driver in New York for thirteen years.

In *Foreign Gods Inc.*, Okey Ndibe unfolds a masterfully-woven tale of human frailty and moral ineptitude as financial demands from Ike's family in Nigeria, mounting debt, a gambling obsession and failed marriage plunge him into a downward spiral of crippling desperation. To escape his plight he decides to steal the statue of Ngene, a war god from a shrine in his village and sell it to *Foreign Gods, Inc.* a gallery that deals in religious artifacts. The commodification of foreign *gods* represents the Western obsession with the exotic yet *primitive* and irresistible art from cultures cast as *the other.* Ike tells the gallery owner how ancient and powerful the god is and that in the olden days, 'the deity led the warriors to wars, and they never lost one' (9). The ill-conceived plan drives the pace of the work and foreshadows how things began to fall apart for Ike and the family that he cannot save in Nigeria.

A compelling feature of the novel is the successful linkage of the past with the present, in a way that skillfully echoes the legacy of Ndibe's mentor, the late Chinua Achebe. Similar to the clash of cultures trope in *Things Fall Apart, a* lengthy, italicized section connects Ngene to the legendary past of Utonki through an account of the intrusion of Christianity and the divisive impact on the villagers. Although many converts are won, Reverend Walter Stanton succumbs to ill health, madness and ultimate demise that symbolize imbalance, seeds of discord and conflict in the village of Utonki in the past as well as the present. Much of the story is set in Nigeria as Ike returns after eleven years absence to witness many changes in the society. In pursuit of the statue of Ngene, of whom his uncle is Chief Priest, Ike observes Christian fundamentalism, and religious hypocrisy that have planted seeds of discord among members of his family to the extent that people accuse others of witchcraft and devil worship.

Foreign Gods Inc. mirrors other contemporary aspects of Nigerian life through the portrayal of characters that, in the struggle to survive turn to drug smuggling, robbery and corruption as means of survival. The husband of his former girlfriend becomes a 'drug mule' and dies when drug-filled condoms burst in his stomach at an international airport. His wife and children are left pitiable and destitute. The author describes the moral corruption of Pastor Uka, the minister who deceives and exploits his congregation in demand for their meager funds. He preys upon their hopes for a better life and works them into religious frenzy and false worship of *himself* as the divine messenger and his voice as the voice of God.

Ndibe critiques the mindless obsession of Nigerians with the trappings of Western society. When visiting the lavish mansion of a former friend, Tony Iba, Ike notes the garish, ostentatious and ridiculous show of wealth, the source of which is unknown. His friend invites children to the *poor people's TV room* to watch old reruns of Michael Jordon's basketball games. Everyone, including the servants is mesmerized by the storied wealth of celebrity sports figures in the USA and imagines outlandish ways to spend their imaginary millions.

A feminist evaluation of the novel reveals the plight of all the Igbo women portrayed. None of them emerges as a strong character and their lives are torn asunder by the violence, betrayal and immorality of the men around them. They are depicted as emotionally and economically dependent, living as appendages to the men. Ike's paternal grandmother is the only credible figure among the women to whom Ike remains attached. Some of the most comical elements of the novel are the caricature and stereotypical portrayal of the crude and emasculated African-American women, prominently, Bernita, who Ike marries for a green card.

Foreign Gods, Inc. rings true to the salient features of African fiction through a vivid rendering of sights, sounds, places, and behaviors of people in Nigeria. Ndibe effectively captures the nuances of Igbo life through the generous use of proverbs, Pidgin English, Igbo language and customs. Despite the familiarity of *home,* as the reader follows Ike on his questionable and tortuous mission, it becomes clear that he is utterly disconnected from his people as a consequence of dislocation and diaspora existence. When he meets his mother after more than a decade, they are both engulfed in darkness, spiritually and materially. Long before the ending of the novel the reader senses that Ike is lost not only to himself but also to his people back home. An unfortunate aspect of diaspora life is that Ike, like many African émigré's in real life, is unable to communicate his alienation, setbacks and failed dreams in foreign spaces. Ike's story is a parable of modern moral crisis and the inability to balance the realities of hybridized existence with familial expectations, and African cultural identity. Ndibe's *Foreign Gods Inc.* is a brilliant work that illuminates the African immigrant dilemma through the dark and desperate avenues of lost cultural integrity, virtue and dignity.

ROSE SACKEYFIO PH.D.
Associate Professor, English
Winston Salem State University
Winston Salem, NC 27127

Mashingaidze Gomo. *A Fine Madness*
Oxford: Ayebia Clarke Publishing Ltd, 2010/Boulder, CO: Lynne Rienne Publishers, 174pp., £9.99/$17.95
ISBN 9780956240149 paper

Anyone reading *A Fine Madness* is likely to be struck first by its title and then to do battle with it. This title encapsulates the passion and emotion that had engulfed the writer over the years. On the one hand, the madness of love is rested on a woman, an older woman, an age-defying older woman and asserts that falling in love with her is 'fine madness'. The woman is defined as Tinyarei that metaphorically is the aged continent of Africa, a continent of great beauty and resources enough to attract the greedy eyes of the Western world that desires to possess her. Gomo states that 'Nature is beautifully mad'; she is surpassingly beautiful and this results in a fine madness for the beholder, mad as exceeding the boundaries of defined consciousness, beyond our limits of sanity and normalcy. This is a love story of a man with his land, his culture, his identity on the brink of extinction and like Okigbo in 'Heavensgate', Gomo gathers the legend before it 'sinks un-gathered into the watery deep' The writer himself being close to death and destruction at all times during his engagement as a soldier pilot, and having delivered death and destruction to others, sees and deeply feels the need to claim his own and preserve it for all eternity. Nature is beautifully mad, a beauty that indulges the lover to undertake dangerous feats of war to protect his beloved. This madness is Gomo's trope and an enduring and endearing one.

A Fine Madness is a new genre of poetic prose with reflexive lamentation and memoirs. The book is divided into thirty-four sections or chapters with stanza blocs of run-on lines. It proves an engaging reading with powerful historical references that define the harsh reality of the African homeland. In his reflections, Gomo raises many great issues of relevance to the continent. He writes that the story of Africa is the 'story of a mother, stripped of all self-respect by neo-colonial barbarism.... The story of Africa standing alone... scantily dressed.... [as] a destitute courtesan subjected to the wiles of Western immorality in which racist legislators vied for a global moral deviation' (17). These and many more are the expressions of victimhood and victimization that abound in the narrative. Gomo forces a re-think of the deplorable African situation and who really may be accountable.

Yes, there was colonialism and African countries won self-rule but with what results? Was neo-colonialism forced on Africans? Ngugi wa Thiong'o explores this topic in his novel *Devil on the Cross* and the co-authored play, *I Will Marry When I Want*. To find who is accountable is a soul-searching task. In the following section, Gomo introduces a comparison between the past and the present, and examines the line of committed warriors that saved the land from the looting colonialists (18). The section portrays Gomo's thoughts and reflections on the fight of African nations for independence. He shows the comparison between the selfless and totally committing fight of liberation by the great-great-great grandfathers and their ultimate sacrifice to the mercenaries of the new generation against their homeland.

Fine madness is madness that is pleasing, joyful, satisfying, fulfilling as refusing a given Christian name as Aaron, Joel or Peter and the priest proclaiming that he was mad, and for him, it was fine madness because he could not abandon the names that his grandfather gave him. Fine madness here translates as proud exhilarating defiance of what negates the Africans' being, values, sense and sensibility, his land and resources, his culture and life. The name in African culture is a social statement and so holds a special reality for the owner.

For Gomo, it is the trauma of war that sharpened his sensibility and creative impulse. He realized that war cannot solve the African problem. This is because 'the way of war... [is] a blood-letting presence that scourges mankind' (29), and on p.47, he states that war is confusion; war cannot be an end in itself. He lists several set-backs to African ascendancy as Education, Poverty, Culture, Politics, Literature and History. There is the need for Africa to re-discover herself anew. The role of the African soldier today is 'to fight the regression of African sovereignty into neo-colonial puppet rule' (41).

Gomo's *A Fine Madness* is indeed fine. It is penned by an angry, concerned and committed home-boy jolted by the ravages and destruction of war in human lives and property, the degradation of the environment and the effect that this had on him which resulted in his poetic prose, deep in meaning, engaging in thought and poignant in style. The trauma, tragedy and pathos that belie his experience forced him into introspection of the real meaning behind the various internecine wars in the continent, in the Congo and Zimbabwe especially. He had to write and he records:

> And I saw time away from home affords one time to reflect on issues
> one cannot effectively reflect on while immersed in them. Certain issues
> demand detachment and solitude. Certain issues demand that one
> should walk away, sit on a mountaintop and watch the action below.
> And certain issues demand that one should watch another person in a
> predicament similar to one's own. (44)

He chose both options, he was a combatant pilot, in similar
precarious situations as other fighters or indeed others affected by
war, and he was also a detached observer watching the actions of
others. This means really that he was privileged. In his argument with
himself, he sought for various solutions to the African situation. One
of such is Reparation from Western powers that enslaved, colonized
and impoverished the continent and he cited examples of the Jew's
Holocaust and Reparation and Settlement (52-3).

A Fine Madness is a love song of an angry lover for one's
homeland, personified as a woman of age-defying beauty. Africa
the motherland, still beautiful in old age but her beauty still attracts
outsiders in morbid continuity. Her charms, seen in her natural
endowment of resources and financial prospects expose her to
rampage and forced exploitation among world powers. But the
reader is bound to see the realization of the Igbo proverb rendered
in translation that 'it is the house rat that informs the bush rat
that there is fish in the fish basket'. This trading of the country's
resources to satisfy a despot's quest for power plays out in civil
warfare. Gomo's panacea to this is massive re-orientation and a
come-back to our cultural values, our histories, songs of valor,
legends. These will re-educate our children on the cost and history
of nationhood and nationalism.

The author treasures his Tinyarei and fights to rescue her from
plundering hands to situate her in her homestead. The soldier's
perspective and plan for achieving this is not by the barrel of the
gun. He advocates a cultural revolution:

> And it struck me that the history of African resistance to European
> conquest and prejudice should not be left to myth and ephemeral folk
> tale alone but in a literary form inculcated into the mental make-up
> of African children as a security vaccine, immunizing black children
> against Eurocentric prejudice, subversion and dominance .... The
> history of African resistance must be versified into nursery rhymes and
> transmuted into extraordinary art for academic study by generations
> contemporary and infinitely remote in future. (27)

The reader will enjoy his descriptive prose and the images it creates. There is some spontaneity in his prose that transports the reader to the various scenes that Gomo evokes as if one is there with him. *A Fine Madness* is a refreshing read and highly commendable.

HELEN CHUKWUMA PH.D
Professor of English
Department of English & Modern Foreign Languages
Jackson State University, Jackson. Ms.

Pede Hollist. *So The Path Does Not Die*
Cameroon: Langaa Research & Publishing Common Initiative Group, 2012, 282pp.
ISBN 9956727377 paper

In post-colonial Africa and the African Diaspora, issues of cultural traditions, material wealth, civilisation, Western education, marriage, family, love, identity and belonging raise political and economic concerns. *So The Path Does Not Die*, Pede Hollist's debut explores the issues as themes in a pulsating and an intricately interwoven narrative. Through the life of the chief protagonist, Faniba, aka Fani, and her relationships in their complex and convolutedly interwoven maze, Hollist lays bare the contradictions and complexities of survival and belonging in a money-driven economy on both mainland Africa and the United States of America.

The writer's prologue to the novel prepares the reader for the intricacies of the over-arching theme of home and belonging and their unusual demands. The prologue is an allegory of a village, Musudugu, far away and long ago, inhabited only by women. In the allegory men tried many times to conquer Musudugu but the brave and patriotic women defended their village. The village was also protected by the Virgin Girl, the daughter of Atala the Supreme. The Virgin Girl in return asked women to keep only one rule: darkness must never cover a man in Musudugu. Only male infants could stay with their mothers in Musudugu until their time of weaning from the breast. The narrator says that Musudugu is a place of harmony, of singing and dancing, and most of all, of caring and sharing. Those who cannot withstand its traditions and rules are free to leave, but they find themselves often returning for its harmony. The story of Musudugu changes when an unusual girl child, Kumba Kargbo is born. She demands to know why men are forbidden in Musudugu. After confronting the village elders she leaves to find out why darkness should not find a man in Musudugu. She meets Atala, the Supreme, who tells her to journey into self so that she may be at home among her people. Upon returning to Musudugu, Kumba destroys the village and mourns the harm and destruction that she has caused.

Immediately after the prologue, the story of Faniba Marah commences as narrated by a third person narrator who uses very accessible everyday language. The tension-filled narrative bursts into life through the heated argument between mother-in-law, Baramusu, and daughter-in-law, Nabou, over Faniba's impending initiation with her age-mates. Baramusu contends that 'si-kool' will not teach Faniba 'to preserve our ways' and 'cook and take care of a husband and children' (2) in order to keep the family intact. Faniba's parents, Nabou and Amadu, who had lost their first daughter Dimusu to initiation, snatch Faniba from the ritual, and surreptitiously leave their home village Falaba for Freetown, Sierra Leone's capital city. The villagers query whether it is wiser to work and preserve 'us and ours' than to preserve 'mine'. Traditionally, Faniba's parents' actions desecrate the people's ideal. The villagers, especially the women, implore God Almighty to punish them for the sacrilege. For Faniba, she would never belong with other women and their unbreakable circle because she never went through the whole initiation process, which outsiders describe as female genital mutilation (FGM).

The flight to Freetown lands Fani in a foster family after her father's passing on since her mother can hardly afford their basic needs. Fani enrols for tertiary education at CC, but is unfortunately sexually molested on the eve of her final college examinations. Her foster sister Edna flies to the United States of America, where they later meet because Fani abandons college before completing her training and leaves for the United States of America, the place of her dream. She has no plans, but resolves to marry for convenience in order to get the green card to stay in the US. She eventually settles in the Washington Metropolitan Area where she meets her urologist fiance Cameroon Priddy, aka Cammy, originally from Trinidad. Cammy is an only surviving child after his older brother died at sixteen from kidney problems. The sad loss of his brother motivates Cammy to become a surgeon.

In exploring Cammy and Fani's love relationship, Hollist examines the ambiguities that surround the adherence to tradition, identity and belonging, especially for the African in the Diaspora. The subject of FGM and Fani's admission to having been circumcised generates tangential attitudes from scientific and cultural perspectives respectively. Fani and Cammy decide to marry, solemnising their relationship by exchanging marriage vows at a public wedding. Unfortunately, skeletons from Fani's past ruin the wedding after which Fani immediately goes back to the war-torn Sierra Leone to look for her people whom she feels she should appease after her parents' cultural desecration early in her teens. Fani returns to a disfigured home and country now filled with child soldiers whose blighted lives of mutilated bodies and minds are metonymic of villages, communities, country and nation of Sierra Leone. Cammy follows Fani to Sierra Leone where she dedicates her life to helping in the rehabilitation of the mentally and physically disabled war victims. The story ends with an Epilogue in which Fani and Cammy's daughter Dimusu-Celeste challenges Fani to change the sad ending to the tale of Musudugu, advocating that men and women should transform society by working together for more wholesome lives for both genders.

Hollist's themes are not new in African literature, yet he distinguishes his talent through the suspense-filled narrative. Through Faniba, Hollist explores what it means to struggle without giving up one's identity as an African and as a woman. He questions what it is that Fani and Cammy overcome that defines their identity, not their professions and accumulated wealth. Hollist exposes how readers and people generally should measure their impact and contributions to make the society a better place, sharing their talents not to accumulate ordinary trinkets, but to polish and make bare the beauty of relationships as depicted through the life of caring and shared pain. In the novel, the story of the strength of Fani and Cammy's characters is measured by their giving up luxurious lives in order to nurture the path of African humanity and dignity. Their contributions are best needed in the war-ravaged Sierra Leone and not the affluent United States. This political statement describes the writer's implied vision – the obligation to rebuild African communities which lies with the very Africans and not with donors and philanthropists. Thus, impliedly, the novel suggests that who you are is to be found in your values, in the baobab tree of your traditions and not others' baobab trees that cannot offer the same quality shade to nurture and nourish lives.

Living true to one's people's ideals creates a lasting peace with one's self and with others and the world. Further, respect for other people and their traditions is what ends up giving Fani and Cammy joy in their relationship and marriage, while reciprocity, giving and taking, water their love tree, in addition to the romance that they share. In pursuing their individual talents, and acknowledging that no two people are exactly alike, they differently give their best to their world. The writer subtly uses Fani and Cammy's relationship to urge Diasporans to give back and plough back into their communities rather than living lives of refugees and enjoying smooth lives whose foundation they never contributed towards.

The most beautiful strength about Hollist's writing is the unassuming approach that he uses to explore very deep subjects using common everyday language. The infusion of African folklore into the prologue and epilogue adeptly packages and trims the narrative's circumference. Cammy and Fani use Creole or Pidgin to show their Trinidadian and African roots respectively. The title of the novel can thus partially get its strength from the characters' pursuits of roots, home, belonging and values that give them dignity and common care for each other as social beings. Written along the lines of traditional folklore whereby virtue is rewarded and villainy punished, the intrusive narrator occasionally shows in the manner that he punishes despicable characters in the narrative. Also, the Black Atlantic that Fani and Cammy discuss towards the end of the novel is a major historical symbol that the novel highlights so that Africans may not forget the landmarks of the ambiguities of the Middle Passage. That Hollist's novel embraces more than mere education entertainment objectives is incontestable. The novel is a must read for lovers, home-makers and home-builders, psychologists, counsellors, educationists, historians, anthropologists, political scientists, traditionalists, artists, film-makers and people in the medical profession – in short, the novel offers a holistic view of what life is about, warts and all, *So The Path Does Not Die*!

RUBY MAGOSVONGWE
A/Chairman
Department of English
Faculty of Arts
University of Zimbabwe

Pita Nwana. *Omenụkọ,* translated into English by Ernest N. Emenyonu

New York: African Heritage Press, 2014, 82pp. ISBN 9781940729176 paper
First published in Igbo language; London: Longman, Green and Co, Ltd., 1933, 94pp.
ISBN 0582636116 paper

The publication in Igbo Language in 1933 of Pita Nwana's *Omenụkọ* was a literary milestone that established the father of the novel in Igbo language. A translation of this first Igbo novel into English by Ernest Emenyonu, Professor and Chair, Department of Africana Studies, University of Michigan-Flint, U.S.A opens it up to the world, especially literary critics and scholars. A biographical novel, *Omenụkọ* is a travelogue of pain and joy. It excels in its didacticism, its realism, its cultural significance and its timeless appeal to the reading world. With its translation into English, it becomes a novel about everyman as he struggles to overcome or accept the burdens of existential conditions that throw him sometimes into joy and at other times into pains but ultimately pulls him to continue on the path of life.

Translation gives the meaning of a text in another language in the way that an author intended the original text to do.

This explanation underlines our appreciation of the laudable achievement of Ernest Emenyonu in translating the novel under review. This effort is an important achievement of the translator whose early interest in the ethnic literature of the Igbo, even as a doctoral student blossomed in the publication of *The Rise of the Igbo Novel* in 1978. It is in Emenyonu's ingenious effort to replace a novel written in the Igbo language with a version in the English language without any loss of information, cultural implications or other details in meaning and indeed style that his excellence lies. In doing this, he takes a revered seat among translators of first indigenous African language novels such as Daniel P. Kunene who translated *Chaka* (*Shaka*, a sotho epic novel) by Thomas Mofolo in 1981 and Wole Soyinka who translated *Ogboju Ode Ninu Igbo Irunmole* into *The Forest of a Thousand Demons: a Hunters Saga* in 1968.

Omenụkọ is a story of a real man, Igwegbe Odum, fictionalized as Omenụkọ, a name that means 'One who acts during a period of scarcity', an attribute which he ultimately lives up to. It is in fifteen chapters. There is a prologue and an epilogue. The translator has also added a very useful foreword.

Omenụkọ's early efforts to rise above the disadvantages foisted on him by deprived parenthood are ruined by the tragic loss of money and articles of trade as he and his porters and apprentices try to cross overflowing River Igwu on their way to an important market in Bende in the present Abia State of Nigeria. Thoroughly exasperated, frustrated and despondent, he sees a life-line in committing a heinous crime against society and the gods in selling his apprentices and even his cousin into slavery. Because he commits an abomination and breaks the harmony of consanguinity, he and his relations become fugitives in Mgborogwu. Here, Omenụkọ is loved to the point of being appointed a regent by the chief of Mgborogwu on the twilight of his life. Fate still deals kindly with Omenụkọ. He becomes prominent and prosperous in a foreign land. His wisdom, integrity, boldness and efficiency, lucidly portrayed, make his colleagues, the people of Mgborogwu as well as the white District Officer accept him as an indisputable and trustworthy leader. When Mgborogwu, his benefactor, dies, Omenụkọ keeps his warrant in trust for his young son, Obiefula.

However, times and circumstances soon begin to remind Omenụkọ that though wealthy and well-received in a foreign land, a stranger must return to his homeland. A thematic summary of the novel in the words of Pita Nwana translated into English is that:

> It is almost like an unwritten law that a man does not forsake his fatherland. Whenever there is a mocking reference to this fact of his status in a foreign land, whether by allusion or indirect hint his desire to return to his homeland becomes a burning issue for him. (1)

Resentment, envy, jealousy and outright confrontation make Omenụkọ desire to go home. But he does not until by patience, tact, benevolence and generosity he secures the freedom of some of the people he sold into slavery including his cousin, Obioha. He also appeases the people, the gods and the land of his birth. Omenụkọ returns home, a rich man ready to serve his community as an intelligent senior citizen.

Omenụkọ is thus a novel of sin, repentance, restitution and acceptance. It is a story of survival through the exercise of courage, initiative and wisdom. It is a story that teaches entrepreneurship, hard work, capitalism, vision and endurance. In the exercise of these attributes, Omenụkọ resembles Robinson Crusoe, the protagonist of an English Literature classic by that name who builds a civilization in a lonely island where he is a lone survivor of a shipwreck and later returns a wealthy man to England.

In *Omenụkọ*, Pita Nwana reveals the intriguing life of Igwegbe through a conscious and disciplined selection of significant events and issues arranged in an understandable classical plot. Filled with unrelieved suspense and motivation, this plot traverses many conflicts and complications to reach a climax in the resentment, antagonism, and physical attack by the people of Mgborogwu on Omenụkọ and a resolution in which Omenụkọ repents and makes restitution.

A good translation should be a close equivalent of the original in terms of the message conveyed, meaning and style. This situation is unmistakable in Emenyonu's translation. Proverbs, the oil with which the Igbo eat words, are captured in abundance. So also are idioms, prayers and incantations. Igbo words and nuances, the peculiar meanings of which may be lost in an outright translation are retained. Where necessary, English equivalents are provided in context. Some examples are 'The hunter whose arrow hits the fast-fleeing deer gets rewarded with twenty arrows' (35), 'A man sitting in the comfort of his home never develops cramps from waiting for a guest' (42); and 'if you treat a child the way you treated his playmates, he would be satisfied' (43).

When the people of Mgborogwu come to Omenụkọ to demand Mgborogwu's 'warrant' for his son, an elder prays for mutual goodwill in spite of the obviously dicey demand and a translation is given thus:

> Earth come and chew kola, our ancestor Mgborogwu come and chew kola. God on high, here is kola for you, kind spirits here's kola. Whoever says I don't deserve what is mine, when he gets his, he won't be fit for it. I am for live-and-let live. Whoever objects to that, let him be denied life. Let the kite perch and let the eagle perch too. Whoever obstructs the other, may his wings break. (26)

And the people affirmed '*Isee*... so may it be,' to each of the prayers above (26). '*Isee*....' (written as *I see*...) is an original Igbo nuance retained as a hallowed conclusion to prayers. Other words retained include 'dibia' – diviner, 'Eze/Ogaranya' – a man of means and 'Nzu' – clay chalk.

Emenyonu also sustains in the *Omenụkọ* translation, vital figures of speech and images. At the site of his tragic loss Omenụkọ moans: 'God Almighty, why have you reduced me to a life where death would by far have been a better choice?' (5). For the families of the men he sold away, 'the tears which were shed in the whole town that day were enough to form a river' (13).

Pita Nwana's *Omenụkọ* is a first and significant novel in Igbo language. It is a *bildungsroman*, a veritable novel of formation and a novel of universal education and socialization. In the course of growing to full consciousness of himself as a mature and functional individual in the society, a protagonist of a *bildungsroman* goes through spiritual and psychological crises that refine him and make him wiser. But it is Emenyonu's adroit translation of this invaluable work into English that opens its merits to the wider world. Thus, Emenyonu reclaims this classic from abandonment in shelves and archives and positions it for more criticism and reception in contemporary scholarship.

PROFESSOR JASPER AHAOMA ONUEKWUSI
Department of English and Literary Studies
Imo State University, Owerri
Imo State - Nigeria

Style in African Literature:
Essays on Literary Stylistics and Narrative Styles
Eds: J.K.S. Makokha, Ogone John Obiero and Russell West-Pavlov
Amsterdam & New York: Rodopi, 2012, 444pp
ISBN 9789042034761 paper

In a beautifully written 'forward' to *Style In African Literature: Essays on Literary Stylistics and Narrative Styles* (2012), Chin Ce re-presents a question that has reverberated in African cultural scholarship for more than half-a-century, on the paradigms for decoding African literature. Chin Ce is apparently uncomfortable with African intellectuals who, he says, 'continue to operate from remote antiquities of western particularities,' and who should endeavour 'to mitigate its basic lack of synthesis in scholarship – that exclusivist attitude that is barely at home with an indigenous linguistic base of interaction with a world language.' Ce's discomfort with the current critical criteria for African literature is the reason he rates *Style in African Literature* superlatively.

Chin Ce's proclamation may sound a little like a piece of

romantic and naïve nativism, but he goes further to clarify his position: 'It is obvious we can fare our cultural products no better by embalming them in mainstream western precepts and, as I have stated in a previous forum, where we simply pander to, rather than transform, hegemonic linguistic and ideological structures for some convenient artistic or financial respite, we are further threatening to bring a whole circle of African heritage to the *cul-de-sac* of 'mutant traditions' (2012: 14). These opening coda in *Style in African Literature* may sound alarmist, but they present challenges to any reviewer of a book of essays on postcolonial literatures in the twenty-first century. The editors of *Style in African Literature* seem enthusiastic in their coverage of significant strands in postcolonial African literary stylistics, particularly within the frames of post-colonial narratology and feminist hermeneutics. Important questions then arise: what does postcolonial narratology consist in? How does one locate the post-ness of the postcolonial 'post'? Is the recourse to linguistics or an audacious embrace of stylistics enough in the decoding of postcolonial narratology? It is sad that not one of the 19 contributions in the book remotely engaged with this issue since the 2005 publication of Gerald Prince's seminal essay, 'On a Postcolonial Narratology.' Beyond postcolonial narratology, what is the place of style in the ideological paradigm of Feminism? What are the specifics of a Feminist hermeneutics?

Russell West-Pavlov and J.K.S. Makokha – two of the three editors of *Style in African Literature* – attempt to respond to some of these questions in the opening essay, 'Introduction: Linguistic Re(turn) and Craft in Contemporary African Literature'. There are indications that the editors are familiar with recent scholarship on postcolonial narratology. The evocation of an illuminating study such as Talib's *The Language of Postcolonial Literatures*, affirm this persuasion. There is no doubt, as the editors observe, that there has been a dearth of scholarship on narrative style in African literature since the seminal challenge from Obi Wali and the impressive efforts of Emmanuel Ngara. It is equally significant to observe that the problem is not so much the unavailability of creative writing as it is the dearth of creative scholarship particularly within the frames of language and style. West-Pavlov and Makokha's 'Introduction' serves its purpose by highlighting the significant strands covered by the book. There are four divisions that cover segments on 'Methodology' as a pivotal element in stylistics; other sections which address literary categories present discussions on fiction, poetry, orature, as well as stylistical issues in African literary drama. Of the nineteen essays in the anthology, two are devoted to the exploration of what the editors classify as 'General Perspectives.' These are Doria Tunca's 'Towards a Stylistic Model for Analysing Anglophone African literatures' and Adesola Olateju's 'Current Issues and Trends in African Verbal Stylistics.' Six essays devoted to the stylistic exploration of selected fictional narratives appear in the next segment. These consist of essays on selected narratives of Buchi Emecheta, Yvonne Vera, Iweala, Kouroma, Tayo Olafioye, Cal de Souza, and Chinua Achebe, written respectively by K.M Matthews, Martina Kopf, Russell West-Pavlov, Adeyemi Adegoju, Shawkat M. Toorawa, and Adeyemi Daramola.

The third segment of *Style in African Literature*, captured by the editors as 'Perspectives on Orature and Poetry,' equally has six essays. There is a compelling resonance of African speech and imaginative nuances in this segment, probably due to the contributors' return to the exploration of style in African poetry and folklore. This is particularly evident in Iwu Ikwubuzor's 'Stylistic Features of Igbo Riddles,' Mikhail Gromov's reading of Swahili poetry, Michael Wainaina's study of Gikuyu popular music, Ogone and Obiero's evaluations of musicals by women, Anette Hoffman's analysis of Malawian praise poetry and Bright Molande's metapoetic interpretation of Chimombo's poetry. The last segment of the anthology, 'Perspectives on Drama and Theatre', consists of four essays: Naomi Nkeala's exploration of female sexuality in Butake's *The Rape*, Chris Wasike's analysis of Ruganda's theatre in Uganda, Victor Yankah's contribution on Ghanaian drama and a revisiting of Ola Rotimi's dramaturgy by Ibrahim Esan Olaosun.

The selections are well-made and carefully placed; each contribution presents an important perspective in the discourse of African literature in these early decades of the 21st century. What seems rather obvious, too, is that the contributions have varying degree of depth, some well researched, others less inspiring but nonetheless relevant in the critical enterprise of the ever-growing African literary scholarship. West-Pavlov and Makokha's 'Introduction' summarizes the energizing qualities of this anthology as well as its infuriating limitations. The 'Introduction' betrays a hurriedly jumbled collection of 'abstracts;' an engagement that has resulted in several non-dignifying sentential structures, syntactical lapses and numerous technical infelicities (see pp. 17, 18, 19, 22, 23, 24, 25, 26 and 27).

Doria Tunca's 'Towards a Stylistic Model for Analysing Anglophone African Literatures' is illuminating. It highlights the theoretical questions that had tended to impede the growth of Stylistics in the study of African literature, just as it illustrates how stylistics could be fruitfully deployed as a practical paradigm in the understanding of African letters. Tunca's essay is particularly refreshing: it not only provides a historical context and thematizes a system of reading that consistently sounds soporific to the critic al literati, but also succeeds in presenting stylistics as a hermeneutical model of reading worthy of our collective embrace. Avoiding the trap of what Stanley E. Fish had identified as 'circularity of arbitrariness' as a basic limitation of stylistic scholarship, Tunca nevertheless recognizes Spitzer's 'philological circularity' – an observation that locates the synergy between stylistics and literature. Tunca locates 'linguistic mimicry' in Adichie's *Purple Hibiscus* as a thoughtless yearning for acceptance: a description that invariably captures the less admirable characters in African narratives who struggle to be more Catholic than the Pope in their embrace of Western values. Tunca's essay immediately evokes memories of F.B.O. Akporobaro's 'African Identity and the Issue of Form and originality in the Modern African Novel,' a study that brilliantly suggests a systematic decoding of structure, language, and content in the reading of the African novel as a genre from the metaphysical, fantastical and quotidian realities and assumptions of African peoples and landscapes.

More problematic is Adesola Olateju's 'Current Issues and Trends in African Verbal Stylistics: The Yoruba Example.' Sample this: 'Today, [however], the trend is that Stylistics goes beyond the background history of an author, or mere identification of stylistic devices. It involves the three profound steps of identification, explanation and interpretation of the stylistic, rhetorical and other [?] devices in the text... This is the more reason why a stylistician is different from either the linguist or literary scholar. For the linguist, his core area is linguistics per se, while for the literary scholar, literary studies. Nevertheless, for the stylistician, he is versatile in both' (sic). This raises a few questions: what are these *other* devices that add to rhetorics and style as basic concerns of the stylistician? Should Mr. Olateju be asking for the widening of the scope of linguistic studies or for the establishment of what he calls a discipline or department of stylistics? What is the need for the further balkanization of humanistic studies in a globalized

21st century research space where interdisciplinarity seems to have found base? In any case, if the research of the Stylistician is neither relevant to the linguist nor to the literary scholar, what then is the use of Stylistics? Mr. Olateju takes literary scholarship back by another century when he returns to a mimetic conceptualization of literature as 'a reflection of societal events and happenings' (65), at a temporal space when literary scholars are battling with the archaeologies of the future (Jameson 2005). This contribution, like the 'Introduction,' certainly would have benefitted from the services of a good proofreader, and more rigorous editing. There is no excuse for the editors to allow the very first sentence of the essay: 'The history of Stylistics as an academic discipline dates back to the 19th century, precisely in the 1950s....' [19th Century: 1950s?] Add this to such awkward and repetitive phrases as: ''literary criticism' has a developmental history of having developed in stages' (59) and 'As far as literary stylistics is concerned, *its method of approach* ...' (63). Note also the omissions on the reference list, including citations on Ojaide and Soyinka, among others.

K.M. Mathew's deployment of what she calls 'Feminist discourse' is particularly interesting. The essay articulates new perceptions of Emecheta's *The Joys of Motherhood* as could be fruitfully be done in a whole lot of other feminist writings by locating narrative semantics through what she submits as 'the examination of discourses within and beyond the text' (88). Mathews' essay is engaging as a fine piece of deconstructive feminism attuned to postcolonial scholarship. Of course, there are a few slips which the editors would have done well to rectify (see pp. 78, 82 and 84). Martina Kopf's exploration of the poetics of trauma in the narratives of the Zimbabwean writer, Yvonne Vera, is equally stimulating. Except for the evident overclaim at the very first sentence of her study, Kopf's essay is not only provocative in its blend of theory and analysis, but also does so within the identification parameters that finally locate metaphor in a semiotics of temporality. West-Pavlov seems persuaded in his reading of the narratives of child soldiers that memorial narrativity appears to more successful when the narrations of the traumatic are less obvious. In other words, he argues, the deployment of the stylistic elements of irony, satire, chiasmus, and the postmodernist dislocation of subjectivity is more plausible.

Adeyemi Adegoju's discussion of mnemic sites in the autobiographical narrative of Tayo Olafioye is an interesting read. The essay's introductory paragraphs show evidence of a scholarship that is familiar with the ancient and re-emerging field of memory as a significant research territory. But Adepoju's exploration of the two linguistic signals of 'naming' and 'imagery' are followed with unequal cadence: only one name – Olu Yaro – seems to be of interest to the author. Iwu Ikwubuzo's 'Stylistic Features of Igbo Riddles' is well-researched and illuminating. Ikwubuzo's meticulous blend of theory and analysis makes a bold departure from the abstractions and speculations that define a number of the essays, particularly with those that address style in fiction. Igbo riddles, one is persuaded to believe, is a stimulating strand of Igbo poetic categories as so painstakingly demonstrated not only at the level of structuration, but also their linguistic and rhythmical cadences. The depth of analysis in this essay is what sets it apart; a feature that Michael Wainaina's 'Stylistic' reading of modern Gikuyu popular songs' almost shares. Wainaina's essay is codified in the subject of his discussion – 'New Wine in Old Wine Skins' – a biblical borrowing that was beautifully deployed in another context of 'stylistic' reading of Osundare's poetry elsewhere by Samson Dare in the 1990s.

Wainaina's contribution is categorized in the six discursive frames he calls didactic, contextualized, extended, problematic, subversive, and dramatic discourses – important paradigms that he manages to theorize within the tenets of the Bakhtinian dialogic imagination. Significantly, Wainaina succeeds in establishing a distinction between the conventional explorations of the antiphonal structures of Orature to a more nuanced 'call and response' cultural mode that anticipated individual and communal participations. Ogone and Obiero's reading of Agnes Mbuta's Luo songs equally reads like a pure literary analysis than a 'stylistic' decoding of the poetic genre of contemporary popular lyrics. There is very little in this contribution that places it within the frame of what the editors have chosen to categorize as style. The authors' categorization of their study as 'Music' heightens our discomfort, as there are no major efforts to take the 'stylistic' evaluations of instrumentation, tonality, performance structures and rhythmic variations of Mbuta's 'music' Particularly refreshing, however, is Anette Hoffman's elaboration on what she calls the 'Chronotopes of the (Post-) Colonial Condition.' Focusing on aspects of panegyric poetry from Namibia, Hoffman's essay presents a reading where eulogistic poetry gets concretized as a machine aesthetically designed for humanistic cogitations. In exploring the nexus between spatiotemporal realities in postcolonial discourse, Hoffman follows Bakhtin in observing that we find in some – or perhaps much – of postcolonial writing a 'synchronic association' where the intrinsic connections of temporal and spatial relationships are so carefully woven that meaning finally emerges more from the *whereness* of the creative incidents than from their *whenness*.

Bright Molande's 'The Art of Chameleon' is an interesting reading of the poetry of the Malawian poet, Steve Chimombo. Molande establishes the admirable deployment of communal mythology in Malawi. The chameleon emerges not just as a forest creature, but one that inspires the artist writing in a state of siege. Malawi, under the dictator, Kamuzu Banda, was a tyrannical state, and it is chastening that Molande would locate the continuing postcolonial condition in Africa within the realms of an eviscerated messiahnism. Mythology takes a privileged position as the liberator is finally emasculated as his people's destroyer, a theme so brilliantly explored earlier by Wole Soyinka in *Idanre*. Molande's essay, like others, too, would have gained from a more rigorous editing: there are occasional deployments of wrong idioms as well as cloudy sentential structures (see pp. 342 and 343 for instance). Incidentally, one of the most perceptive essays in the collection – Naomi Nkeala's feminist reading of Butake's *The Rape of Michelle* is as sensitive as it's beautifully articulated. This is in spite of the author's evocation of conventional analytical codes such as dramatic settings in terms of spatial and temporal topographies, dramatic progressions and characterizations, narrative tone and language, contrasts and binary oppositions, imagery and symbolism, structuration, naming, and the metaphorical figurations of womanhood as nationhood. Nkeala's essay brilliantly incites a perception of style as implicit in the rigorous and meticulous explication of 'narratives' at both their contextual and structural underpinnings. Here, stylistic and literary criticisms converge in the ideological tenets of a feminist poetics that is at once postcolonial and poststructural.

The last three essays in *Style in African Literature* – like Nkeala's study – are devoted to the 'stylistic' reading of selected plays from Uganda, Ghana, and Nigeria. The interest in 'Style' seems however clouded by the dominant politicality of the discourse, particularly evident in Chris Wasike's 'Figuration of 'Troubled Motherhood" and Feminization of the Ugandan Nation in John Ruganda's plays', and in Victor Yankah's reading of Efo Mawagbe's 'In the Chest of a Woman.' Yankah's excavation of Akan mythologies and their transmutation into theatre is very stimulating. On the other hand, Ibrahim Esan Olaosun's 'Incantation as Discourse' focus on just two incantations extrapolated from Ola Rotimi's *The Gods Are Not to Blame* seems uncomfortably scanty in scope, and needed to be beefed up, if not within the play, at least comparatively with another African play. In the final analysis, *Style in African Literature: Essays on Literary Stylistics and Narrative Styles* remains essentially what it is: an assemblage of perspectives. One is left with the unpleasant feeling, however, that 'Stylistics' as a field of academic enquiry is still a less confident, eclectic blend of critical formalism, linguistic structuralism, structuralist poetics, poststructuralist feminism, and even the exegetical recourse to postcolonial mythologies – whether or not the scholar is obsessed with the Hallidayan codifications of stylistic features or fascinated with the postcolonial narratology of Gerald Prince's persuasion. On the whole, what seems important is not so much that the derided literati of Africa's postcolonial imagination should search for relevance in a linguistic paradigm struggling to 'Re(turn),' but that the professed Stylisticians of this literary minefield should demonstrate more rigour and vigour in ensuring that Stylistics not only enjoys a 'Re(turn)', but also a reinvigoration.

OSITA EZELIORA, PHD
Senior Lecturer, Olabisi Onabanjo University
Ago-Iwoye, Ogun state, Nigeria.

Maik Nwosu and Obiwu (eds) *The Critical Imagination in African Literature: Essays in Honor of Michael C. Echeruo*
New York: Syracuse University Press, 2015, 289pp
ISBN 9780815633877 paper

The Critical Imagination in African Literature: Essays in Honor of Michael J.C. Echeruo is a handsome book, but that is not what makes it stand out among the roll of this year's publications on African literature. It is that it is an apt book in honor of one of the most distinguished figures in modern African literature, Michael J.C. Echeruo. It is the culmination, or perhaps in fact, the result of the valedictory symposium held by the English department, Syracuse University, New York, in honor of Echeruo on his retirement from the academy after fifty years of productive and stellar scholarship. Michael Echeruo began his academic career at the University of Nigeria, Nsukka, on the foundation faculty of English when it opened in those early and hopeful years of Nigeria's independence from Britain. He went to Cornell from 1962 to 1965, where he earned his PhD in English and American literatures, on the strength of his dissertation, 'Joyce Cary: Dimensions of Order', work which represents what Chukwuma Azuonye has described as the 'Africanist tilt of the occidentalist focus'of Echeruo's early scholarship. He returned to Nsukka in 1965, to resume his job as a lecturer in English, teaching Elizabethan and Jacobean Drama. With the civil war in Nigeria between 1967 and 1970, Echeruo took the side of the Easterners, and worked in the war bureaucracy as the Director of War Information for the secessionist state of Biafra, enmeshed in what for most Igbo like him was a war of survival against a federal onslaught that sacked Nsukka in August 1967, and literally uprooted Echeruo and his fellow university men till the end of the war in 1970. At the end of the civil war, Echeruo returned to the University of Nigeria as Senior Lecturer and Head of English, and was later appointed Professor and Dean of Arts, until he left for the University of Ibadan in 1974, to assume the chair of English, and Dean of the Arts and later Dean of the Postgraduate school. Echeruo thus became the first Nigerian chair of English in two of its oldest universities, until he left Ibadan in 1980, to become the foundation President/ Vice-Chancellor of the new Imo state University, from 1980 to 1988. He was visiting professor from 1988 to 1990, at Indiana University, and the University of California, Los Angeles, until he was appointed the William Safire Professor of Modern Letters at Syracuse University, New York, from which he retired, becoming emeritus in 2010.

The Syracuse symposium organized to honor and celebrate Echeruo's distinguished academic life staged over the stretch of half a century drew many eminent scholars, including his peers and younger colleagues – and took into account Echeruo's multivalent work as a poet, critic, and historian of ideas. Echeruo's distinguished body of work covers areas as diverse as Elizabethan and Restoration drama, particularly Shakespeare; the Victorian English novel, particularly Conrad and Joyce Cary, 18th and 19th century African and African Diasporic literature and culture; modern African literature; literary nationalism; Igbo language and Drama, and cultural history, particularly with his groundbreaking book, *Victorian Lagos* (1977). Aside from his accomplishments as a literary critic, Echeruo is also highly regarded for his achievements as a poet of considerable weight. He is one of the major pioneer African modernist poets who emerged in the 1960s, in an era that included his friends like the poet Christopher Okigbo, J.P. Clark, Wole Soyinka, and Gabriel Okara in Nigeria. Echeruo's early significance as a poet is indicated in the fact that he won the first All-Africa poetry prize in 1963, beating the South African poets, Arthur Nortje and Dennis Brutus. His two published poetry collections, *Mortality* (1968), and *Distanced* (1975), established Echeruo firmly in the canon of modern African poetry. However, as Azuonye has equally noted, in spite of Echeruo's remarkable and pioneering presence, 'since the mid-1970s, there has been a noticeable decline in notices on Echeruo's presence on the African literary scene. Not surprisingly, in 2008, Owomelaya Oyekan, in the *Columbia Guide to West African Literature in English since 1945* (p. 102) even begrudges him a place among modern West African creative writers... there seems to be a total eclipse of Echeruo's name in the most recent anthologies, and entries under his name in literary biographies (e.g. Gikandi 2002) are begrudgingly brief and sketchy.'

This seems to be the main reason for this book – *The Critical Imagination* – a move to, in part, restore Echeruo's place, as one of the true *eminence grise* of African literature. Obiwu does an exact job of this in his laudatory opening essay in the collection 'Cultural Icon: Michael Echeruo and the African Academy', in which he strives to place Echeruo in his proper historical context. The point is in the striving, for beyond Obiwu's panegyric on Echeruo, there must be a place in this special focus for a more hardboned analysis of Echeruo's work. Nonetheless, this opening essay offers a very close introduction to Echeruo, in ways that allow a proper entry to the larger concerns of the collection, properly outlined in Maik Nwosu's prefatory statement, to 'gesture toward an ethos that is part of a global or human cognitive map...toward the expansion or reinvention of that tradition' (xi). It is all very 'Echeruoan'. Maik Nwosu's main contribution to the collection of essays, 'The Figuration of the Un' proposes the generative presence of a unique semiotic matrix, the 'Un'; in my reading, a negative sign of the order, or global dimensions of world literature. To put it a little more simply, Nwosu navigates, with a rather complex language, the shape of transnationalism, and the value of 'World Literature'. Theoretically, as Morse Peckham has famously argued, 'any sign can elicit all responses'; and the sign of the 'Un' in Nwosu's essay, I think may need to be fleshed out a bit more to do just that, in this intriguing and indeed resourceful, and perceptual reading of the semiotic behavior of the 'Un' as the controlling force in the historical interpretation of the African text, in its category as World Literature. Rashna B. Singh essay, 'The Vortex of the Expulsion', explores the place of the Indo-African imaginary, given its complex and often troubled, and perhaps even invisible place as part of what is generally discussed as African literature. It is a timely inclusion in the debate that expands the very yardage claimed by the Indian experience of the African world to which it is linked. The contribution of that experience in the work done by Rajat Neogy the Ugandan-Indian intellectual who founded the *Transition* magazine in Kampala in 1961, the novelist Peter Nazareth (*The General is Up*), Jameela Siddiqi's (*The Feast of the Nine Virgins*), and Mira Nair's film (*Mississippi Masala*), among many, exemplify the texture of that aspect of the African imagination, but the historic moment of Indian expulsion from East Africa, particularly in the Amin regime, has given rise, in Singh's reading, to what might be a new genre of African literature – the literature of its Indian diaspora. For while the Asian African expulsion might have displaced that community, it has also dispersed exilic memory – the idea of home as a 'moveable place' as well as a 'mythical place'. Singh's conclusion ties down the real thrust of her exploration: 'An imaginary must be grounded in a physical place and perceptual reality, and for the children of exiles that reality is no longer Uganda but rather the mostly Western countries where their parents settled. Uganda, however, replaced India as the land of mythic origin.' Obiwu's essay, 'Jacques Lacan in Africa' places Lacan's work in the context of his African travels, but while it is bold in its claim that Africa may be a source of Lacanian psychoanalysis, the essay is in need of a connecting center to all the strands that the essayist attempts to pull in summoning Freud, Jung, Charles de Gaulle, Gide, and Hannibal, and their various connections to Africa, in Lacan's work. It does often take an imaginative leap for the reader to fuse together these various interconnected relationships that this essay summons to establish 'Lacan and psychoanalytic theory in the discourse of the continent and its diaspora'. It is easy to question the audacity of some of its claims, for example, on the explication of Lacan's 'theory of reading': 'The eaten book, however, neither displaces nor substitutes the hunger and, therefore, comes at the cost of *jouissance*'

(89). What is that but verbal obliquity, that makes the essay elliptic in places. But it is in its very sum an original reconsideration of Lacanian sources.

Bojana Coulibaly's '(Re)Defining the Self through Trauma in West African Short Fiction' and Heather Hewett's 'Rewriting Human Rights' in my view mine through rather old questions about agency and the African condition, and leave little room for theoretical reconsiderations. Other contributors, like Chielozona Eze in 'The Postcolonial Imagination and the Moral Challenges of our Time', Glen Bush's 'Survivalist Autobiographies', Kanchana Ugbabe's 'Rebellion as a Narrative Strategy in South African Women's Writing', Sule E. Egya's 'Dialogism, African Poetics, and Contemporary Nigerian Poetry', and Dul Johnson's 'Confronting Politics through History: A Reading of the Historical Novels of Ayi Kwei Armah and John Edgar Wideman', add in various interesting ways to the wealth of this collection of essays in honor of a distinguished African man of letters. *Critical Imagination in African Literature* is appropriately summed up in the special report, 'The Michael J.C. Echeruo Valedictory Symposium' by Maik Nwosu and Obi Nwakanma, a fitting conclusion to a, broadly speaking, very articulate body of essays. The essays in a general sense, celebrate Echeruo's accomplishment, but not by any direct reference to his work. It is an anthology which rather projects the trajectories of Echeruo's scholarship abstractly. Perhaps that is the only limitation of this book: it fails to situate Echeruo wholly, by examining his own work in critical terms. Inclusion of essays that directly explore Echeruo's work would have enriched this collection, and made *The Critical Imagination in African Literature* an even more satisfying book. All the same, there can be no doubt that this book is an important addition to the body of African literature.

OBI NWAKANMA, PHD
English Department
University of Central Florida,
Orlando, Florida, USA